Management for Professionals

The Springer series *Management for Professionals* comprises high-level business and management books for executives. The authors are experienced business professionals and renowned professors who combine scientific background, best practice, and entrepreneurial vision to provide powerful insights into how to achieve business excellence.

More information about this series at http://www.springer.com/series/10101

Alan Okros

Harnessing the Potential of Digital Post-Millennials in the Future Workplace

 Springer

Alan Okros
Canadian Forces College
Toronto, ON, Canada

ISSN 2192-8096   ISSN 2192-810X   (electronic)
Management for Professionals
ISBN 978-3-030-25725-5   ISBN 978-3-030-25726-2   (eBook)
https://doi.org/10.1007/978-3-030-25726-2

This Springer imprint is published by the registered company Springer Nature Switzerland AG
The registered company address is: Gewerbestrasse 11, 6330 Cham, Switzerland

Acknowledgements

This volume is drawn from engaging, collaborative research conducted by thirty-seven academics and graduate students over a three-year period. Each made a valuable contribution: some by producing integrative summaries drawing across multiple sources; others by being willing to leap off conceptual cliffs to present provocative ideas; and, a few who served as academic curmudgeons who challenged assertions and predictions. Their original reports along with our many informative meetings and discussions provided a rich foundation for this book. My thanks to each and, in particular, Ryan Zade and Christian Leuprecht for their assistance in pulling all of the ideas together into a coherent manuscript.

Project Director

Alan Okros

Contributing Editors

Ryan Zade
Christian Leuprecht

Incorporating Research by

Peter Bradley, Ph.D., Royal Military College
Victor Catano, Ph.D., St. Mary's University
Arla Day, Ph.D., St. Mary's University
Danielle Charbonneau, Ph.D., Royal Military College
Lobna Cherif, Ph.D., Royal Military College
Brenda Fraser, Defence Research and Development Canada
Sarah Hill, Ph.D., Royal Military College
Tara Holton, Ph.D., Defence Research and Development Canada
Karen Koundakjian, Ph.D., Defence Research and Development Canada
Daniel Lagace-Roy, Ph.D., Royal Military College
Christian Leuprecht, Ph.D., Royal Military College
Damian O'Keefe, Ph.D., St. Mary's University
Eric Ouellet, Ph.D., Canadian Forces College
Grazia Scoppio, Ph.D., Royal Military College
Rebecca Tiessen, Ph.D., University of Ottawa

François Vachon, Ph.D., Université Laval
John Verdon, Defence Research and Development Canada
Randall Wakelam, Ph.D., Royal Military College
Marianna Balakhnina, University of Ottawa
Sandra Berg, Royal Military College
Cindy Chamberland, Université Laval
Leigha Covell, M.Ed., Queen's University
Jonathan Dixon, St. Mary's University.
Ariel Garneau, Royal Military College
Ken Hill, Queen's University
Katherine Labonté, Université Laval
Amanda MacDonald, St. Mary's University
Alexandre Marois, Université Laval
Samantha Penney, St. Mary's University
Denise Scott, University of Toronto
Shauna Smith, St. Mary's University
Victoria Tait, Carleton University
Shaun Tymchuck, Royal Military College
Leigha Tregunna, Queen's University
Ryan Zade, Queen's University

This research was supported by a Defence Research and Development Canada Technology Investment Fund grant (14ap06).

Contents

Part I

Surfing the Digital Tsunami

The Future is Closer than You Think
—Anon

This book offers employers insights into the characteristics that the next generation of employees are likely to bring with them when they enter the workforce. The toddler depicted below is not only being amused with the tablet but already starting to master the new alphabet of the digital environment. We asked a fairly basic question: what will be the implications for employers of youth that will be raised immersed in a ubiquitous digital environment? The observations in this book suggest that key emergent factors will require employers to change their organization to fit the characteristics of new employees rather than having these new individuals fit the existing corporate status quo—and many employers will have to anticipate this shift well before our happy toddler is ready to enter the full-time workforce; the future is closer than it would appear (Fig. I.1).

As a basis for our work, we know that employers fully recognize that optimizing the individual and collective contributions of their workforce is key to success. While many organizations will use the slogan 'people are our most important resource', what they really mean is the 'right' people: those who not only possess required skills sets but, in exchange for the benefits offered, bring the desired motivation, creativity and attitudes that their employer expects from them. The evolution from the industrial era to the information age has been accompanied by a commensurate shift from physical labour and manual dexterity to greater importance being placed on the intellectual skills of knowledge workers and the behaviours of individuals as ambassadors of corporate values.

To ensure that they have the 'right' people, organizations invest in attracting, developing and engaging the ideal employees: optimizing the fit between the person and the organization. To do so, all facets of organizational functions need to be aligned. This requires work practices, leadership styles, human resource policies and organizational culture which are fully integrated through coherent policies,

Fig. I.1 Changes influencing today's youth

programmes and processes. Those who fail to do so create conditions that can lead to the unproductive effort, demoralized employees and dysfunctional teams—and ultimately organizational failure.

Positioning an organizational for success has to start with the manner in which new talent is attracted and oriented. For many employers, the primary philosophy applied to manage new employees is to focus on selecting those who are the best fit with the current corporate culture and work environment and, once hired, providing them with initial orientation, training sessions or on job supervision to assist them to learn how to work within the established corporate policies, procedures and management styles. The general expectation tends to be that new employees will learn to fit in by adapting to well-established work routines and getting accustomed to how business is done. In addition to reading through the corporate handbook and memorizing the organization's 'mission, vision and value statements' that are conveniently on display, new employees are expected to draw on the expertise of those who have been around for many years hence acquiring the approved narrative of 'who we are, where we came from, what we stand for'.

While this well-established approach to creating an effective workforce is likely to be retained at some level by many organizations, our research has identified two emergent factors that will cause a growing number of employers to have to change the organization to fit the new employees rather than having these new individuals fit the existing corporate status quo.

First, demographic projections for many developed nations paint a bleak picture.[1] Given low fertility rates, most of these nations rely on the combination of net immigration and high labour force participation rates to increase their population

---

[1]Among others, see the national projections of the UK Office of National Statistics, US Department of Labor and Australian Government Treasury. For updated global statistics, see the

and grow their labour force. In recent years, Canada has led the G7 nations in percentage population growth[2]; however, in 2016, there were 4.4 million Canadians aged 15–24 and 4.9 million people aged 55–64 suggesting an unhealthy balance for labour force growth (Fields et al. 2016). Further, when projections for declining participation rates[3] and potential slowing of net immigration[4] are combined, the forecast for the period 2011–2036 is not positive. Under scenarios for moderate immigration and participation rates, the total number of those aged 15–64 in the workforce would grow by only 4.4%, while the population would increase by 27.7%. Under the scenario of low immigration, the size of the workforce would actually shrink by 3.3%.[5]

Although many projections for the USA have suggested that the overall work-force would continue to grow,[6] economists and financial officials have identified that proposed policies for immigration and employability of some residents without US citizenship could result in pressures in the US labour force.[7] When combined with the continued drops in the fertility rate and labour force participation, the US is moving much closer to Canada and other developed nations. As has been predicted in many of these countries, employers will soon have to seriously engage in the battle for talent.

Second, and the focus of this book, is the nature of talent that will enter the labour market. As our toddler and the tablet illustrate, the evolutions in the digital environment will result in the youth of today being raised in a different environment than their predecessors. We propose that they will bring quite different skills, attitudes, beliefs and expectations to the workplace of tomorrow. Noting the quote often attributed to Bill Gates that '640K of memory ought to be enough for any-one',[8] it is fully recognized that predictions of the future can be problematic; nonetheless, our research provides insights into the current youth cohort with the recommendation that decision-makers would be prudent to consider the implica-tions. When placed in the context of what we see as significant disruptions in the economy and workplace due to the evolving digital environment, we conclude that the 'digital post-Millennials' will possess the critical skills to 'surf the digital

---

projections by the International Labour Organization or the Organization for Economic Cooperation and Development.

[2]See Statistics Canada data for 2011–2016 at: http://www.statcan.gc.ca/daily-quotidien/170208/cg-a001-eng.htm.

[3]Forecast to decline from 67% to between 59.7 and 65.6%; see Martel et al., Statistics Canada Report 11-0110-X for labour force participation projections to 2031.

[4]See Morency et al. (2017) Statistics Canada Report 91-55-X for population projections to 2036.

[5]Data are extrapolated from the two reports listed above using the median projected participation rate of 61.2% from and Tables A4.1, A4.2 and A4.3 from Morency et al. (2017).

[6]A summary of current US Labour Force projections is accessible at: https://www.census.gov/content/dam/Census/library/publications/2015/demo/p25-1143.pdf.

[7]In February 2017, then US Federal Reserve Chair Janet Yellen commented on the potential adverse impact of proposed policy changes at: https://www.banking.senate.gov/public/index.cfm/2017/2/the-semiannual-monetary-policy-report-to-the-congress.

[8]As cited in James E. Fawcette's Editorial, the full quote is: 'When we set the upper limit of PC-DOS at 640K, we thought nobody would ever need that much memory'.—William Gates, chairman of Microsoft InfoWorld, 7(17), p. 5, 29 April 1985.

tsunami'. While nobody will be fully prepared for future events, the informed should be the least unprepared for the coming changes including adapting to harness the skills of today's youngsters are likely to have when they join the full-time workforce.

Overview of Research

Over a 4-year period, a group of academics and graduate students at several Canadian universities along with defence research scientists peered into the future to understand the youth cohort and to develop plausible implications for employers. As a key component of the Canadian Department of National Defence (DND), Defence Research and Development Canada (DRDC) conducts research across a broad spectrum of areas to provide DND, the Canadian Armed Forces, other government departments and the public safety and national security communities with the knowledge and technological advantage needed to defend and protect Canada's interests at home and abroad. Under the title "Harnessing 21st Century Skills", DRDC provided funding for a research team comprised of academics from several universities including faculty at the: Royal Military College of Canada, Canadian Forces College, St. Mary's University, Université Laval and the University of Ottawa as well as research scientists working in DRDC.

In all, 37 scientists, academics and graduate students with diverse backgrounds in social sciences and the humanities drew on a wide range of academic literatures, scoured websites and blogs and conducted qualitative and quantitative analyses to examine the environment in which the current youth cohort is being raised. While our team was composed primarily of Canadian researchers, we drew on a full range of sources with particular attention to the literature relevant to the USA and, where of value, comparisons to Europe and the leading industrialized nations. This comprehensive research was then used to generate plausible predictions of the characteristics these individuals are likely to possess by the time they enter the workforce. Our ideas were tested through presentations at various academic conferences and the inclusion of designated 'academic curmudgeons' on the team who were tasked with challenging colleagues' assertions of major changes in youth characteristics or suggestions of sweeping generalizations applied to all of the same age. In total, our team generated 17 research reports, presented 30 conference papers and are in the process of submitting journal articles and producing book chapters and a second edited volume.

This volume presents an integration of all of the work conducted with reference to the specific reports that members produced. Copies of contributor's research reports can be obtained from the lead researcher Dr. Alan Okros. Our focus in this book is on providing insights that may be used to monitor evolutions, anticipate changes and initiate timely responses. As such it is written primarily for practitioners. The second edited volume being produced also draws on the various reports generated under this project with an emphasis on theory, specifically, to determine whether empirical research supports current theories and whether or how these theories apply across national contexts.

In conducting our analyses and developing the ideas for this volume, we are fully aware of several limitations in the work we present. We recognize the dangers of attempting to peak into the future especially when considering human behaviour. A key concept presented in the first chapter, however, is that, by integrating a number of different perspectives and 'weak signals', one can identify factors that have the potential to create a 'tipping point' when what exists today will significantly alter. While it is not possible to identify exactly when these changes will occur or what the resultant 'new order' will look like, we have endeavoured to develop plausible hypotheses with some indicators that the informed can monitor to anticipate and understand changes as these emerge.

A focal point of our analyses is today's youth. As academics, we also fully acknowledge that any effort to characterize who young people will be when they enter adulthood is a risky proposition. The personal circumstances surrounding any child's upbringing along with the choices each person makes when growing up will have a significant impact on who they will be when entering adulthood. Further, there are multiple factors that can be used to differentiate subgroups including nationality, gender, ethnicity, socio-economic status or a host of other valuable and meaningful characteristics. Thus, we recognize that variations will remain when comparing one individual to another.

Our work, however, is informed by two perspectives related to concurrent continuity and change. First, while youngsters growing up will have many experiences that will be highly similar to those that their parents and grandparents encountered, they will also encounter marked differences in context that have the potential to alter the impact of these experiences. As an illustration, girls and boys will continue to be exposed to a range of social signals as to what are deemed 'appropriate' roles, behaviours and attitudes for their assigned gender that will be broadly similar to the nature of gendered identities projected on previous generations. These continuities, however, will be accompanied by newer discourse, images and cues that indicate that gender is more fluid than even their parents were exposed to.[9] We have focused on the implications of these subtle shifts particularly in contexts where those of a similar age are likely to have shared experiences that will differ from those their elders encountered—and we believe to have identified several.

Second, people generally interpret events with an assumption of continuity. Particularly as adults, we tend to fit our observations to our already well-defined expectations of how the world works and we often do not recognize evolutions until these have produced major or disruptive changes to the stereotypes, schemas or taken-for-granted assumptions on which we draw.

Together, these two perspectives related to continuity and change serve to frame the analyses conducted and, we suggest, the conclusions that the reader may draw. Those who seek to find evidence of continuities will find plenty of indicators to support that assumption; however, we suggest that it is more important to look for,

---

[9]For a presentation of continuity as represented in children's toys, see Blakemore and Centers (2005) and for a presentation of evolving perspectives on gender fluidity, see Huston (2015).

and understand, the indicators of change. Much of our presentation is intended to present examples where the informed observer will realize that they are encountering indicators that do not fit the patterns that they are used to. We have extended our work to suggest how these changes may affect the world of work and what employers may consider as appropriate responses when they realize that changes are happening.

This volume will present key findings from the research conducted by starting with three chapters that present the foundation for our analyses. We posit the rise of the information age as having a significant impact on young people—and employers. Thus, the first chapter provides an expansive environmental scan of the changes that are or may be occurring due to evolutions in the digital environment. Given our focus on the youth cohort, the second chapter presents a critical consideration of the current literature on the generational theory and cohort analyses. Some suggest that it may be plausible to forecast future implications for the youth cohort by examining experiences that are shared at a similar age, while others use these analyses to differentiate among those of a similar age. The third chapter examines the other key area where the youth cohort will have shared experiences; their schooling and the significant evolutions occurring in not only what they are learning but how they are learning to learn. Drawing on these first three chapters, the second part will examine the key characteristics that the youth cohort may bring to the workplace including aspects of their: key skills and twenty-first-century competencies; identity, social skills, values and attitudes; and goals and expectations in life and work. The final part with two chapters will examine future implications for organizations with an emphasis on those who have (to date) retained structured, hierarchical approaches. Recommendations will be provided for employers to consider as they prepare for their future.

References

Australia. (2004). *Australia's demographic challenges.* Canberra: Government of Australia. Retrieved from http://demographics.treasury.gov.au/content/_download/australias_demographic_challenges/html/adc-04.asp.

Blakemore, J. E., & Centers, R. E. (2005). Characteristics of boys' and girls' toys. *Sex Roles, 53*(9/10), 619–633.

Fawcette, J. E. (1985). Give me power. *InfoWorld, 7*(17), 5.

Fields, A., Uppal, S., & LaRochelle-Côté, S. (2017). *The impact of aging on labour market participation rates.* (Report 75-006-X) Ottawa: Statistics Canada.

Huston, M. (2015). None of the above: An emerging group of transgender people is looking beyond "man" and "woman." *Psychology Today*, 9 March 2015. Retrieved from https://www.psychologytoday.com/articles/201503/none-the-above.

Madouros, V. (2006). Projections of the UK labour force, 2006 to 2020. *Labour market trends, 114*(1), 13–27. Retrieved from https://www.ons.gov.uk/ons/rel/lms/labour-market-trends-discontinued-/volume-114-no-1/projections-of-the-uk-labour-force-2006-to-2020.pdf.

Martel, L., Malenfant, E. C., Morency, J. M., Lebel, A., Bélanger, A., & Bastien, N. (2011). *Projected trends to 2031 for the Canadian labour force.* (Report 11-0110-X). Ottawa: Statistics Canada.

Morency, J. D., Malenfant, E. C., & MacIsaac, S. (2017). *Immigration and diversity: Population projections for Canada and its regions, 2011 to 2036.* (Report 91-551-X). Ottawa: Statistics Canada.

Toossi, M. (2013, December). Labor force projections to 2022: The labor force participation rate continues to fall. In United States Department of Labor, *Monthly labor review.* Retrieved from http://www.bls.gov/opub/mlr/2013/article/pdf/labor-force-projections-to-2022-the-labor-force-participation-rate-continues-to-fall.pdf.

The Digital Environment

1

> *In this electronic age we see ourselves being translated more and more into the form of information, moving toward the technological extension of consciousness.*
>
> —Marshall McLuhan

Introduction

The microprocessor has drastically changed how we live, work, and play. Computers and video game consoles are now as much a part of the home as the television. Smartphones and ubiquitous apps provide instance access to information in virtually any location. This digital evolution has accelerated owing to the development of communication technologies that allow these processors to network and exchange information; the 'internet of things' as exemplified by the Internet and mobile devices. Post-Millennials are the first generation to be born into a truly digital age: many were introduced to the world when their parents posted their sonogram on Facebook. Our central argument is that the ubiquity of these connected technologies throughout their formative years will make the digital environment the most significant factor that will serve to differentiate members of this cohort from those before them.

To appreciate how the digital environment will influence current and future generations, we sought to develop a comprehensive understanding of how this environment is going to affect societies at large. As John Verdon's elaborates,[1] we conducted a broad and integrative futures analysis that moves beyond descriptions of the ways in which digitization may change how we live, work and communicate

---

[1]Verdon's ongoing analyses and posts are currently accessible at: http://johnverdon-friday-thinking.blogspot.ca/ and "The Wealth of People for the 21st Century" at http://www.johnverdon.com/.

© Springer Nature Switzerland AG 2020
A. Okros, *Harnessing the Potential of Digital Post-Millennials in the Future Workplace*, Management for Professionals, https://doi.org/10.1007/978-3-030-25726-2_1

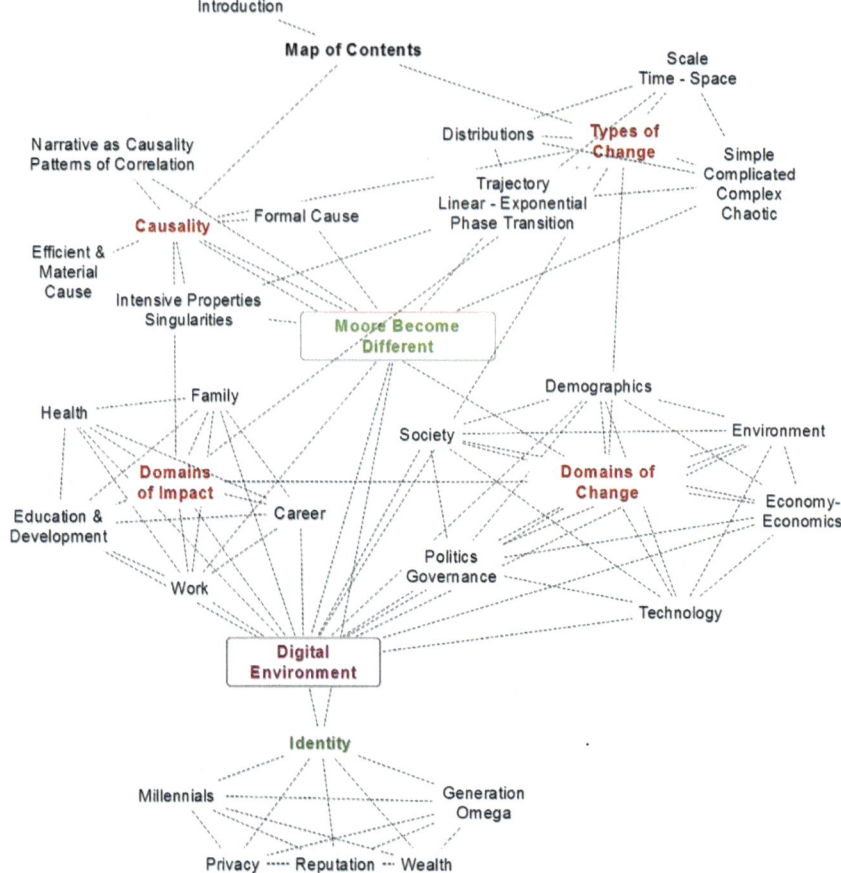

Fig. 1.1 Mapping of topics related to the Digital Environment

to positing that the emerging digital environment will serve as a fundamental change in the conditions of change and will result in significant adjustments beyond making our personal lives more convenient or our business practices more efficient. We concluded that the disruptive effects of the evolution of the digital environment are likely to create fundamental changes in social order and the nature of the lives most people will live.

Figure 1.1 illustrates the range of literatures, topics and perspectives that Verdon cross connected and integrated in his assessment of the evolving digital environment. This chapter summarizes the key conclusions and inferences drawn from his analyses.[2]

---

[2]See also Verdon (2010), Verdon et al. (2009) and Okros et al. (2011).

Our reference to the digital environment extends well beyond common references to the Internet as the medium for searching, posting and exchanging information. To a large extent, the vast majority of Internet usage today is to allow us to conduct our lives faster or easier while still retaining the fundamental nature of our interactions be these personal, social, commercial, political or other (Brody, 2009; Raimi & Wellman, 2012). The expanding and increasingly integrated array of sensors, transmitters, storage and retrieval capacities and embedded analytical capabilities are leading to a future where virtually everything of importance can be measured, shared and analysed through automation (Brynjolfsson & Saunders, 2009; Carr, 2009). This concept of the *digital* extends to the biological as life becomes an information science coded through DNA, while matter becomes 'hackable' at the quantum level (Tocchetti, 2014; Verdon, 2010). The Internet of Things connects a vast array of everyday objects allowing them to send and receive data (forecast to comprise over 50 billion devices by 2020 and 100 trillion by 2035). In involving to the 'Internet of Everything', the power of this interconnectivity is likely to change virtually all aspects of how we live our lives (Greenfield, 2006; Kelly, 2008). By enabling intelligent processing of massive amounts of data, it is possible that most facets of human existence will be conducted, facilitated or mediated on or, at least, through, the digital environment (Denning, 2001). In this context, the next evolutions will be powerful, disruptive forces of change.

We might consider the driving forces behind this rapid socio-technological change as *Attractors* that provide both static and kinetic impetuses behind system stability and system transformation (Verdon, 2010). While our focus remains on understanding the implications of the digital environment on today's youth, we will present a holistic understanding of how digital evolutions may influence all of society. This chapter will start by providing a discussion of three key topics: attractors, futures analyses and an understanding of conditions of change. We will then provide a brief summary of the ways in which the digital environment is likely to have a profound impact on the nature of our society and human existence writ large. The final portion will apply our considerations to examining the potential implications for today's youth.

Attractors, Systems of Organization and Transaction Costs

The most profound social revolutions in human history have arisen whenever a technology comes along that lowers transaction costs.—Cory Doctorow

Verdon's contends that entities or systems (biological, social or physical) that exist in dynamic, complex contexts will seek to find the most efficient way to organize so as to survive and, ideally, flourish. Often this most efficient form of existence is based on an 'attractor' that served to enable the entity to create, maintain and replicate itself. A simple example is a soap bubble: regardless of the shape used to create a bubble, the particles will quickly form into a sphere as the most efficient form to exist. The concept of minimal surface area represents one of the boundary conditions that generate an attractor based on efficiency. Many existing social institutions and organizational characteristics represent the application of attractors of efficiency that are normally based on identifying either an optimal or sufficing way to perform the function and, in social systems specifically, to reduce transaction costs.[3] Transaction costs include a number of key variables that create the boundary conditions that sustain hierarchy as an attractor of efficiency (Benkler, 2006; Doctorow, 2012). These variables include the time, effort, resources and missed opportunities created by conducting activities in a certain way (Williamson, 1981).

While commonly recognized in the business sector, transaction costs are a key consideration in many disciplines. As an illustration, representative democracy represents one of the most efficient ways for societies to govern themselves and can be traced back to a time when humanity recognized that gathering the entire clan for every significant decision was inefficient (Graeber, 2004). As clans became larger, the transaction costs (stopping the hunt, ceasing to gather food, leaving the fire unattended) became too great, and, therefore tasks, became specialized as the area of activities expanded (Tudge, 1999). In this way, over time, we have created a range of systems that are organized to minimize transaction costs and are based on often unrecognized attractors of efficiency (Goldsmith & Eggers, 2004; Strayer, 2005).

The key conclusion reached in our analyses is that evolutions in the digital environment are fundamentally lowering transaction costs across a wide array of social functions that, in turn, will alter the underlying attractors leading to new ways of organizing systems and conducting our affairs. To understand how and why these will occur and, why these are likely to come as surprises to many, it is necessary to consider futures analyses and the nature of change.

Futures Analyses

> You can't connect the dots looking forward. You can only connect them looking backwards, so you have to trust that the dots will somehow connect in your future. —Steve Jobs

We have a strong tendency to assume that tomorrow will be much like today. Even when faced with significant disruptive shocks, whether environmental, economic or social, we make the assumption that, over time (and usually fairly quickly) 'things will get back to normal' (Taleb, 2001). This worldview assumes a 'normal' and that it will remain static (DeLanda, 1997, 2012; Schwartz, 2003). With a more nuanced perspective, most of us recognize that many conditions around us are changing

---

[3]To the extent that a system is bounded, constrained and predictable, we tend to search for optimal outcomes; to the extent that it is complex, dynamic and unpredictable, we tend to look for sufficing outcomes. The literatures on complex adaptive systems and wicked problems are informative, see Okros et al. (2011).

however we tend to see these changes as linear and incremental.[4] Those in major cities are likely to agree with the notion that 'my commute to work in five years will take a little longer than it does today' but few would opine that there will be no need to commute to work in five years as neither work nor commuting will exist as we know it now.

In our analyses,[5] we argue that evolutions in the digital environment will result in sharp breaks or disruptive changes in key aspects of our society and social functioning that many, at present, cannot anticipate. While our assessment of the impact of the digital environment has similarities with foresight analysis, the work conducted goes beyond trend analyses or scenario testing to examine the plausible interactions across a wide range of conceivable future developments. In this integrated analysis the potential for fundamental shifts in our society and in ourselves becomes apparent. In this way, our analysis outlines large scale patterns that are useful in anticipating plausible trajectories of change that, in turn, enable us to ask better questions of the present and to be better prepared for events in the future as these patterns unfold.

Changes in the Conditions of Change

> Humans can only grasp change at the rate they experience it.
>
> Advantageous—http://www.imdb.com/title/tt3090670/

In considering the implications of plausible future events, our thinking is informed by Taleb's (2001, 2007) conceptualization of black swans. Taleb uses the 16th Century metaphor of black swans to highlight how people will impose hindsight logic to suggest that major surprise events could have been or should have been anticipated. Although once considered impossible (in Europe), the existence of black swans becomes entirely plausible in retrospect (once Europeans visited Australia). Taleb argues that we need to address major surprise events (which he characterises as rare, disruptive and only predictable retrospectively) by seeking to create robust conditions to mediate the consequences of negative events and optimize the outcomes from positive ones. We suggest that many individuals, social institutions and organizations and, in particular, employers, ought to develop the capacity to capitalize on the types of disruptive social, economic and personnel changes that we see on the horizon.

In this regard, we caution that it is not just objects in the mirror that are closer than they may appear; both the driverless car and 3D printing have moved from scientific 'pipedreams' to reality with astonishing speed. When we do recognize

---

[4]For an illustration see Smil (2012).

[5]For an excellent presentation of foresight analysis as an important analytical tool as well as a summary of many outputs of these analyses, see the Government of Canada Policy Horizons website currently accessible at: http://www.horizons.gc.ca/eng.

that important changes are occurring, we tend to assume that we can see the implications relatively quickly. The creation of the Uber rideshare/taxi service is a good example. The core of the current commercial model posits the company dispatcher as the key link between the potential passenger and a licensed taxi driver. With the Uber model, this crucial role is replaced by automation, therefore, it displaces not only the dispatcher but also the licensed professional driver. But this is not the end state. In turn, the driverless car/automated vehicle may replace the Uber driver and could lead to the emergence of door-to-door publicly run mass transit. Thus, Uber should be understood as a stepping stone in the transition to a future state that we, as of yet, have not grasped.[6] As an illustration, the average car is parked for 95% of the day; what are we going to do with all of the space currently devoted to commercial parking garages and home driveways if these are no longer needed?[7]

In essence, our analyses make the case that the digital environment is a change in *the conditions of change*. New boundary conditions generate new attractors of efficiency that increasingly give primacy to anything that lowers the costs involved in generating and seizing opportunity. The nature of change is likely to have profound effects on societies writ large (Castells, 2000; Wellman, 2001). Many key institutions such as the health care system, public safety, policing, justice and education are based on a model of expert knowledge; professionals performing a unique service for society based on having mastered a body of knowledge and practice developed over years of intensive study.[8] Applications focussed on unique professional expertise (such as IBM's *Watson*, *Ross* for legal studies and *AlphaGo* beyond gaming) are not just changing how professionals conduct their business but also how society acquires the desired outcomes of good health, community safety, justice and education.

The central challenge when confronted with *changes in the conditions of change* is a lack of predictability. Just as the invention of the printing press eventually enabled the development of public education and consequently, violent revolutions throughout Europe, the inventions arising from the emerging digital environment will lead to similar disruptive social changes that can neither be accurately foreseen nor managed using current methods.

---

[6]An illustration come from the French Revolution. The Comité de salut public (Committee of Public Safety) served as an interim/transition form of governing between the previous *ancien régime* (rule by the Bourbon monarchs) and what would emerge as the form of government in France of today (see Allen, 2011).

[7]http://www.reinventingparking.org/2013/02/cars-are-parked-95-of-time-lets-check.html.

[8]In these cases it is the professional model that serves as the attractor of efficiency. These professions are struggling to maintain the status quo in the face of a new attractor of wide spread, easily accessed knowledge.

Evolutions in the Digital Environment

The Future Ain't What It Used To Be—misattributed to Yogi Berra[9]

The intent of this section is to make the case that imminent and fundamental changes in society, politics, economics and other key social arenas have the potential to challenge almost all current organizations and institutions as well as fundamentally altering the nature of work and the primary source of our wealth, human capital (Benkler, 2006; Davenport, 1999; Fontela, 2002). While we face a future we cannot yet fully imagine, this section provides some more concrete indicators or 'weak signals' of changes that are already unfolding and briefly describes some of the key shifts that are already consequential.[10]

Demographics and Age Inflation

The dramatic reversal of the traditional population age pyramid is not only the consequence of the baby boom bulge but also represents an unprecedented demographic situation in the developed nations of the 21st Century (Goda & Shoven, 2008). In conjunction with other trends (e.g. science/technology and medicine), as a society, we are heading into unchartered territory. We are developing new social structures that contain stages of life that have not been experienced or researched before (Oeppen & Vaupel, 2002). We are seeing the advent of a society with a quarter of its population over 'retirement' age, and yet still healthy and actively involved in their communities. Globally, the highest national-level life expectancies continue to increase almost linearly (increasing about 3 months every year) and showing no sign of leveling off (Lutz, Sanderson, & Scherbov 2004). With the cost of DNA sequencing likely to fall below $500,[11] we will see a phase transition in our approach to health and health research. In the coming decades, we will continue to live healthy, longer and more productive lives.

These demographic changes will not only change social structures but will also contribute to increasing social complexity. We are seeing increasing number of unique blended, extended and networked families with the emergence of 'Families of Choice' where individuals opt to form close, emotional ties with acquaintances rather than biological relatives (McCarty & Edwards, 2011). Redefining the nuclear

---

[9]It is more accurately attributed to Paul Valery as either "The future, like everything else, is no longer quite what it used to be" or "The trouble with our times is that the future is not what it used to be."

[10]With the caveat that there are numerous assessments being conducted in this area on a daily basis, we offer the work published by Policy Horizon's Canada as of value; see in particular Meta Scan 3: Emerging Technologies accessible at: http://www.horizons.gc.ca/eng/content/metascan-3-emerging-technologies-0.

[11]See the July 2016 summary of the costs of genome sequencing accessible at: https://www.genome.gov/sequencingcosts/. Media reports indicate some companies are suggesting the cost could reach $100: https://www.forbes.com/sites/matthewherper/2017/01/09/illumina-promises-to-sequence-human-genome-for-100-but-not-quite-yet/#2ba44045386d.

family structure has had numerous corollary effects, including, for some, redefinitions of the self and identity with, in particular, a corresponding extension of the period of socially defined 'youth'. Furthermore, most nations will continue to urbanize. Relatedly, the advent of the global 24/7 society is challenging traditional local rhythms. Technology is blurring boundaries between previously well-defined environments such as work and home. Network technologies and highly urbanized populations allow an ever-increasing range of social relations, exchanges, and choices that will enable the development of more socio-cultural interdependencies, tensions and individuals with multiple allegiances and antagonisms.

The confluence of increasing life-expectancy, age inflation, and low fertility rates (possibly accelerated through bio-medical, scientific and technological advance) has significant implications for dramatic change in social structure including:

- An extended and productive retirement—what will the Boomers do regarding community, political involvement and activism?
- A greater range and complexity of family structures—increasing number of four generational, multi-marriage, blended/extended/networked families
- Novel and un-researched life stages as mass numbers of people reach extended age while still healthy, engaged in the world and seeking to remain productive
- An extended period of socially defined 'youth' with further delays in achieving common markers of adulthood such as leaving the parental home, completing education, having children, getting married or buying a home.

Biotechnology and the Quantified Self

Biology is now an information science—whether the matter at hand is genes or chemicals. This is due, in part, to the convergence of many sciences forming the bio-cogni-nano-info technologies (the technologies arising from biological, cognitive, nano-and-smaller-scale, and the computational-data and artificial intelligence sciences). As these sciences and technologies continue to converge, new capabilities emerge resulting in ever more powerful computational-algorithmic-visualization technologies (Roco, Bainbridge, & Whitesides, 2013).

Smart devices especially wearables and/or sensor-based-apps and sensors embedded in virtually all products we use are tracking personal and other forms of behavioral information (Verdon, 2010). These apps support an increasing array of means to monitor health, behavior and social behaviours. By incorporating lessons learned from games and social physics, these data can help people find new forms of motivations to support their aims and their health.[12] The combination of information already available on the Internet, data arising from self-monitoring (e.g. the

---

[12]For illustrations, see Pentland's work at: http://socialphysics.media.mit.edu/ and that of Huamyze at: http://www.humanyze.com/.

quantified self) and the emergence of social platforms that enable extended support networks is already transforming how medical practitioners engage with clients as well as their families and support networks.[13] Medical professionals are facing the pressure to treat their patients and clients as equal partners who are empowered with self-knowledge.

These advances are accelerating the increasing use of robotics, artificial intelligence and telepresence. Robots will not only become fully integrated into surgical and other specialist teams but are also augmenting staff in hospitals, hospices and other care facilities and will play a significant role in home care. Providing specialist health services and care remotely through telepresence is already being enabled by robots and communication technologies allowing health professionals to provide real-time services including surgery, therapeutic counseling and more. In the next decade, these technologies will enable higher quality and more efficient delivery of medical services.[14]

New technologies are also benefiting from open-source and 'do it yourself' (DIY) movements and becoming the domain of emerging citizen scientists, inventors and entrepreneurs. Genetics and biotechnology labs are being created with advances demonstrated with the implantation of DNA nanobots in the bloodstream to detect and destroy cancer cells.[15] Other technologies on the horizon include regenerative medicine for creating tissue as blood vessels, bone/cartilage, organs/valves and skin and are not just grown in a 'vat' but produced through 3D printing.[16] In the next decade, virtual and augmented reality will enable the development of immersive environments for new forms of learning, interaction and healing between patients and health services.[17]

The emerging technology of the digital environment will expose the hidden aspects of not only our daily life but also the workings of our body, brains, minds and relationships—the rise of the transparent self—with a much greater expectation of deep individual assessment (medical, genetic, psychological, developmental, etc.). In conjunction with computational sciences, cognitive sciences are advancing the capabilities of language translation, artificial intelligence, software and increasingly capable robotics. These will have considerable implications for what people will expect in relation to training/development, education and related

---

[13]Here see Duncan Watts' 'The Organizational Spectroscope' at: https://medium.com/@duncanjwatts/the-organizational-spectroscope-7f9f239a897c#.gurew5ttg.

[14]For one illustration, see Ross Crawford, Anjali Jaiprakash & Jonathan Roberts, 10 Feb 2016 Robots in Health Care Could Lead to a Doctorless Hospital: http://singularityhub.com/2016/02/10/robots-in-health-care-could-lead-to-a-doctorless-hospital/.

[15]See DNA Nanobots Precisely Target And Shrink Tumors, Without Any Side Effects; accessible at: http://www.iflscience.com/health-and-medicine/dna-nanobots-precisely-target-and-shrink-tumors-without-any-side-effects/.

[16]See 3D Printing Of Human Organs With The Use Of Stem Cells; accessible at: https://humanlimbregeneration.com/3d-printing-of-human-organs-with-the-use-of-stem-cells.

[17]See Betsy Isaacson's article A Fitbit For Your Brain Is Around The Corner Newsweek 3 April 2016 accessible at: http://europe.newsweek.com/human-brain-eeg-technology-neuroscience-443368?rm=eu and David Eagleman: Can we create new senses for humans? accessible at: https://www.youtube.com/watch?v=4c1lqFXHvqI.

systems including those involved in the maintaining and evolving of any organi-zation's occupational structure (Doidge, 2007). To ease the human burden and amplify human capability, the cognitive sciences will hold the key to the necessarily human-centric design of the person-system interface in the developing ubiquitous digital environment.

This brief exploration of current and emerging biotechnology shows that we are approaching a *change in the conditions of change* that goes beyond how we proactively maintain health, to how we understand ourselves and ultimately, how much we manipulate the human body. At its most radical, biotechnology anticipates fundamental improvement or enhancements of human capability and more choices about how we choose to be or become—to the point of challenging our definitions of what it is to be human.

Additive Manufacturing and Artificial Intelligence

The boundaries between 3D printing, robotics, information-as-Big-Data (bits), and artificial intelligence are blurring at an accelerating pace.[18] The future, near- and long-term, involves the continual development of intelligent robotics (software/hardware) that are able to assemble themselves and other things out of elemental components to provide an ever increasing range of services—including the conduct of scientific explorations and discovery.[19] The concept of 4D printing is one of creating 'smart materials' that can change their shape or nature or even self-assemble into material forms with new, emergent properties.

Not only are computers becoming more powerful with computing paradigms being developed based on new forms of hardware (neural, memristor, quantum chips) but the "Big Data" emerging from the proliferation of sensors is also enabling new forms of algorithmic analyses. These are facilitating computational intelligence via machine learning, deep learning, neural networks, model-free analyses and more (Mullins, 2009).[20] Applications of these capabilities are evident in all domains from autonomous drones, image recognition to stock market trading and health care diagnosis. Within the next decade, we will see new forms of interacting with the digital environment enabled by voice, gesture and even thought.[21] Many of our transactions with businesses and appliances are already

---

[18]See The underestimated impact of the convergence of AI, IoT and big data analytics at: https://www.i-scoop.eu/convergence-ai-iot-big-data-analytics/.

[19]See Who will own the robots at: http://www.technologyreview.com/featuredstory/538401/who-will-own-the-robots/?utm_campaign=newsletters&utm_source=newsletter-daily-all&utm_medium=email&utm_content=20150616.

[20]While the label Big Data is indicative of the sheer volume of data that can be assembled, the term is indicative of the more integrative understandings, conclusions and predictions that can be drawn from these data. The new forms of algorithms need to manipulate these data are increasingly referred to as data analytics.

[21]See Device that can literally read your mind invented by scientists at: http://www.independent.co.uk/news/science/read-your-mind-brain-waves-thoughts-locked-in-syndrome-toyohashi-japan-a7687471.html.

becoming accessible via our mobile and wearable devices. For example, in 2015, the Associated Press wrote ten times more articles using artificial intelligence than human authors.[22] Another example is IBM's Watson beginning to advise U.S. veterans in making decisions such as where to live or what insurance to buy. Watson also advises chefs, scientists and lawyers. The claim from IBM is that Watson assists/augments the work people have to do—enabling counselors, salespeople, chefs, paralegals, researchers and many more to be more productive. In the next decade we will see whether this technology replaces or assists people.

In terms of transaction costs, these advances will provide a rather fundamental challenge to the entire array of business activities related to designing, producing and selling products and services to consumers. We found Jeremey Refkin's (2014) ideas on zero marginal cost to be compelling and concur with his assessment of a fundamental change from an economics of scarcity toward the need to develop a new economic paradigm of managing abundance. Thus, not only are entire sectors of employment likely to be displaced but that the fundamental role of the business sector in providing us with the goods that we seek to obtain is going to be replaced with new systems. Again, we are much closer to the Star Trek 'replicator' than many recognize.

Energy and the Learning Curve

We are now on the threshold of a phase transition (a change in the conditions of change) in relation to the energy that powers societies. The speed of the transition will be two-fold—one dimension based on the exponential drop in price/performance of solar and other renewables and the other dimension involves the shift in investment from traditional energy resources towards renewables. Investment money is already beginning to shift based on the inherent risks of a competitive return on investment (McCrone, 2017).

A common feature of all emerging technology is the learning curve that is used to help assess the future change in costs. The essential point is that the more a technology is used, built or implemented, the cheaper the technology is to produce (Papineau, 2006). Photovoltaic energy is the fastest growing energy source with continued declines in cost (Fu, Feldman, Margolis, Woodhouse & Ardani, 2017). Although it continues to depend on energy storage technology to attain its real potential, its price is at parity with current electricity sources. Changes in coal, oil or gas cost trajectories have become irrelevant as renewable energy sources approach become cheaper while technological improvements in efficiency, installation and distribution accelerate. A key contributing factor in the emerging new energy paradigm will involve a shift in investment from the traditional energy sector to the renewable energy sector (McCrone, 2017).

---

[22]See http://www.theverge.com/2015/1/29/7939067/ap-journalism-automation-robots-financial-reporting.

Based on current trajectories, the energy invested to install solar energy is estimated be returned within six months and by 2030 will surpass the energy invested-returned ratio of oil and gas (Philibert, 2011). Despite the fact that solar and wind energy will be cheaper than coal or natural gas within a decade, the current key question is persistent continuous supply of energy in the face of discontinuous supply of sunlight and wind energy (Hulac, 2015). This means that energy storage is now a key enabling technology. However, energy storage costs have decreased exponentially for over two decades. Using a model of a 20% learning curve per doubling of capacity, analysts have projected that Lithium-ion batteries will reach 5 cents/kilowatt-hour by 2030.[23]

While much of the focus of current thinking regarding energy is on the shift from carbon-based to alternate sources with related changes in how power is used, the more critical shifts will occur in who owns new sources and who benefits from these. While the economic impact on petro-states such as Canada are becoming clear, we have not yet identified the relationships between States, corporations or individuals in the production and usage of new energies let alone the ways in which these will fundamentally change how our societies function.

Knowledge Creation, Social Computing and the Collaborative Commons

We have highlighted significant changes occurring in the realm of data creation; a similar revolution is occurring in the domain of knowledge creation. The key is social computing, which is a general reference to the intersection of social behaviour and computational systems. One use of social computing involves social media where software is used to create platforms, social conventions and contexts; blogs, email, instant messaging, social network services, wikis, social bookmarking and tagging and other 'social software' applications (Barnaghi et al., 2015). These platforms provide a space and a structure for shaping social interactions.

There is a sense of social computing that has to do with computations carried out by 'masses' of people. This involves some of the ideas popularized in Surowiecki's (2005) 'Wisdom of Crowds': collaborative filtering, online auctions, prediction markets, reputations systems, and even some massive multiplayer online games. New fora for knowledge creation such as Galaxy Zoo (astronomy), FoldIt (biology: enzymes) and EteRNA (biology: RNA) are examples where experts are harnessing the capacities of large groups (crowdsourcing knowledge) and reducing transactions costs with Wikipedia representing the best example of a collaborative knowledge commons where millions of users come together to both update and draw on the accessible information. This idea is presented as:

---

[23]http://rameznaam.com/2014/09/30/the-learning-curve-for-energy-storage/ and http://reneweconomy. com.au/2014/stored-electricity-heads-to-0-05kwh-by-2030-39889 It is important to note that other storage technologies are also progressing.

...the vision of the Creative Commons – a collaboration and knowledge governance framework is nothing less than realizing the full potential of the evolving digital environment: universal access to research, researchers, learning and full participation in a culture of knowledge flow to drive a new era of development, growth and productivity - http://creativecommons.org/about[24]

Underlying these evolutions are changes in how we validate, control and update knowledge. At present, our society uses mechanisms such as peer-reviewed journal articles or approved school/university curricula to standardize 'the truth' and many organizations and institutions rely on formal publications (policies, rules sets, guidelines, doctrine) to govern day-to-day practices. Control over the use of knowledge is, in fact, the key attractor of efficiency that has led to the creation of the entire function of 'middle management' in hierarchical organizations. A focus of all institutions is to maintain legitimacy both in the eyes of internal and external audiences (Scott, 2001; Shirky, 2008).[25] The ability for individuals to apply, generate, and exchange knowledge without mediation by the 'experts' or 'authorities' means more self-directed collaboration (Carr, 2009; Hagel et al., 2010). While ensuring that knowledge flows from where it is created to where it is needed, self-directed collaboration is challenging existing control mechanisms and sources of power (Brafman & Beckstrom, 2006; Fairtlough, 2008). Keeping human efforts aligned to higher level effects, while simultaneously promoting agility and innovation, will require more types of responsible autonomy enabling permission-less or self-directed collaboration within increasingly complex environments (Bunge, 2007; Varian & Shapiro 1998).

Beyond requiring organizations to develop new methods of collaborative governance to harness human knowledge or capital, the evolutions in social computing and knowledge creation will serve as the leading edge of significant changes that will affect today's youth. As will be developed more fully in the following chapter on Education, we are already seeing fundamental shifts in not only what children are learning in school but also how they are learning and how they are learning to learn.

Summary of Major Changes

This section outlines five major domains experiencing changes in the conditions of change: Demographic, Biotechnology, Manufacturing, Energy and Knowledge. In each domain, the trajectory is toward new attractors with profound implications for social and economic structures. When considering the likely rise of cheap energy, extreme customization in manufacturing, Big Data-Algorithmic-Intelligence creating the Internet-of-Everything, and the technological domestication of DNA with new advances in gene therapy—it is impossible not to imagine some deeply fundamental changes in the future. The consequences are already evident, although still

---

[24]Reprinted under Creative Commons licensing at: https://creativecommons.org/policies/#license.
[25]See our reports produced by Ouellet & Balakhnina and Chap. 8 for further analyses.

nascent: self-driving cars, intelligent logistics and supply chains, new forms of currency and mediums of exchange and massively distributed energy. The central implication is an increasing shift from centralized control structures to distributed, networked and self-organized systems in many domains, including:

- Governance—with increasing enablement of participatory engagement
- Leadership—from a mythic-meme of individual heroism to one of co-created futures
- Work—more forms of social computing and distributed enterprises—harnessing pro-sumers[26] to engage in continually evolving form of work, rather than hiring labor for stable predetermined jobs
- Energy—Distributed production of solar, wind, and other renewal, cheap forms of energy
- Mass Transit—driverless vehicles to access models of transportation
- Business—Pro-sumer, Distributed and Commons-Based models
- Education—assembling forms of curiosity-driven educational models such as MOOCs, Youtube, etc.
- Currency—new form of distributed post-sovereign-central bank models of currency institutions
- Capital—from extraction of raw resources to creative human productive capacity
- Accounting—ubiquitous value recording and automated accounting capacities
- Health—Quantified Self, IoT-sensors and Bio-social-computing.

Our central argument is that these evolutions have already started to alter many facets of our lives and will increasingly serve as major disruptive forces that will require new ways of organizing and regulating our personal, social, economic and political affairs. These same forces of change will present us with the new attractors that will in turn generate further new systems. Although it would be impossible to posit the form that these systems will take at this stage, we are suggesting that it is of benefit to start to anticipate changes, and it is of paramount importance that we ensure that the youth of today are prepared to deal with these. Thus, having presented our expansive assessment of the possibilities arising from evolutions in the digital environment, the final section in this chapter will look at the current state of the digital environment with an emphasis on the youth of today.

Where Are We Today?

In summarizing our integrative analyses of the evolving digital environment, we started by stretching beyond what we can confidently know or project to suggest that our society is on the precipice of a fundamental *change in the conditions of*

---

[26]The term pro-sumers refers to the fact that individuals will concurrently be producers and consumers in key areas such as new knowledge, current events, energy and what are now, commercial goods and services.

change that will take us in directions yet to be sensed or recognized. We presented major changes occurring in five key domains with illustrations as to the ways in which these are likely to affect our lives. This final section will bring the focus back to the present day with a short summary of how youth are engaging with their digital surroundings.

Internet Access and the Digital Divide

Internet access has continued to increase in the majority of the globe with US and Canada ranked around 20th in the world in 2016 with the same 88.5% penetration rate, which is just above the mean of 87% for advanced economies.[27] While statistics on the use of smartphones continue to evolve rapidly, as a marker of the fastest growing medium to access the Internet, 72% of American adults and 67% of Canadian own a smartphone again comparable to the mean of 68% for advanced economies. Several reports note that usage by key sub-groups in both countries is reaching the saturation point and that the gap in penetration rates between developed and developing nations is narrowing quickly.

Perhaps nothing illustrates the current context better than the estimates of the information shared in an average minute. An excellent illustration is presented in Fig. 1.2 depicting an analysis of the content shared via popular digital media.

In assessing the impact of the internet on youth, sweeping generalizations are to be avoided. Belonging to an age cohort by no means defines the individual nor will we suggest that all youth have equal access to technology or, when they do, share equal experiences. There exists a "digital divide" between those who have access to technology and those who do not (Boiling et al., 2012; Sciadas, 2002) although some identify the divide as between those who have and those who have more (Paulas, 2016). In many countries, including the US and Canada, Internet penetration in rural and northern communities is less than in urban and suburban centres; however, governments are attempting to close this gap through access in schools.[28] Further, access to the Internet is stratified by income. According to Statistics Canada in 2014, nearly all families within the top income quartile had access to the Internet at home, while only half of families in the lowest quartile had similar access. US data are similar with 93% of households earning over $75,000 having

---

[27]For Internet penetration see: http://www.internetlivestats.com/internet-users-by-country/ and for international comparisons see: http://www.pewglobal.org/2016/02/22/smartphone-ownership-and-internet-usage-continues-to-climb-in-emerging-economies/.

[28]Chen et al. (2014) reported that 99% of Ontario schools reported providing access to computers with 80% reporting access starting in kindergarten. In the US, President Obama's ConnectED initiative is intended to provide Internet connectivity to 99% of American schools by 2018.

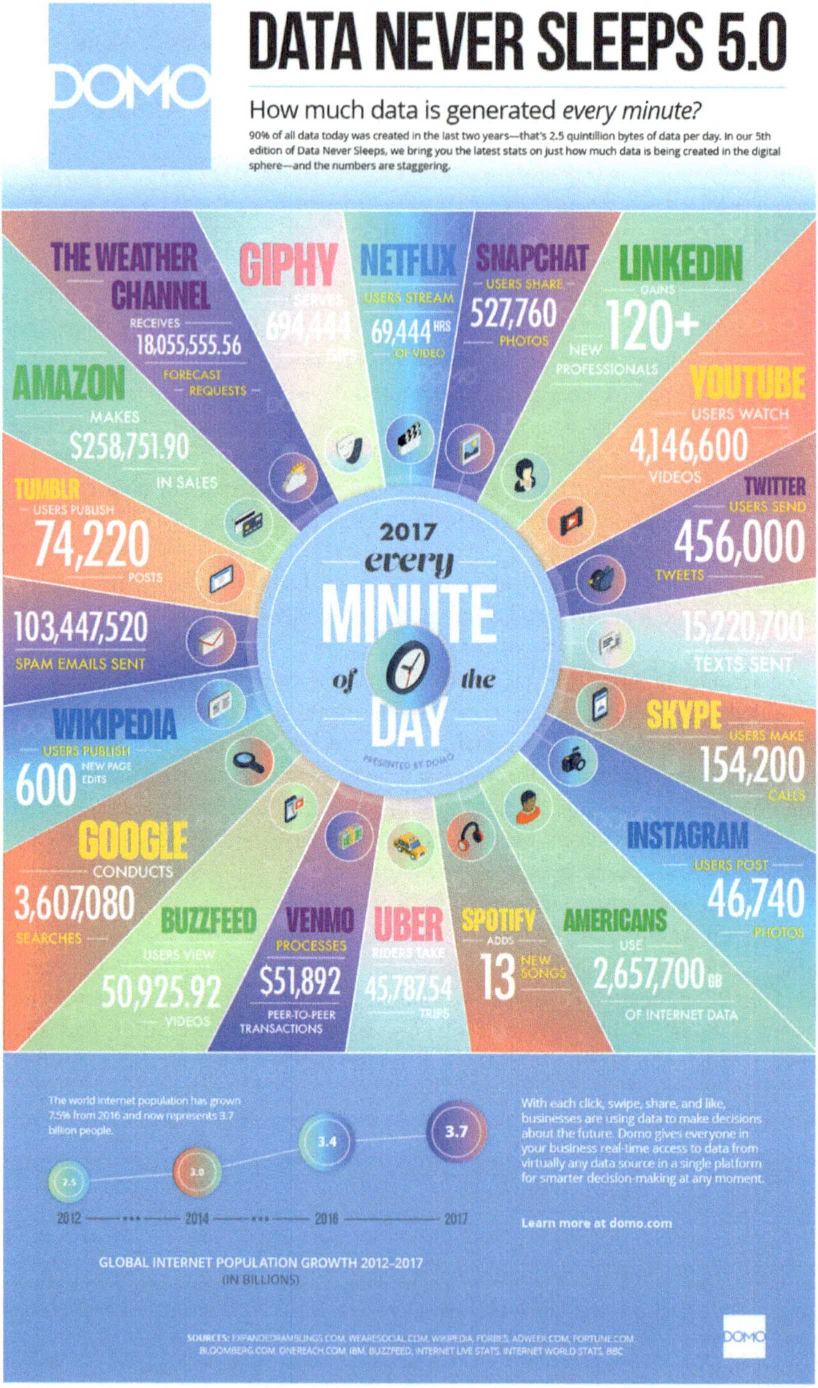

DATA NEVER SLEEPS 5.0

How much data is generated *every minute?*

90% of all data today was created in the last two years—that's 2.5 quintillion bytes of data per day. In our 5th edition of Data Never Sleeps, we bring you the latest stats on just how much data is being created in the digital sphere—and the numbers are staggering.

THE WEATHER CHANNEL
RECEIVES
18,055,555.56
FORECAST REQUESTS

GIPHY
SERVES
694,444 GIFS

NETFLIX
USERS STREAM
69,444 HRS
OF VIDEO

SNAPCHAT
— USERS SHARE —
527,760 PHOTOS

LINKEDIN
GAINS
120+ NEW PROFESSIONALS

AMAZON
MAKES
$258,751.90
IN SALES

YOUTUBE
USERS WATCH
4,146,600 VIDEOS

TUMBLR
USERS PUBLISH
74,220 POSTS

TWITTER
USERS SEND
456,000 TWEETS

103,447,520
SPAM EMAILS SENT

15,220,700
TEXTS SENT

WIKIPEDIA
USERS PUBLISH NEW PAGE EDITS
600

SKYPE
USERS MAKE
154,200 CALLS

GOOGLE
CONDUCTS
3,607,080 SEARCHES

INSTAGRAM
USERS POST
46,740 PHOTOS

BUZZFEED
USERS VIEW
50,925.92 VIDEOS

VENMO
PROCESSES
$51,892
PEER-TO-PEER TRANSACTIONS

UBER
RIDERS TAKE
45,787.54 TRIPS

SPOTIFY
ADDS
13 NEW SONGS

AMERICANS
USE
2,657,700 GB
OF INTERNET DATA

2017
every
MINUTE
of **the**
DAY
PRESENTED BY DOMO

The world internet population has grown 7.5% from 2016 and now represents 3.7 billion people.

2.5 — 3.0 — 3.4 — 3.7

2012 — 2014 — 2016 — 2017

GLOBAL INTERNET POPULATION GROWTH 2012–2017
(IN BILLIONS)

With each click, swipe, share, and like, businesses are using data to make decisions about the future. Domo gives everyone in your business real-time access to data from virtually any data source in a single platform for smarter decision-making at any moment.

Learn more at domo.com

SOURCES: EXPANDEDRAMBLINGS.COM, WEARESOCIAL.COM, WIKIPEDIA, FORBES, ADWEEK.COM, FORTUNE.COM, BLOOMBERG.COM, ONEREACH.COM, IBM, BUZZFEED, INTERNET LIVE STATS, INTERNET WORLD STATS, BBC

◄ **Fig. 1.2** Illustration of Amount of Data Usage

high speed access at home as compared to 53% for those earning less that $30,000.[29] Kassam et al. (2013) also identify a divide between those who do and do not use technology—by preference or lack of computer literacy—regardless of accessibility.

A key area of differentiation across both age and income groups pertains to the use of technology. When comparing older to younger individuals, the most common usage shifts from email, banking and shopping to games and online gaming to social media. The implications of these differences in use for younger individuals will be discussed next.

Teens as Digital Natives and the Rise of Social Media

As this connected world emerged during the time when Millennials entered their teens and young adulthood, many Millennials have developed characteristics that are assumed to apply to the future disposition of Post-Millennials. Accordingly, much of this section describes the relationship between the Millennial and Post-Millennial generations and the digital world.

The Millennial generation distinguishes 'traditional' from 'digital' generations (Strauss & Howe, 2000). Many Millennials have had access to digital technology since childhood. Only once Millennials grew older did telephones become unplugged, digital music devices replace the compact disc, and the high-pitched tones of a telephone modem were silenced (Rainer & Rainer, 2011). For many as adults, modern technology is thoroughly integrated into their professional, social, and academic lives (Pew Research Center, 2015). Millennials' embrace of technology can likely be traced to their childhoods: many parents who put their children at the centre of their lives were eager to provide these early devices for them, and, in doing so, seeded their embrace of technology as adults.

From their earliest moments, the majority of Post-Millennials were exposed to mature technologies: instant messaging, wireless Internet, and computers of exponentially greater speed and power than those from the 1990s. As we will present in subsequent chapters, for most in this generation, the Internet is a social construct as much as it is a tool. They can be 'connected' to billions of individuals, terabytes of data, and an evolving online culture. With the emergence of social media in the first years of the 21st century, socialization for young people can now be intertwined by access to, and use of, technology. To be sure, socialization occurs in many traditional fora including with family in the home, friends on the playground and cultural and community events, however, easy access to the digital environment for many means that social media are increasingly used for making sense of their real-life experiences. In our work, social media is defined as the

---

[29]Based on the 2018 Pew Research "Internet/Broadband Fact Sheet" accessible at: http://www.pewinternet.org/fact-sheet/internet-broadband/.

digital structure and the resulting products of services that allow individuals to create and share information while building or maintaining relationships between users. At the time of publication, Facebook, Twitter, Instagram, Reddit and Tumblr are among the most popular social networks in the world.[30]

The vast majority of Post-Millennials have embraced social media and technology in all aspects of their lives. Lenhart (2015) found that 92% of young American respondents accessed social media at least once a day with 24% reporting accessing 'almost constantly'. Internet access is no longer restricted to the home computer; many in this cohort have access to multiple, connected devices such as smartphones, laptops, and tablets. Access to a mobile device is almost a given among the cohort and forms an integral part in Post-millennials' social interactions. Smart phones can be used to access the Internet, play games, and listen to music, but research indicates that many Post-Millennials use their devices mainly to engage on social media.[31] Even when interacting face-to-face, the social lives of this cohort can be tied to technology such as through sharing text messages to discussing the latest meme or Internet sensation. This pervasive technological influence transcends enabling daily obligations; whether the individual is fully aware of it or not, technology is increasingly integrated into the ways that they socialize, learn, and interact with the world around them (Rainer & Rainer, 2011). As Mack states (2012): "This generation takes for granted a world of smartphones, tablets and high-speed wireless Internet—24/7 digital connections. They're also wired to socialize digitally, which is reshaping how kids communicate and with whom."[32]

How ingrained is the digital world in the DNA of post-Millennials? Nearly 40% of Canadian students who owned digital devices revealed that they sleep with their devices so that they can engage with their peers at any time; including 20% of those in Grade Four (Steeves, 2014). One might conclude that Post-Millennials are slaves to their phones, and they are lacking in social skills due to their preference for digital communication. This complaint is particularly pronounced amongst the Boomer generation, who are less familiar with technology, or Generation X, who according to Leuprecht et al. (2016), take issue with Millennials' social media etiquette. We argue the opposite: that Post-Millennials are socially engaged, and that it is 'socialization' that is changing. Much of the literature we reviewed suggests that young Millennials and Post-Millennials socialize in a different way than their elders. Millennials rely on technology and social networking sites to solidify friendships with peers (Pempek et al., 2009). These young people effectively communicate with their multiple peers at once through their devices, often a short sentence at a time. This method speaks to the Millennial and Post-Millennial preference for finding efficiency through multitasking, a trait discussed in Chap. 4.

---

[30]Drawn from: Top 15 Most Popular Social Networking Sites and Apps [February 2018] accessible at: https://www.dreamgrow.com/top-15-most-popular-social-networking-sites/.

[31]https://www.commonsensemedia.org/research/zero-to-eight-childrens-media-use-in-america-2013/key-finding-2%3A-kids%27-time-on-mobile-devices-triples.

[32]Quoted in the post "Gen Z: Digital in their DNA—Study examines attitudes and tech habits of teens and tweens, and their parents" 1 May 2012, accessible at: https://www.jwt.com/en/worldwide/news/genzdigitalintheirdnastudyexaminesattitudesandtechhabitsofteensandtweensandtheirparents/.

Another indicator of the changing nature of socialization is the emergence of new methods of civic engagement. Usage of the Internet for socialization amongst younger cohorts extends beyond a circle of friends: Millennials and Post-Millennials are reported to use technology to engage with both their local and the global communities (Cone Inc., 2006; Stauss & Howe, 2000). The ability to dedicate leisure time and leverage the Internet to collaborate and coordinate on matters of civic importance—the sum of which Shirky (2008) has termed "cognitive surplus"—may be how Post-Millennials will volunteer in the future.[33]

Technology has also changed how many in this generation learn about significant events. The Internet now allows for news to be understood beyond the lens of traditional media: users are able to glean insights from media outlets from across the globe, first-hand accounts, videos, blogs, and online conversations including real time events with a cacophony of multiple concurrent opinions being shared. Many turn to the free, online information depositories such as Wikipedia (which in and of itself is a social media site) as these serve to unite communities passionate about dissemination of information. This access to information, along with the ability to triangulate different sources, has the potential to empower many Post-Millennials to observe and analyze the world around them from a multitude of perspectives.

This is not to say that they will. Indeed, a real concern we and other researchers have found pertains to digital "echo chambers", where social groups and online exposure only serve to reinforce shallow viewpoints, limiting exposure to broader, alternate or contradictory views as well as the recent phenomenon of 'fake news'. If "the medium is the message", then sites such as Facebook and Twitter can embed assumptions and influences through the presentation and perception of the content generated by their users and influenced by the advertisers who actually generate their profits. In this regard, we found recent US studies to be of interest. In assessing Twitter usage in the United States, Colleoni et al. (2014) found Democrats and Republicans on the site exhibited levels of political homophily: their social media feeds resemble partisan echo chambers more than lively debate. Bakshy et al. (2015) examined whether Facebook's system of highlighting posts on a users' homepage inadvertently creates such an echo chamber. They found that, although Facebook's algorithms play a role, the primary source of homophily on that site is the user: 'Facebookers' read *what they want* to read. Similarly, in their analyses of the spread of misinformation on Facebook, Del Vicario et al. (2016) concluded that homogeneity and polarization of views were the greatest contributors to the degree of spread.

Concerns about the darker side of digital social interaction grow larger when considering online discussion boards or commenting systems where a user need not be identified: the relative anonymity the Internet permits allows individuals to present their opinion (often rather aggressively) without ever having to formally articulate or defend their point of view or even acknowledge that other perspectives exist. When mixed with vitriol, social media gives birth to digital 'trolls'. In this

---

[33]Clay Shirkey—TED Talk accessible at: https://www.ted.com/talks/clay_shirky_how_cognitive_surplus_will_change_the_world?language=en.

regard, we noted that a number of major news outlets have deleted the 'below the line' option for individuals to post comments on stories. We will expand on this issue in Chap. 5 with additional considerations of the 'darkside' of the internet for teens. Thus, while some have seen on-line fora as a key tool in creating the spaces for broad sectors of society to exchange opinions, the anonymity provided often serves to create the opposite effects of entrenched and often inflamed views with limited tolerance for, let alone, understanding of, alternate perspectives. As a final comment in this regard, Verdon posits the evolutions of the digital environment as the end of the concepts of anonymity or privacy as we current know these with a return to social orders based on the premise that everybody does (or can) know everything about anybody. As with many of the topics addressed in this volume, to a large extent, only time will tell how the Post-Millennials will learn to navigate through, and make sense of, the information environment.

Finally, to reprise the digital divide(s), as much as access to technology is not uniform, there may be a divide forming with regards to social media. The emergence of social media has changed the nature of the digital divide (Haight et al., 2014). They believe that demographics influence the adoption of social media, which accordingly creates 'new divides' between those with or without access to technology, those able and unable to use said technology, and between those who engage in social media and those who do not. It remains to be seen how the socialization process will differ between those 'plugged in' and those 'unplugged' however our analyses identified that the key question to consider is what the world will be like when Internet access is invisible because it is ubiquitous.

Conclusion

This chapter has provided the key highlights from our broad and integrative futures analysis, which leads us to conclude that the emerging digital environment will serve as a fundamental change in the conditions of change and will serve to create significant alterations in social order and the nature of the lives most people will life. We outlined five major domains experiencing changes in the conditions of change—Demographic, Biotechnology, Manufacturing, Energy and Knowledge. In each domain, the trajectory is toward a new 'attractor of efficiency' with profound implications for social and economic structures. A key challenge is that neither the new attractor nor the resultant new systems, structures or implications are, as yet, apparent. As has happened when civilizations have gone through significant social upheavals, what is clear is that there will be a period when individuals and institutions as collectives will seek to maintain the existing approaches and their social legitimacy while others will be seeking to replace these with something new—and that these changes will cut across an array of social, economic, political and community domains.[34]

Moving to the present, it is apparent that most in the current youth cohort are living a 'connected' life. While they may not literally have digital in their DNA, they most certainly are immersed in a digital world. We will provide additional analyses of the implications in subsequent chapters but will note that, while some lag their peers in access and usage based on predictable factors, virtually all are aware of the digital environment and even those who do not have ongoing access interact with others who do. Thus, regardless of their personal usage, this evolving digital environment is influencing them all. We will provide more of our analyses on how in subsequent chapters, however, we see the Post-Millennial cohort as likely to exhibit many of the characteristics observed in the Millennials who entered the digital world as they moved into their late youth and young adulthood. This next generation, however, has the capacity to communicate in a different way: briefly, digitally and, sometimes, to a global audience. Today's youth have the ability to understand, react, and contribute to world events from a plethora of sources. Similarly, Millennials are also able to use technology to volunteer in communities of all sizes. Whether they will use this access to broaden their horizons or broadcast a narrow viewpoint remains to be seen. With access to incredible amounts of information, socialization, devices, and media, many Post-Millennials are becoming adept multitaskers. As we will develop further, when employed, we expect many to increasingly use technology to facilitate collaborative work environments and increase workplace efficiency. In embracing this efficiency, employers will likely be concerned with building a globally-minded workforce, adapting processes to a cohort of multitaskers, and adapting to the privacy risks associated with the first truly connected generation.

References

Allen, D. W. (2011). *The institutional revolution: Measurement and the economic emergence of the modern world*. Chicago: University of Chicago Press.

Bakshy, E., Messing, S., & Adamic, L. A. (2015). Exposure to ideologically diverse news and opinion on Facebook. *Science, 348*(6239), 1130–1132.

Barnaghi, P., Sheth, A., Singh, V., & Hauswirth, M. (2015). Physical-cyber-social computing: Looking back looking forward. *IEEE Internet Computing, 19*(3), 7–11.

Benkler, Y. (2006). *Wealth of networks: How social production transforms markets and freedom*. New Haven: Yale University Press.

Brafman, O., & Beckstrom, R. A. (2006). *The starfish and the spider: The unstoppable power of leaderless organizations*. London: Penguin.

Brody, M. (2009). Understanding our digital universe: Unleashing natural forces. In *Proceedings IEEE International Conference on Digital Ecosystems and Technologies*, IEEE Press, http://www.michaelbrodie.com/documents/_Research_MLB_Presos_Publications_Confs_Our_Digital_Universe_DEST09_UnderstandingDigitalUniverse.pdf.

---

[34]For a provocative presentation, see Jordan Greenhall's Situational Assessment 2018: the Calm Before the Storm, accessible at: https://medium.com/deep-code/situational-assessment-2018-the-calm-before-the-storm-5a0bd014ec84.

Brynjolfsson, E., & Saunders, A. (2009). *Wired for innovation: How information technology is reshaping the economy*. Cambridge: MIT Press.

Bunge, R. (2007). *Using Crowd Power for R&D*. Wired accessible at: http://www.wired.com/techbiz/media/news/2007/07/crowdsourcing_diversity.

Carr, N. (2009). *The big switch: Rewiring the world from edison to google*. New York: Norton.

Castells, M. (2000). *The rise of the network society*. Oxford: Blackwell Publishers.

Chen, B., Gallagher-Mackay, K., & Kidder, A. (2014). *Digital learning in Ontario schools: The 'new normal'*. Toronto, ON: People for Education. Retrieved from http://www.peopleforeducation.ca/wp-content/uploads/2014/03/digital-learning-2014-WEB.pdf.

Colleoni, E., Rozza, A., & Arvidsson, A. (2014). Echo chamber or public sphere? Predicting political orientation and measuring political homophily in twitter using big data. *Journal of Communication, 64*(2), 317–332.

Cone Inc. & AMP Insights. (2006). *Millennial cause study—The Millennial generation: Pro-social and empowered to change the world*. Retrieved from http://blogthinkbig.com/wp-content/uploads/Cone-Millennial-Cause-Study-La-hora-de-cambiar-el-mundo.pdf.

Davenport, T. O. (1999). *Human capital: What it is and why people invest it*. San Francisco: Jossey-Bass.

De Landa, M. (1997). *A thousand years of nonlinear history*. New York: Zone Books.

De Landa, M. (2012). Emergence, causality and realism. *Architectural Theory Review, 17*(1), 3–16.

Del Vicario, M., Bessi, A., Zollo, F., Petroni, F., Scalaa, A., Caldarellia, G., et al. (2016). The spreading of misinformation online. *Proceedings of the National Academy of Sciences of the United States of America, 113*(3), 554–559.

Denning, P. J. (2001). *The invisible future: The seamless integration of technology into everyday life*. New York: MaGraw-Hill.

Doctorow, C. (2012). Disorganised but effective: How technology lowers transaction costs. *The Guardian*. Retrieved from http://www.theguardian.com/technology/2012/jun/21/how-technology-lowers-transaction-costs.

Doidge, N. (2007). *The brain that changes itself*. New York: Penguin.

Fairtlough, G. (2008). *Open secrets! Innovation through openness*. Axminster, UK: Triarchy Press.

Fontela, E. (2002). From the wealth of nations to the wealth of the world. *Foresight, 4*(1), 6–12.

Fu, R., Feldman, D., Margolis, R., Woodhouse, M., & Ardani, K. (2017) *U.S. solar photovoltaic system cost benchmark*. Golden, CO: National Renewable Energy Laboratory.

Goda, G. S., & Shoven, J. B. (2008). Adjusting government policies for age inflation. In John Shoven (Ed.), *Demography and the economy*. Chicago: University of Chicago Press.

Goldsmith, S., & Eggers, D. W. (2004). *governing by network: The new shape of the public sector*. Washington D.C.: Brookings Institution.

Graeber, D. (2004). *Fragments of an anarchist anthropology*. Cambridge, UK: Prickly Paradigm Press.

Greenfield, A. (2006). *Everyware: The dawning age of ubiquitous computing*. Berkley, CA: Peachpit Press.

Hagel, J., Brown, J. S. & Davison, L. (2010). *The Power of Pull: How Small Moves, Smartly Made, Can Set Big Things in Motion*. London: Basic Books.

Haight, M., Quan-Haase, A. & Corbett, B. A. (2014). Revisiting the digital divide in Canada: the impact of demographic factors on access to the internet, level of online activity, and social networking site usage. *Information, Communication & Society, 17* (4), 503–519.

Hulac, B. (2015) Strong future forecast for renewable energy. *Scientific American*, 27 April 2015.

Kassam, A., Idling, M. & Hogenbirk, P. (2013). Unraveling the digital divide: Time well spent or "wasted"? *Education and Information Technologies, 18* (2), 215–221.

Kelly, K. (2008). Predicting the Next 5000 Days of the Web. TED Talks at http://www.ted.com/index.php/talks/kevin_kelly_on_the_next_5_000_days_of_the_web.html.

Lenhart, A. (2015). *Teen, social media and technology overview 2015*. Washington: Pew Research Center.

Leuprecht, C., Skillicorn, D. B., & Tait, V. (2016). Beyond the Castle Model of cyber-risk and cyber-security. *Government Information Quarterly, 33*(2), 250–257.

Lutz, W., Sanderson, C. W., & Scherbov, S. (2004). *The end of world population growth in the 21st century: New challenges for human capital formation & sustainable development.* London: Earthscan.

McCarty, J. R., & Edwards, R. (2011). *Key concepts in family studies.* New York: Sage.

McCrone, A. (2017). *Global trends in renewable energy investment.* Frankfurt: Frankfurt School of Finance & Management.

Mullins, J. (2009). Memristor minds: The future of artificial intelligence. *New Scientist, Issue 2715.*

Oeppen, J., & Vaupel, W. J. (2002). Broken limits to life expectancy. *Science, 296*(5570), 1029–1031.

Okros, A. C., Verdon, J., & Chouinard, P. (2011). *The meta-organization: A research and conceptual landscape.* (DRDC CSS TR 2011-13). Ottawa, ON: Defence Research and Development Canada.

Papineau, M. (2006). An economic perspective on experience curves and dynamic economies in renewable energy technologies. *Energy Policy, 34,* 422–432.

Paulas, R. (2016) *The digital divide is about much more than access.* Pacific Standard Newspaper https://psmag.com/the-digital-divide-is-about-much-more-than-access-6cf366bbee68#.7wi7pbrju.

Pempek, T. A, Yermolayeva, Y. A., & Calvert, S. L. (2009). College students' social networking experiences on Facebook. *Journal of Applied Developmental Psychology, 30*(3), 227–238.

Pew Research Center. (2015). *Comparing Millennials to other generations.* Retrieved from http://www.pewsocialtrends.org/2010/02/24/interactive-graphic-demographic-portrait-of-four-generations/.

Philibert, C. (2011). *Solar energy perspectives.* Paris: International Energy Agency.

Raimi, L., & Wellman, B. (2012). *Networked: The new social operating system.* Cambridge: MIT Press.

Rainer, T., & Rainer, J. (2011). *The Millennials: Connecting to the largest generation.* Nashville, TN: B&H Publishing Group.

Refkin, J. (2014). *The zero marginal cost society: The Internet of things, the collaborative commons, and the eclipse of capitalism.* New York: Palgrave Macmillan.

Roco, W. S., Bainbridge, B. T. & Whitesides, G. (2103) *Convergence of knowledge, technology and society: Beyond convergence of nano-bio-info-cognitive technologies.* London: Springer.

Schwartz, P. (2003). *Inevitable surprises: Thinking ahead in a time of turbulence.* New York: Gotham Books.

Sciadas, G. (2002). The digital divide in Canada. Ottawa, ON: Statistics Canada.

Scott, W. R. (2001). *Institutions and organizations.* New York: Sage.

Shirky, C. (2008). *Institutions versus Collaboration.* TED Talks at http://www.ted.com/index.php/talks/clay_shirky_on_institutions_versus_collaboration.html.

Smil, V. (2012). *Global catastrophes and trends: The next fifty years.* Cambridge: MIT Press.

Steeves, V. (2014). Young Canadians in a Wired World, Phase III: Life Online. Ottawa: ON, MediaSmarts.

Strauss, W., & Howe, N. (2000). *Millennials rising: The next great generation* (3rd ed.). New York: Vintage Books.

Strayer, J. R. (2005). *On the medieval origins of the modern state.* Princeton: Princeton University Press.

Taleb, N. N. (2001). *Fooled by randomness: The hidden role of chance in life and in the markets.* New York: Random House.

Taleb, N. N. (2007). *The black swan: The impact of the highly improbable.* New York: Random.

Tocchetti, S. (2014) *How did DNA become hackable and biology personal? Tracing the self-fashioning of the DIYbio network*. Unpublished PhD thesis, The London School of Economics and Political Science.

Tudge, C. (1999). *Neanderthals, bandits and farmers: How agriculture really began*. New Haven: Yale University Press.

Varian, H., & Shapiro, C. (1998). *Information rules: A strategic guide to the network economy*. Boston: Harvard Business School Press.

Verdon, J. (2010). Stewarding engagement, harnessing knowledge: Keeping the future in reserves. *Journal of Military and Strategic Studies, 12*(4), 70–125.

Verdon, J., Forrester, B., & Wang, Z. (2009). *The last mile of the market: How networks, participation and responsible autonomy support mission command and transform personnel management*. (DGMPRA TM 2009-022) Ottawa, ON: Director General Military Personnel Research and Analysis.

Wellman, B. (2001). The rise of networked individualism. In L. Keeble (Ed.), *Community networks online*. London: Taylor & Francis.

Williamson, O. E. (1981). The economics of organization: The transaction cost approach. *The American Journal of Sociology, 87*(3), 548–577.

Generational Theory and Cohort Analysis

2

Occasionally in history, massive demographic change combines with relentless technological change and, within a generation, society altogether changes. Today we are living in such an era.
—Mark McCrindle

Introduction

As highlighted in the McCrindle quote and presented in the preceding chapter, the confluence of several major drivers of change have the potential to result in significant transformations in our societies, particularly in our economy and workplaces. Key in our analyses is developing an understanding of the qualities and values that youth cohorts will bring to the workforce. We do so through the lenses of generational theory and cohort analyses. The first focuses on those of the same age(s) while the second considers groups based on important shared characteristics. So, those between the certain ages (e.g., those 15–30) are a generation while those currently attending college or university are a cohort. Social scientists examine both but nuance assumptions, limitations and analyses.

Socio-demographic research has pointed to significant generational shifts due in part to the striking differences between the youth of the 1960s (the first wave of the Boomers coming of age) in comparison to those of similar ages in the preceding decades. More recently, there has been a growing interest and debate surrounding differences across various generations across the academic literatures, news media, and the Internet giving rise to a literature on generational theory. The previous chapter highlighted that, within the youngest generation, the vast majority are being influenced by changes in the digital environment. Thus, our focus is on this cohort within this generation. There are important reasons for considering how the next wave of those entering adulthood might be different from those before them. The

© Springer Nature Switzerland AG 2020
A. Okros, *Harnessing the Potential of Digital Post-Millennials in the Future Workplace*, Management for Professionals, https://doi.org/10.1007/978-3-030-25726-2_2

initial portions of this chapter will provide an overview on how social scientists attempt to understand specific groups through generational theory and cohort analysis. Drawing on this work, the subsequent portion will present a summary of the descriptions of the current generations with a focus on Canadian and American demographics.[1] The more detailed analyses of the digitally engaged cohort within the youngest generation will be provided in subsequent chapters.

Generational Theory

> Each generation imagines itself to be more intelligent than the one that went before it, and wiser than the one that comes after it. —George Orwell

The premise of generational theory is that those of a similar age share formative experiences that can produce important and widespread commonalities in personal traits and that there probably will be a degree of meaningful differentiation in comparison to groups of different ages. While some authors use this approach to conduct retrospective analyses to explain why an age group appears to share key characteristics, others suggest that it is possible to forecast the emergence of shared traits across a group based on assessments of the impact of key experiences or events. As highlighted in the first illustration below, some extend these ideas to posit a cycle that continues across successive generations. We highlight the work of Stauss and Howe with key critiques of their theory.

Strauss–Howe Generational Theory

Perhaps the best-known work on generational theory comes from William Strauss and Neil Howe as described in *The Fourth Turning* (1997).[2] Within, they define a social generation as lasting approximately 20 years with individuals experiencing four life stages over an 80-year span: childhood, young adulthood, midlife, and elderhood. Significant historical and socioeconomic events occurring during childhood help to shape the attitudes and worldview of the group. As a generation moves from their youth into young adulthood, Strauss and Howe argue that they will attempt to remedy a "problem" facing the previous generation of young adults. They will go on make correction during their midlife and then fulfill their social role as guiding elders as members of the previous generation pass on. Based on this theory, many have interpreted Strauss and Howe as providing an approach to predicting key characteristics of future generations.

The core to the Strauss and Howe work is their understanding of social cycles and group responses. Based on their historical analyses, they argue that society

---

[1]This chapter draws on several of the reports produced under our project.
[2]This discussion also draws on Strauss and Howe (1993, 2000).

undergoes a cycle they call a "saeculum." These saeclua have been of varying length throughout history. The saeculum, in turn, are divided into four "turnings:"

1. Each saeculum begins after a *Crisis*: a cataclysmic event, such as an economic crisis, war, or social upheaval. This marks the beginning of the *High* turning: society seeks strong institutions in response to the crisis, at the expense of individualism.
2. The second turning is an *Awakening*: strong institutions give way as the next generation seeks to move from social cohesiveness towards personal, spiritual, and cultural autonomy.
3. *Awakening* is followed by *Unravelling*. While individualism continues to flourish—perhaps to excess—institutions continue to weaken and begin to become volatile. The new civic order begins to decay as society moves closer to crisis.
4. Finally, society enters the *Crisis* stage. In response to a new cataclysm, authority and institutions are restored, while individualism gives way to a communitarian view of society and societal institutions are rebuilt. This fourth turning and its founding crisis defines the beginning of a new saeculum.

Strauss and Howe (1997, p. 84) posit these turnings form as a pattern based on which each generation fits one of four archetypes.

1. *Hero* generations are born after an *Awakening*, during an *Unraveling*. They are protected by their parents as children and emerge as "team-oriented... optimists." During their midlife, they are "energetic [and] overly-confident," and grow to become politically powerful elders.
2. *Artists* are born during a *Crisis*. Their parents are also protective of these children during the crisis. They are generally conformists during their young adulthood. During their midlife, they are "process-oriented... leaders," and become thoughtful elders.
3. *Prophet* are born during a *high* after a *crisis*. They are the most "parented" of all the generations. They become adults and emerge as wise elders during the next *crisis*.
4. *Nomads* are born during an *awakening*. Their parents are much less involved with their children than during the other turnings, leading to a feeling of alienation during their time as young adults. They exhibit pragmatic leadership during the *crisis* of their adulthood, leading to a reputation as tough elders.

In sum, Strauss and Howe argue that each generation is born during a turning, which then defines their archetype. They suggest that members of the same archetype will develop common characteristics as a result of the socioeconomic conditions and societal evolutions that they encounter throughout their lives.

Strauss and Howe identify turnings from 15th to 18th century England, and American history to today. Yet, it is unclear if these patterns hold for non-European and other linguistic groups. Further, their work is inherently retrospective and has yet to demonstrate any predictive capacity. McCrindle (2011) makes several observations that serve as indirect critiques of the Strauss–Howe generational theory. In an age of rapid technological advancement and a movement to childbirth and marriage later in life, biological definitions can no longer properly capture the nuances within each generation. McCrindle and others contest that as technology rapidly advances, defining a generation by their shared experiences over decades may generate too broad a category. Instead McCrindle advocates for a sociological definition, eschewing biological taxonomies for classifying each generation.

Our research sought to examine whether the Strauss–Howe generational theory could be of use when applied to a new context by applying the main tenets to examine the student protest movement that occurred in Quebec in 2012.[3] We tested the Howe and Strauss descriptors and concluded that some urban Millennials from Quebec have displayed the predicted 'hero' archetype attributes suggested by the theory but others clearly did not. From this, and much of our other research, we do not support the idea of cyclical patterns in generational effects, and lack confidence in using the Strauss–Howe generational theory for predicting future group characteristics.

Ultimately, the value of the Strauss–Howe generational theory is to provide a method to examine the interactions between groups of individuals and broader social conditions suggesting that, in certain circumstances, some within an age group will seek to significantly change or subsequently reinforce aspects of social order. If such actions are broadly supported by peers, their beliefs, values and actions can come to define the generation. As McCrindle (2011, p. 21) acknowledges, "the broader point holds true—each generation is a factor of its times and a reaction to the generation that went before it".

Holly Agati

In her review of generational theory, Agati (2011) considered the gap in existing research by looking at generational variables and characteristics. Agati claims that the relationships and interplay between four generational variables—time interval, cohort, period, and attitude—and several personal and societal attributes need to be examined in a systematic way. They include:

1. *Time interval effects* that can distinguish generations as distinct periods that are decades-long. Building on McCrindle's critique, there is challenge as to how to delineate one generation from another. For instance, how does one explain any similarities or differences between one born at the end of one generation from another born at the beginning at the next?
2. *Cohort effects* consider the influence of historical events on a generation. Agati challenged the assumption that those who experience an event together in their childhood will develop a common understanding of the occurrence and share a similar response. For instance, she found that the reaction by Millennial Americans to 9/11 were based on how directly this event affected their family.

---

[3]Further information is contained in the three reports produced by Charbonneau and Garneau.

Although the knowledge of 9/11 was widespread, she concluded that it did not influence this generation uniformly.

3. While Strauss and Howe's theory emphasizes a sense of belonging to a generation, Agati undertook a small study that suggests that people identify most closely with their immediate peers with strong influences from family. She suggests that generations appear to develop as a kaleidoscope rather than in distinct groupings.

4. The final variable—*common attitudes*—builds on the previous variables that inherently lead to the conclusion that common values and attitudes may be shared by sub-groups within a generation; hence that a generation is a collection of 'sub-generations'.

Finally, Agati identifies that more work needs to be done to determine whether family values and attitudes persist throughout life. Another potential avenue identified for further research is to examine how socioeconomic status—urban versus rural, poor versus rich, availability of education—influences different sub-groups within a generation.

Our analyses found Agati's work to be informative and influenced our assessments of how to understand generations; the importance of examining sub-groups rather than seeking to draw broad pan-cohort conclusions; and, the need to consider a host of individual differences in factors ranging from socio-economic status through family characteristics to national differences and geographic location within the same country.

Morris Massey

Although he does not provide a generational theory *per se*, Massey's (1979) work provides a conceptual framework from which an individual and their peers are said to develop values; a process that may lead to a shared worldview by a cohort. He defines three periods of differing influences:

1. The *imprint* period lasts until the age of seven, where values are absorbed and accepted from external sources, particularly parents. By accepting everything as a truth, we develop a core belief of right from wrong; however, these are easily influenced by traumatic events.

2. The *modelling* period lasts between the ages of eight and thirteen, where blind acceptance moves to emulation. Influence of one's parents is supplemented—and perhaps overcome—by external mentors, such as teachers.

3. Finally, the *socialization* period lasts between the ages of 13 and 21. Here the individual emerges, seeking out friends and other young people similar to them. These friends, along with mass media, become driving influences in their lives.

He also notes the impact of "Significant Emotional Events," both personal and societal, that can have a significant influence on the worldview and values of an individual at any stage of their development. The impact of 9/11 in our discussion of Agati's work is a common referent of such an event and, in fact, is one that many American researchers cite as likely having long term effects on a person's values, particularly on younger individuals.

Massey's framework influenced our assessments of several factors and, in particular, our considerations of how wider access to social media at younger ages might be shifting the age ranges with his modelling and socialization occurring earlier in life as well as expanding some of the external influences that become important during his third socialization phase. As with the 9/11 effects and, more recently, reference to the impact of the 2008 economic recession, his work also provided a strong caution that unforeseen events can have a significant influence on many people, especially those affected by these events.

In sum, we did not find the literature on generational theory to be sufficient to apply directly to our analyses; both Agati and Massey highlighting the importance of understanding shared experiences. Our extension is that, while most youngsters in US and Canada are experiencing common influences from the digital environment and, in the next chapter, formative education, not all are. Based on our assessment of generational theory, we concluded that the more informative approach would be to consider cohort analyses.

Cohort Analyses

There are differences across academic disciplines in how each understands cohorts and the methodologies for cohort analyses; medicine, sociology and management studies vary significantly.[4] Our work is focussed on social cohorts: as per Agati and Massey, those who have had similar social experiences during the same period of time. While social cohorts can be defined independent of age, the vast majority of the literature relevant to our research blends the notions of age groups and shared experiences. Thus, social cohorts are generally seen as those of similar ages with common social experiences.[5] In our research, we found the work by Canadian sociologist and pollster, Michael Adams to be most informative.

Michael Adams

Michael Adams has been polling attitudes and values in Canada since 1970 and in the United States since 1992. In *Fire and Ice* (2003), Adams found that, despite the argument by some that Canadian and American societies are converging, their

---

[4]To return to the notion of Big Data, the growing field of behavioural analytics blends approaches used in psychology with those from management studies.

[5]Noting that this can lead to some authors and many in the media or posting on line using generations and cohorts interchangeably.

respective value systems are diverging.[6] He found that American society as a whole was moving towards traditional conservative values, while Canadians headed in the opposite direction. In addition, each Canadian generation was found to be more idealistic and open-minded than their American counterparts, the Canadians rejecting what they saw as 'outdated' norms and institutions and with a strong sense of self-reliance and self-sufficiency.

Adams has undertaken comprehensive work on the presence of sub-groups within Canadian generations. In his best-selling *Sex in the Snow* (1997), Adams paints what he calls a "psychographic geography of Canada." To do so, he uses the *système cofremca pour suivre des courants socio-culturels* (3SC system) survey technique. Adams employs a psychographic approach that emphasises the study of groups or market segments in the population who are defined by their values and resulting lifestyle choices. For Adams, individual drive and desires trump, but do not completely dominate, demographic effects. The 3SC system allows multivariate clustering and mapping on a two-dimensional grid (Fig. 2.1). The first axis measures one's emphasis on individuality, from outward looking and socially focused to inward-focused and individualistic. The second axis considers a value system, ranging from a traditionalistic, conformist, and somewhat exclusionary view of the world to one that is more accepting, modern, and tolerant. In this way, Adams presents his work using tables with four quadrants, where the "average individual" lies in the centre.[7]

The 3SC approach can locate a subgroup within this map, and in doing so generally define their value system. This analysis can be both static and dynamic: in addition to pin-pointing a cohort, it can track the evolution of the values of a group over time, essentially transforming a point into a vector. For Adams, the real strength of the psychographic approach is that it reveals a number of subgroups or "tribes" within each generation, defined by their common space within the map. These points may diverge from the point occupied by the generation as a whole. Using Canadian and US data, Adams has identified 18 tribes contained within the Elders, Boomers, Generation X, and Millennial generations.

Adams attempts to address gendered differences in his work, an angle generally overlooked by many generational theorists. This is an important consideration: it is only recently that women have made significant gains towards social equality; a feminist critique would theorize that almost the entire period of Strauss and Howe's work as male-centric and constructed on masculine perceptions of events, characteristics, and traits. Nevertheless, Adams notes that differences between the sexes are minor compared to the differences between the 'value tribes' themselves. Accordingly, he suggests that the values of men and women are converging and there are no meaningful sub-group differences by gender.

---

[6]Some have argued that Canada and the United States share similar values; see, Francis (2013).
[7]In some of his reports and presentations the quadrants are 'centred' using norms from Canadian data (which shift US data points up and to the left) while in other instances these are based on norms from US data (which shift Canadian data down and to the right). Personal communication: Alan Okros/Michael Adams 11 February 2015.

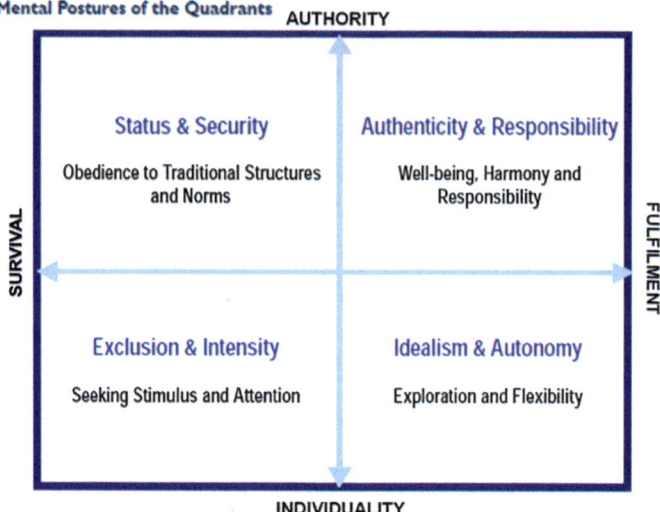

Fig. 2.1 Michael Adams/3SC map

We found Adams' work to be of value as it addressed a number of the issues raised in our review of generational theorists. His analyses do address differences across generations as well as providing comparisons between the United States and Canada; however, the two strongest contributions from his work are the presentation of important ways in which sub-groups of the same age can differ and the consideration of gender differences. As Adams and *Environics* have recently extended their work with younger Canadians including finding some gender differences, we will return to some of the more recent findings in subsequent chapters.

Other Measures of Cohort Changes

Researchers generally see a new social cohort emerging whenever there has been at least a substantial behavioural change displayed; shared significant historical experiences; and/or, a significant change in live births per year (Erickson, 2008; Strauss & Howe, 2000; Rainer & Rainer, 2011; Tapscott, 1998). Others believe the basis of changing traits amongst younger cohorts is a function of the parenting received hence they focus more on significant shifts in family structure or context (Loveless & Holman, 2006). Finally, some define generations by observations of differences in responses to attitudinal surveys suggesting that marked changes in attitudes serve as important indicators of social differentiation (Taylor, 2014). We saw the consistency across several authors on behavioural change and historical experiences as of relevance as was the work on parenting styles. Changes in fertility rates were assessed as of less importance and the analyses conducted by Leuprecht, Skillicorn and Tait (2016) indicated that analyses based on responses to attitudinal surveys need to be examined closely before making broad conclusions.

Current Generations

Children have never been very good at listening to their elders, but they have never failed to imitate them. —James Baldwin

While our assessments of generational theory and cohort analyses indicated that it is of greater importance to consider individual or sub-group differences amongst those of the same age, we also recognized that there is a significant literature that describes characteristics of those within defined age groups. Whether accurate or not or whether applicable to any specific individual or not, we recognize that these descriptions or stereotypes can influence how others see individuals of a certain age. Further, as with other broad group characterizations such as nationality, ethnicity or religious affiliation, these common descriptions are neither static nor uncontested; rather, they are in a constant state of evolution as the members of these groups seek to influence how others perceive them and as mediators such as the news media, academics, entertainers and authors/playwrights portray them. With this social reality in mind and recalling the caveat that these descriptions provide simplistic indicators of a few aspects of any one individual's identity, we sought to provide a summary of how current generations are defined and described.

Cohort Definitions

We examined different approaches to gauge a consensus on the timing, and general characteristics of modern generations. As Table 2.1 describes, the temporal definitions for each generation can vary, but the categorizations are generally well-defined and the cohort size relative to the overall population is about the same in the United States and Canada.

Notwithstanding the relatively arbitrary selection of the year to indicate the beginning and ending of each generation, most see each lasting about two decades. Recent work suggests that current youth cohorts can be differentiated in shorter periods with some authors reporting group differences in as short as ten years (Taylor, 2014).

As Table 2.2 demonstrates, some broad conclusions or generalizations have been drawn about those currently in the workforce.[8] As a significant event can influence attitudes and values, some refer to the Millennial cohort as split between those who entered the workforce prior to the 2008 economic recession and those

---

[8]Common references for older groups are: the Silent Generation (1925–1945), the Greatest Generation (1910–1925) and the Lost Generation (1890–1910).

Table 2.1 Generation ranges and population sizes

Common Title	Boomers	Generation X	Millennials	Post-Millennials
Range of dates	1940–1960; 1943–1960; 1946–1962; 1946–1963	1960–1980; 1961–1981; 1963–1980; 1965–1976; 1965–1980	1977–1994; 1977–1997; 1980–2000; 1981–2002; 1984–2006	Born early 1990s; born after 1997; born after 2000; born after 2006
Canada	9 million +	7 million	8 million	5 million +
United States	70–80 million	45–55 million	65–75 million	61 million

Table 2.2 Broad generational characteristics

Generation	Boomers	Generation X	Millennial (Gen Y)
Born in	Mid 40s–early 60s	Early 60s–early 80s	Early 80s–early 2000
Shaping influences	Television, the Cold War, the Vietnam War, student activism, the FLQ crisis, feminism, space travel, and stay-at-home moms	The energy crisis, the war on drugs, technology's first wave, fall of the Berlin Wall, AIDS, working mothers, and rising divorce rates	Explosion of technology and media, 9/11, the Columbine shootings, multiculturalism, and a variety of family structures
Values	Standing out and recognition	Flexibility, honesty, feedback, and work-life balance	Strong leadership, concern for community, structure, fair-play, diversity
Approach to work	A driven service-oriented team player who does not want to be micro-managed. They live to work	Independent, self-reliant, unimpressed by authority and focused on self-development. They work to live	Self-confidant, optimistic, outspoken, collaborative. They blend work and personal life
Career motto	Education plus hard work equals success	Invest in portable career skills	Multi-track or die!

who entered after as these two subgroups have experienced rather different careers to date.[9]

Using the 3SC system, Adams identified twelve psychographic tribes within three Canadian generations, each with their own motivations and value systems as shown in Table 2.3. Adams has also identified four tribes for Canadian millennials that we will consider below.

---

[9]Amongst others, see the Harvard survey at: http://www.iop.harvard.edu/Spring-2014-HarvardIOP-Survey.

Table 2.3 Adams' tribes, elders to generation X

Group	Psychographic type	% of adults	Size of group	Motivation	Key values
The elders (age 70+)	1. Cosmopolitan Modernists	6	1.4 million	Traditional institutions and experience-seeking	Global world-view; respect for education; desire for innovation
	2. Rational Traditionalists	15	3.5 million	Financial independence, stability and security	Religiosity; duty; guilt; deferred gratification; primacy of reason; respect for tradition and authority
	3. Extroverted Traditionalists	7	1.7 million	Traditional communities, institutions and social status	Religiosity; duty; fear; deferred gratification family; respect for tradition and institutions
The boomers (age 50–69)	4. Disengaged Darwinists	18	4.3 million	Financial independence, stability and security	Fear; nostalgia for the past
	5. Autonomous Rebels	10	2.4 million	Personal autonomy and self-fulfilment	Belief in human rights; scepticism of institutions; suspicion of authority; freedom; individuality; respect for education
	6. Connected Enthusiasts	6	1.4 million	Traditional and new communities, and experience-seeking	Family; community; hedonism; immediate gratification
	7. Anxious Communitarians	9	2.1 million	Traditional communities, institutions and social status	Family; community; fear; duty; need for respect
The gen Xers (age 35–49)	8. Thrill-Seeking Materialists	7	1.7 million	Traditional communities, social status and experience-seeking	Desire for money and material possessions; desire for recognition, respect and admiration
	9. Aimless Dependents	8	1.9 million	Financial independence, stability and security	Fear; desire for independence
	10. Social Hedonists	4	900,000	Experience-seeking and new communities	Aesthetics; hedonism; sexual permissiveness; immediate gratification
	11. New Aquarians	4	900,000	Experience-seeking and new communities	Egalitarianism; ecologism; hedonism
	12. Autonomous Post-materialists	6	1.4 million	Personal autonomy and self-fulfilment	Freedom; respect for human rights

Integrated Summary

The following are brief descriptions of each of the generations highlighting characteristics that commonly ascribed to those in the age group. Again, the reader is cautioned to remember that these descriptions should be understood to apply to most but not all of those in the age group.

Boomers

Begala (2007) once called the Boomers the "most self-centered, self-seeking, self-interested, self-absorbed, self-indulgent, self-aggrandizing generation in American history." As the children of the "Greatest Generation" (those who fought in the Second World War), the Boomers number between 70 and 80 million in the United States and over 9 million in Canada (Brinckerhoff, 2007; Espinoza, 2012; Statistics Canada, 2012; Espinoza, Ukleja & Rusch, 2010).

The majority of the Boomers were raised in a traditional household by stay-at-home mothers (Rainer & Rainer, 2011). Through the new medium of the television, they collectively witnessed events including: the women's and civil rights movements, the war in Vietnam, the assassinations of John and Robert Kennedy, the moon landing, and the Beatles (Brinckerhoff, 2007; Espinoza, 2012; Lancaster & Stillman, 2002; Meister & Willyerd, 2010; Tapscott, 1998) and, in Canada, Trudeaumania (Peters, 2000). As adults, the Boomers experienced an unprecedented period of economic growth, giving credence to the American dream: with hard work, you can be anyone you want to be. The sheer size of the cohort may drive the Boomer's ambition, competitiveness and materialistic tendencies in an effort to stand out among their peers (Crampton & Hodge, 2007).

The Boomers were the largest cohort when Adams wrote *Sex in the Snow*. As shown in Table 4.2, he defined four Boomer tribes in Canada:

1. The "Disengaged Darwinists" comprise the largest group within the Boomer generation and are torch bearers for the traditional values of their parents.
2. "Connected Enthusiasts" are more proactive than their Darwinist peers, embracing new experiences while actively seeking instant gratification.
3. "Anxious Communitarians" are grounded and identified by their relationship with their communities.
4. Finally, "Autonomous Rebels" seek autonomy and self-fulfilment, push for human rights and are skeptical of authority.

Generation X/13ers

Generation X – or 13ers as Strauss and Howe call them—are those born between the mid-sixties and the early eighties. Falling birthrates in North America starting in the mid-sixties led to a much smaller cohort vis-à-vis the Boomers: Generation X accounts for approximately 45–55 million Americans and 7 million Canadians (Brinckerhoff, 2007; Lancaster & Stillman, 2002; Meister & Willyerd, 2010; Rainer & Rainer, 2011; Statistics Canada, 2012; U.S. Census Bureau, 2013; Wiggins, 2012). Many of these children were raised by Boomers.

Rearchers have noted that Generation X's childhood was marked by a shift from involved parenting towards, arguably, a less child-friendly and more parental-centric environment. According to Strauss and Howe (1993, p. 57), this generation was raised by parents that put themselves ahead of their children and, at worst, "expressed moral ambivalence where a child sought clear answers, expected a child to respond too young to real-world problems, hesitated to impose structure on a child's behavior, and demonstrated an amazing (even stupefying) tolerance for the rising torrent of pathology and negativism that engulfed a child's world." As women increasingly entered the workforce, family income rose. However, with both parents now working, many Generation X'ers were "latchkey kids" coming home to empty houses at the end of the day. This generation also saw skyrocketing divorce rates. Their teenage years were marked by rising crime and drug use rates and falling SAT scores that some suggest may have been a function of their absent parents (Tolbize, 2008). Together, they came of age during the AIDS epidemic, the fall of the Berlin Wall, and the end of the Cold War. Privy to the 24-hour news cycle, conflicts in various regions of the world were beamed directly into the televisions of this generation, reinforcing their characteristic cynicism and distrust of authority (Drago, 2006).

Generation X entered the workforce during a time of job shortages and corporate layoffs. Unlike their parents—who often stayed with one or a few companies for their careers—Generation X became accustomed to frequent job changes, self-employment, or entrepreneurism (Brinckerhoff, 2007; Espinoza, 2012; Lancaster & Stillman, 2002; Martin & Tulgan, 2006; Meister & Willyerd, 2010). They generally value a work-life balance much more than the proceeding generation, advancing policies such as paid parental leave, sabbaticals from work, and using technology to occasionally work from home (Cone Inc. & AMP Insights, 2006; Espinoza, 2012).

Michael Adams split Canadian Generation X into five tribes: "Thrill-seeking Materialists" (1.7 million), the "Aimless Dependents" (1.9 million), the "Social Hedonists" (900,000), the" New Aquarians" (900,000), and the "Autonomous Post-Materialists" (1.4 million). As a group, they are much more focused on immediate gratification, self-fulfillment and experience-seeking. According to Adams, they are on "the leading edge in the movement away from traditional values." In *Sex in the Snow*, Adams predicted New Aquarians and the Autonomous Post-Materialists as being those most likely to lead society into the future. While other tribes are driven by money and independence, these groups seemed to exhibit an outward focus on values such as egalitarianism and human rights.

Millennials/Generation Y

For both the Millennials and Post-Millennials, we present brief generalities drawn from a range of sources. In subsequent chapters, we will draw on specific research to explore many of these assumptions and related critiques in depth, including the digital and educational environment, learning styles, sociability, identity, and their interactions with the workplace. Thus, this and the following sections are best read as a broad 'portraits' of how these two generations are perceived.

There is no consensus on the size of the Millennial cohort. There are two generally accepted time frames for this generation: from the late 70s to the mid-90s or between the 1980s and the early years of the 21st century. For our purposes, we will use the later time period counting the Millennials as having been born up to 2005. By any definition, Millennials make up over a quarter of the population in the United States and nearly as much in Canada.[10]

Many Millennials experienced a different childhood than their Generation X elders. Perhaps owing to a desire to be more present than their own parents, the guardians of Millennials tended to be highly engaged. Often called 'overprotective' or 'helicopter parents,' Millennials grew up with parents who were seen as focussed on giving their children an ideal life, protecting them from harm, and encouraging them to seek out their passions from an early age (Rainer & Rainer, 2011). In short, Millennials are described as used to being the centre of attention and having developed a confident, goal-oriented approach to life. Accordingly, the youth and young adulthood of Millennials has been marked by a reversal of many of the trends seen during Generation X, including rising test scores and falling youth crime rates.

As adults, Millennials are described as committed to their parents and family. They also value community and volunteerism. Strauss and Howe (2000) suggest that Millennials might be the most socially-oriented generation since World War II. They are seen as being comfortable relying on peers and parents for support, and prefer to work in groups, sharing goals and failures. Their friendships are increasingly part of large social groups, as opposed to small cliques. Their proclivity towards group settings can be a result of their parents and teachers emphasizing teamwork, whether it be in the classroom, on the baseball diamond, or within an after-school club.

Technology is affecting the way the Millennial generation has evolved. With the widespread penetration of the Internet into homes in the 1990s, many Millennials have had access to computers and online materials since an early age. The adoption of cellular telephones became widespread as Millennials became teenagers and young adults. They grew up, and continue to develop, in an increasingly interconnected world, where they experience events and communicate with their peers in real time, regardless of their location. The greater connectivity provided by the Internet may explain the increasing emphasis Millennials place on community over

---

[10]For 2015 US Census data, see: http://www.census.gov/newsroom/press-releases/2015/cb15-113. html.

individualism. Technology has allowed for their "helicopter" parents to remain in contact with their children throughout their day, creating what some argue to be the "world's longest umbilical cord" between Gen X parents and their now adult Millennial offspring (Stafford & Griffs, 2008).

Research indicates that Millennials are generally concerned about inequalities generated by wealth, the environment, and other political and social issues. They are more tolerant and appreciative of the diversity of race, gender, and sexuality than any generation before (Stafford & Griffis, 2008). For Millennials, encountering diversity is the norm although as we will present, not all embrace it. Greater exposure to diversity is facilitated by social networking, creating a greater and instantaneous attachment to a community of shared experiences. Finally, some looked beyond their own borders: the civic-minded qualities of this generation extend to the global community (Rainer & Rainer, 2011). In extending the Howe–Strauss generational theory to this cohort, some suggest the Millennials should be powerful leaders in addressing global challenges as their adulthood continues.

Our research indicates that the Millennial preference for group settings has extended into the workplace. They normally appreciate a diverse, collegial, and team-based work environment. This generation's concept of work-life balance is to blend them together. As multitaskers, they prefer flexibility in their lives. Millennials are hard workers, although they may not be suited to the nine-to-five workplace. They highly value pay, but also look for other incentives, such as training, learning opportunities, pension, health, and other benefits, the opportunity for rapid advancement, and recognition for their contributions. As a globally-minded generation, many Millennials appear to purposely seek out employers who have the same values as themselves. Some argue that their desire to have an impact on the world influences choices as they decide on a career path (Ehlert, Senn, Kling, & Beers, 2013).

A common refrain among Boomers is that Millennials lack respect for authority. Indeed, they have a number of traits that may run counter to their elders. As Millennials have been entering the workforce from a home setting where they were often the centre of attention, they have encountered a different environment at work. Research indicates that Millennials expect to be nurtured, move up the corporate ladder quickly, be involved in the decision-making process, and expect access to their managers (Rainer & Rainer, 2011; Taylor, 2014). Their upbringing with the "information superhighway" brings with them a sense of entitlement for information (Ng, 2010), even those facts deemed by management to be beyond their pay grade. They are seen as disliking bureaucratic, pyramid-like corporate structures, preferring a much more "flat" environment. It is unclear how loyal Millennials are to their organizations, but they nevertheless expect to have multiple employers throughout their careers (Stuart & Lyons, 2008).

Michael Adams has identified six tribes within the Canadian Millennial cohort:

1. The largest group—38% of all Millennials—find themselves among the "Bros & Brittanys." They focus on generating income to support their lifestyle beyond the workplace: staying on top of the latest trends and the newest technologies,

seeking out excitement and embracing of risk taking, being active consumers, and enjoying escapes from the daily grind.

2. "Engaged Idealists" make up 19% of the cohort. They are creative, progressive, socially engaged, and energetic. They seek fulfillment through work but also look for opportunities to make the world a better place;

3. Another 19% represent the anti-culture "Lone Wolves" tribe. They are disconnected from society, even skeptical of it;

4. "New Traditionalists" embody conservatism, faith, family, and not surprisingly, a move towards the traditional values. They represent 10% of the cohort;

5. "Diverse Strivers"—at 10%– are ethnically diverse, intense, love crowds, social status, the latest fashions, and are driven to succeed in all aspects of their lives; and,

6. The smallest group, the "Critical Counterculture" represent activists with strong political views, a civic perspective on society, both at home and abroad.

Generation Z/Homelanders/Post-Millennials/IGen/Gen We/Gen Me/Founders/Gen C

We considered the issue of the label to be attached to the current youth cohort. While the use of Boomers is nearly universal and GenX is the norm for that age group, there is a split in popular usage between Gen Y versus Millennials and a plethora of phrases for the youngest cohort. While, at one level, picking a single identifier is just a variation of 'name the baby', we chose to use Post-Millennial. This reflects our assessment that Millennial is used more often than Gen Y. Concomitantly, our choice reflects the broad conclusion we have reached that this current youth cohort will be at the forefront of significant changes across our society and economy. We therefore will use *Post-Millennial* with linkages to conceptual postmodernism to reflect a significant shift away from an established ontology and towards an acceptance of pluralism and diverse ways of knowing and being. We argue that the Post-Millennials will be more than just 'junior' Millennials.

Although the delineation between the Millennial and Post-Millennials remains unclear, we know that Post-Millennials are currently in their youth or, potentially, starting their teenage years. The Post-Millennial population is roughly 61 million in the United States and over 5 million in Canada (Espinoza, 2012; Statistics Canada, 2012; U.S. Census Bureau, 2013). Little rigorous academic study has been published on this group, although we noted that perspectives on who they are and what they value do exist in marketing research, news media coverage and online exchanges. Again, this section provides a summative portrait of how the Post-Millennials are being described.

We found a common trend across the literature: Millennials and Post-Millennials are seen to share several similarities. They will likely continue to value diversity, social responsibility, volunteerism, and teamwork. Social media and the Internet will play a significant role in their upbringing and the formulation of common values; nearly every child today has access to a computer or tablet and can master the technology as early as the age of six (Irvine, 2010). Coupled with the ubiquity of technology, this generation may become attached to their electronic devices as technology becomes their primary outlet for creativity and for developing relationships with the world around them. Indeed, Post-Millennials may redefine "social skills" away from person-to-person contact and towards Internet etiquette and communication.

Their career expectations may also be similar to those of Millennials: an emphasis on accomplishments rather than hours worked, thriving in a collaborative work environment, and experiencing multiple career changes during their working years. One source, however, notes that this next generation might be much more loyal to their boss and the corporate vision than the Millennials.[11]

Building on their generational theory, Howe has termed these youngsters "Homelanders" for their tendency to view society with "greater public urgency and emergency, both at home and around the world" (Irvine, 2010). He speculates that Post-Millennials will be industrious and lack the sense of entitlement that characterizes the Millennials. In *Millennials Rising* (2000), Strauss and Howe predicted that their archetype will be similar to those before the Boomers, the "G.I. Generation." Applying the Howe–Strauss cycle, this generation was born during "crisis" and will become "artists." It is plausible that the ramifications of the financial crisis of 2008 could form the basis for a crisis event and, in the United States, it will take time to determine in what ways national dialogue, particularly in the political domain, may influence young people. To the extent that their predication is borne out, they could be overprotected children, grow into conformists during their young adulthood, be part of a move towards individualism as adults during an "awakening", and finally become sensitive and liked elders.

Conclusion

This chapter introduces the broad frameworks of generational theory and cohort analyses as a means to, at a minimum, examine groups and/or describe those of similar ages and, as some authors posit, to project key characteristics of groups into the future. These broad generalizations by no means define any individual. Several authors point to likely significant intra-generational variations owing to age, socioeconomic status, parenting styles, and technological diffusion. Despite the shortcomings of current generational theory, broad social factors and shared experiences can influence how a group of people close in age and, in particular, sharing key experiences, interact with society and develop values. Of greater importance, while any accurate understanding of attitudes, perceptions and values

---

[11]See the summary of the "Worldwide Study Comparing Gen Y and Gen Z Workplace Expectations"; accessible at: http://millennialbranding.com/2014/geny-genz-global-workplace-expectations-study/.

needs to consider factors such as income, gender, ethnic identity and specific community, we recognized that each age group is likely to acquire labels, ascribed characteristics and broad stereotypes that, whether accurate or not, will influence how others see them and, in return, how members of the defined group will see themselves and others. Accordingly, we believe it is a useful exercise to present these brief portraits to identify perceived commonalities and shared experiences. Our subsequent analyses will examine these in more detail to determine how we might generate reasonable descriptions and plausible predictions regarding the current youth age group as they enter early adulthood and move into the workforce. Our focus is on those in their adolescence or just entering their teenage years hence individuals who will enter the workforce starting in about ten years. Given their current ages, the Post-Millennials are currently in school thus the following chapter will examine the ways in which evolutions in the digital environment are affecting education and learning.

References

Adams, M. (1997). *Sex in the snow: Canadian social values at the end of the millennium.* Toronto: Viking.

Adams, M. (2003). *Fire & ice: The United States, Canada and the myth of converging values.* Toronto, Canada: Penguin.

Agati, H. A. (2011). *The millennial generation: Howe and Strauss disputed.* (Doctoral dissertation). Retrieved from ProQuest Dissertations and Theses. (Accession Order No. ATT 3492308).

Begala, P. (2007, January 29). The worst generation or, how I learned to stop worrying and hate the boomers. *Esquire,* 123–124.

Brinckerhoff, P. (2007). *Generations: The challenge of a lifetime for your nonprofit.* Saint Paul, MN: Fieldstone Alliance.

Cone Inc. & AMP Insights. (2006). *Millennial cause study—The Millennial generation: Pro-social and empowered to change the world.* Retrieved from http://blogthinkbig.com/wp-content/uploads/Cone-Millennial-Cause-Study-La-hora-de-cambiar-el-mundo.pdf.

Crampton, S. M., & Hodge, J. W. (2007). Generations in the workplace: Understanding age diversity. *The Business Review, 9*(1), 16–23.

Drago, J. P. (2006). *Generational Theory: Implications for Recruiting the Millennials.* Carlisle, PA: U.S. Army War College.

Ehlert, R., Senn, K, Kling, C., & Beers, R. (2013). It takes more than a major: Employer priorities for college learning and student success. *Liberal Education, 99*(2). Retrieved from https://www.aacu.org/publications-research/periodicals/it-takes-more-major-employer-priorities-college-learning-and.

Erickson, T. (2008). *Plugged In: The Generation Y Guide to Thriving at Work.* Boston: Harvard Business Press.

Espinoza, C. (2012) *Millennial Integration: Challenges Millennials Face in the Workplace and What They Can Do About Them.* Unpublished PhD Thesis, Antioch University: Retrieved from https://etd.ohiolink.edu/rws_etd/document/get/antioch1354553875/inline.

Espinoza, C., Ukleja, M., & Rusch, C. (2010). *Managing the Millennials.* Hoboken, NJ: Wiley.

Francis, D. (2013). *Merger of the century: Why Canada and America should become one.* Toronto: HarperCollins.

Irvine, M. (2010, June 11). Newest-generation label: Who are you? *The Denver Post.* Retrieved from http://www.denverpost.com/headlines/ci_15273047.

Lancaster, L. C., & Stillman, D. (2002). *When generations collide: Who they are. Why they clash. How to solve the generational puzzle at work.* New York, NY: Harper Collins.

Leuprecht, C., Skillicorn, D. B., & Tait, V. (2016). Beyond the Castle Model of cyber-risk and cyber-security. *Government Information Quarterly, 33*(2), 250–257.

Loveless, A., & Holman, T. (2006). *The family in the new millennium world voices supporting the "natural" clan.* Westport, Connecticut: Praeger Publishers.

Martin, C., & Tulgan, B. (2006). *Managing the generation mix: From urgency to opportunity* (Expanded 2nd ed ed.). Amherst, MA: HRD Press.

Massey, M. E. (1979). *The people puzzle: Understanding yourself and others.* Reston, VA: Reston.

McCrindle, M. (2011). *The ABC of XYZ: Understanding the global generations* (2nd ed.). Bella Vista, Australia: McCrindle Publication.

Meister, J. C., & Willyerd, K. (2010). *The 2020 workplace: How innovative companies attract, develop and keep tomorrow's employees today.* New York, NY: Harper Collins.

Ng, E., Schweitzer, L., & Lyons, S. (2010). New generation, great expectations: A field study of the Millennial generation. *Journal of Business & Psychology, 25*, 281–292.

Peters, J. (2000). *Just Watch Me: Trudeau and the '70s Generation* (Documentary). ICanadian Materials: Manitoba Library Association.

Rainer, T., & Rainer, J. (2011). *The Millennials: Connecting to the largest generation.* Nashville, TN: B&H Publishing Group.

Stafford, D. & Griffis, H. (2008). *A Review of Millennial Generation Characteristics and Military Workforce Implications.* Arlington, VA: Center for Naval Analysis.

Statistics Canada. (2012). *Canada at a Glance 2012.* Ottawa, ON: Statistics Canada.

Strauss, W., & Howe, N. (1993). *13th gen: Abort, retry, ignore, fail.* New York: Vintage Books.

Strauss, W., & Howe, N. (1997). *The fourth turning: An American prophecy—what the cycles of history tell us about America's next rendezvous with destiny.* New York: Broadway Books.

Strauss, W., & Howe, N. (2000). *Millennials rising: The next great generation* (3rd ed.). New York: Vintage Books.

Stuart, A., & Lyons, D. S. (2008). *Millennials in the workplace.* Halifax, NS: Knightsbridge Robertson Surrette. Retrieved from http://www.kbrs.ca/insights/millennials-workplace.

Tapscott, D. (1998). *Growing Up Digital. The Rise of the Net Generation.* New York: McGraw Hill.

Taylor, P. (2014). *The next America: Boomers, Millennials, and the looming generational showdown.* New York: PublicAffairs.

Tolbize, A. (2008) *Generational Differences in the Workplace.* University of Minnesota: Research and Training Center on Community Living.

Wiggins, G. L. (2012). *A descriptive analysis of generation Y employees working in Georgia State Government: Implications for workforce planning.* (Doctoral dissertation). Retrieved from ProQuest Dissertations and Theses. (Accession Order No. ATT 3544061).

Education and Learning

3

> *The illiterate of the 21st century will not be those who cannot read and write, but those who cannot learn, unlearn, and relearn.*
>
> —Herbert Gerjuoy

Introduction

By the time today's youth enter the fulltime workforce, the majority will have completed 14–16 years of schooling thus making their time in the classroom second only to the amount spent with parents and family.[1] Formal education, of course, is more than just developing basic literacy skills or acquiring factual knowledge. The influence of teachers in shaping how young people see the world is a key component in Massey's work on understanding how generations develop and how they come to be differentiated from those before them. While we have noted earlier that the vast majority of students in public schools are being provided access to computers, the key question is: what are the consequences of an increasingly digitized learning environment? Thus, the focus of our analyses and this chapter is on understanding how access to the digital world is changing the nature of the educational experience and learning outcomes. Our key conclusion is that the most profound effects will not be in what these students will have learned but how they will have learned to learn.

---

[1]We acknowledge that some children experience home schooling or alternate means of education.

© Springer Nature Switzerland AG 2020
A. Okros, *Harnessing the Potential of Digital Post-Millennials in the Future Workplace*, Management for Professionals,
https://doi.org/10.1007/978-3-030-25726-2_3

21st Century Skills

> We are currently preparing students for jobs that don't yet exist using technologies that haven't been invented in order to solve problems that we don't even know are problems yet.
> —Did you know[2]

As reflected in the 'Did you know?' quote, a number of academics and educational organizations have called for major changes to the curricula taught across all levels of formal education. The central argument behind the call for changes in education is that evolutions in the digital environment are requiring individuals to develop new skillsets to be successful across the range of personal, social, community and especially work activities that they will face in the future. While acknowledging the continued importance of core learning such as verbal and numerical literacy, oral communications or problem solving, our analyses revealed two significant changes in the objectives of educational activities. The first is that the contexts in which traditional skills will be used have changed in significant ways. As an example, while collaboration and team work may still start with pre-schoolers learning to share toys, the types of collaborative activities and the nature of teamwork expected by the time they reach adulthood will be complex and multi-faceted and often mediated by the digital environment. Thus, teachers are changing how collaborative skills are developed.

The second factor is the emergence of new skill sets with digital and media literacy as two obvious competencies that now need to be mastered. As highlighted in our scan of the digital environment, the sheer amount of material being created and accessed on line is giving rise to what is being called 'digital disorder' or 'content clutter.'[3] Individuals, including children, have to learn to sort fact from opinion or, often having to interpret 'fact-ion' due to the volume of data, information and knowledge (and opinion) that is being generated and made accessible.[4] A critical factor in this regard is the erosion of current systems to review, critique and organize knowledge with much of this information becoming accessible and entering common usage without having gone through processes such as the peer-review associated with academic journals or the cataloguing associated with the Dewey Decimal System.[5] More than ever, young people are having to make sense of a kaleidoscope of knowledges and need to develop the skills to be able to navigate a changing learning environment.

---

[2]A plethora of "Did You Know" and "Shift Happens" posts are available particularly on YouTube. The original quote is credited to a presentation in August 2006 at Arapahoe High School in Centennial, Colorado.

[3]See Susan Gunelius' blog post The Cost of Content Clutter Infographic accessible at: http://aci.info/2013/11/06/the-cost-of-content-clutter-infographic/.

[4]For essays on the challenges of making sense when facts are blurred with fiction, see Johansen & Sondergaard (2010).

[5]Albeit beyond the scope of this book, the debate of the Dewey Decimal System as imposing specific worldviews at the expense of others. Hope Olson's (2002) critique The Power to Name presents examples such as classifying pregnancy under the heading of disease and lynching under the heading of law enforcement.

In this context of preparing students for a changing learning environment, a number of initiatives have been undertaken to articulate new approaches to developing what are generally referred to as 21st Century skills. Frameworks for this new skillset have been published to inform educators in many countries including: Partnership for 21st Century Skills (2007), Organization for Economic Cooperation and Development (2005), Texley (2007); and Canadians for 21st Century Learning and Innovation (2012) alongside government leaders and international organizations including the United Nations Educational, Scientific and Cultural Organization (UNESC), which additionally tackles key ideas in policy development amongst member states.

Of these initiatives, our assessment is that the Partnership for 21st Century Skills (P21) framework is the most developed with others providing areas of increased emphasis in certain of the domains contained in the P21 framework. P21 was formed in the United States in 2002 with the goal of developing a framework for teaching the skills required for today's students to succeed as adults. The group brought together the American Federal Department of Education, the State Educational Technology Directors Association (SETDA), the International Society for Technology in Education (ISTE), teaching professionals, academics, and business leaders. In their vision of the next century of learning, traditional subjects—mathematics, sciences, languages, and history, for instance—will continue to form the core of any curriculum. Nevertheless, this foundation will not be enough for the modern learner: traditional academic subjects must be interwoven with interdisciplinary themes representing issues that Post-Millennial will face as adults, such as environmental literacy and global awareness. Students will also need to develop new learning skills that they present as the 4Cs to complement the 3Rs: Critical thinking & problem solving; Communication; Collaboration; and Creativity & innovation.[6] These aptitudes are seen to be important to enable the next generation of students to become life-long learners hence able to acquire new knowledge in the rapidly-changing 21st Century digital environment. P21 also identifies the life and career skills needed to prepare students for the workforce that include: flexibility and adaptability; initiative and self-direction; social and cross-cultural skills; productivity and accountability; and leadership and responsibility.

Consistent with our overall theme of understanding the implications of the evolving digital domain, the 21st Century Skills frameworks all emphasize the ability to work, understand, and interact within the digital environment. Although this begins with basic competency in using digital technology, it extends to media and information literacy: understanding the context and implications of the information generated by these tools. We found the work by Jenkins, Clinton, Purushotma, Robinson, and Weigel (2006) on the types of intellectual activity needed to comprehend digital content and media to be informative. Rather than simply focusing on describing technical skills, they emphasize (Jenkins et al., 2006, pp. 4):

---

[6]While Reduce, Reuse, Recycle may be the 3Rs many are familiar with, the longer standing reference is to Reading, wRiting and aRithmatic.

- Play   The capacity to experiment with one's surroundings as a form of problem-solving
- Performance   The ability to adopt alternative identities for improvisation and discovery
- Simulation   The ability to interpret and construct dynamic models of real-world processes
- Appropriation   The ability to meaningfully sample and remix media content
- Multitasking   The ability to scan one's environment and shift focus as needed to salient details.
- Distributed Cognition The ability to interact with tools that expand mental capacities
- Collective Intelligence The ability to pool knowledge and compare notes with others toward a common goal
- Judgment   The ability to evaluate the reliability and credibility of different information sources
- Transmedia Navigation The ability to follow the flow of stories and information across multiple modalities
- Networking   The ability to search for, synthesize, and disseminate information
- Negotiation   The ability to travel across diverse communities, discerning and respecting multiple perspectives, and grasping and following alternative norms

In addition to the P21 initiative in the US, educators and policy makers across a wide range of countries have recognized the need to significantly update both the content and communication of modern teaching. Some states are assessing the UK initiative to introduce computer coding in primary schools and several organizations are further encouraging girls to develop these skills.[7] In Canada, the P21 4Cs and identified life and career skills have been integrated into 7 Cs: Creativity, innovation and entrepreneurship; Critical thinking; Collaboration; Communication; Character; Culture and ethical citizenship; and, Computer and digital technology (C21, 2012). We found the Pellegrino and Hilton (2012) summary of the various frameworks to be of value:

- The Cognitive Domain includes three clusters of competencies: cognitive processes and strategies; knowledge; and creativity. These clusters include competencies such as critical thinking, information literacy, reasoning and argumentation, and innovation.

---

[7]For an illustration of the objectives and resources for teaching coding across all grades, see the Edutopia site at: http://www.edutopia.org/topic/coding-classroom. For a presentation in the Australian context; see Leon Sterlings article "An education for the 21st century means teaching coding in schools", accessible at http://theconversation.com/an-education-for-the-21st-century-means-teaching-coding-in-schools-42046.

- The Intrapersonal Domain includes three clusters of competencies: intellectual openness; work ethic and conscientiousness; and positive core self-evaluation. These clusters include competencies such as flexibility, initiative, appreciation for diversity, and metacognition (the ability to reflect on one's own learning and make adjustments accordingly).
- The Interpersonal Domain includes two clusters of competencies: teamwork and collaboration; and leadership. These clusters include competencies such as communication, collaboration, responsibility, and conflict resolution.

We will explore how these aptitudes are developed through formal education in the following section; later, we will focus on the competencies that will be critical for success in the 21st century workplace.

Shifting K-12 Pedagogy

> Surface changes in education will not equip students for the 21st Century: Change is needed at the core of educational practice.—Shifting Minds 3.0

Beyond developing broad frameworks, those arguing for the development of 21st Century Skills are presenting new methodologies that call for significant changes in pedagogy (C21, 2012; Jenkins et al., 2006; P21, 2007; Pellegrino & Hilton, 2012).[8] To prepare for future courses and the complexities and interconnectedness of today's society, they believe that students should learn the conceptual underpinnings and assumptions behind core content. This includes actively addressing misconceptions they might bring to the classroom especially, as already highlighted, those that can be formed from visiting Internet websites. An important concept is that students should be encouraged to be inquisitive and to investigate core content critically. To do so, they need to collaborate with other students and learn from mentors of all types. This approach should enable 21st Century learners to use their skills to create and transform knowledge for meaningful purposes.

Researchers have concluded that the model of simple transmission of knowledge is no longer acceptable and will not develop new skills needed for today's evolving society and workplaces (Bozalek et al., 2013; Dearn, 2010; Schols, 2012). Recent research is concluding that, in addition to increasing student learning, an inquiry-based approach can motivate students to learn and advance their problem solving and critical thinking skills.[9] Thus, pedagogy is shifting away from 'siloed'

---

[8]Pedagogy refers to an array of teaching strategies that support intellectual engagement, connectedness to the wider world, supportive classroom environments, and recognition of difference while promoting the wellbeing and confidence of students, teachers and the school community. http://education.qld.gov.au/curriculum/learning/teaching/technology/pedagogy/index.html.

[9]For ongoing presentation of relevant research and resources in the Canadian context, see the Canadian Education Association website at: http://www.cea-ace.ca/research-publications/other?field_publications_author_nid=6784&tid=All.

learning with a specific block of time dedicated to an individual core subject to multi-subject, integrated learning. Further, many Post-Millennials are more likely to conduct their learning activities in group contexts; the days of pupils sitting in rows of individual desks taking notes or working on problem sheets are numbered. These shifts require increased resources including access to new technologies, funding to retain excellent teachers and, most crucially, time for teachers during the school day.

Given these pedagogical shifts, Post-Millennials will experience a much more fluid classroom than preceding generations with increased focus on the development of 21st Century Skills through project-based activities, inquiry-focussed learning, interdisciplinary teaching and individualized education. Central to this shift is a move away from the traditional textbook-lecture teaching model towards project- and problem-based instruction, including self-learning with guidance from a teacher (C21, 2012; P21, 2007). This type of instruction includes introducing students to realistic, real-world problems. Projects present complex, multidisciplinary problems that are designed to require critical thinking skills, collaboration, written and oral communication and problem-solving skills thus presenting the learning experiences needed to develop the necessary 21st Century Skills (P21, 2007; Pearlman, 2009).

An individual's success in the classroom—and in later life—also increasingly depends upon many factors including learning styles, learning needs, multiple intelligences, and learner preferences (Crumpacker, 2001; Saeed, Yang, & Sinnappan, 2009). We found that accepted pedagogy continues to evolve from the "sink or swim approach" to "individualized" or "differentiated" education. This means abandoning "equal" treatment regardless of ethnicity, gender or ability towards a teaching style that emphasizes the importance of addressing each student's needs and beliefs, while celebrating strength through diversity in the classroom (Egbo, 2009). This enables a pupil to understand material according to their strengths, abilities, and learning style rather than forcing their education into a specific path (P21, 2007). When best practiced, students receive personalized learning opportunities and individualized access to technology based on the student's passions, strengths, weaknesses and interests (C21, 2012). Accordingly, teaching at the elementary level more closely approximates coaching than professing: teachers are expected not only to instruct students, but also to support and mentor them using individually tailored approaches.

In our analyses of the ongoing pedagogical evolutions to develop 21st Century Skills, three key factors stand out. First, the expansion of curricula to develop the analytical capabilities to connect declarative knowledge to real world contexts. Second is increased emphasis on interdisciplinary learning. Third, and most critical, is the shift away from teacher directed learning and towards student-group exploration with peer and teacher support. Thus, far more than in previous years, learning will be exploratory, shared and creative. By facilitating this learning environment, 21st Century curricula are reinforcing the importance of *learning how to learn*, rather than learning by rote. Through encouraging students to explore and challenge assumptions, they will be better prepared for the transformations in the nature of work that will arise from digital evolutions, and by facilitating group learning, students will be better prepared to work in teams and understand issues in a broader cultural context.

Our conclusion is that, when properly resourced, supported by schools and embraced by students, this transformation in 21st Century curricula will better prepare students for their future workplaces. We recognize that inequities will continue to exist in all three of resources, school support and student engagement however offer a few optimistic perspectives. First, P21 highlights that the key shift is in philosophy and that altering the nature of pedagogy experienced by students does not have to be resource intensive. They provide a series of "Exemplars" with short case studies to demonstrate how changes can be affected. Their description of Title 1[10] Katherine Smith Elementary School in San Jose, CA provides an illustrative example.[11] Second, US research is challenging common perceptions that ineffective parenting is a significant factor in explaining poor educational outcomes for children in low income families leading to recommendations for shifts in the strategies used to improve these outcomes (Oser, Beck, Alvarado, & Pang, 2014; Watkins & Howard, 2015).

Technology and the Digital Classroom

We have reached the end of squeezing good out of an outdated school system.—Michael Fullen

We found that these pedagogical shifts are occurring in tandem with the emergence of the digitized classroom. For students, technology in the classroom can motivate success by leveraging the enthusiasm that many Post-Millennials hold towards the digital world. For those students who have Internet access at home, digital technology provides an opportunity to access experts within a global community. Students are also increasingly creating their own content online: websites, online profiles, multimedia art, and participating in online collaborative projects (C21, 2012). P21 researchers argue that students' enthusiasm for digital technology extends to their schoolwork. For example, the National School Boards Association found that half of students with online access say they use social networking services to talk specifically about schoolwork. Embracing these new technologies will build an education system that "connects to student's lives" (P21, 2007).

Multimedia presentations can introduce a lively and interactive method to explore content. Advanced scientific technology can support and encourage interest in the important sectors of science, technology, engineering and math (STEM). An Internet connection can facilitate distance learning and foster relationships by connecting students to interactive online multimedia and by increasing their

---

[10]Under US Department of Education programs, Title 1 schools are identified as having high numbers or high percentages of children from low-income families and receive funding to help ensure that all children meet challenging state academic standards: https://www2.ed.gov/programs/titleiparta/index.html.

[11]Accessible at: http://www.p21.org/exemplar-program-case-studies/1623.

exposure to cultures beyond their community. Online learning can allow students to interact with individuals or groups across the world that bring different skills, cultural experiences, and perceptions. Online learning also provides students with a number of different tools such as messaging services, wikis, blogs, and podcasts that allow students to collaborate, create, publish, subscribe, and share information (Arnett, 2012; Fullen, 2012; Saeed et al., 2009). Technical innovation will provide even more opportunities for digital learning through gaming and gamification of learning content, the use of "big data" to inform teaching practices, 3D printing in the classroom and wearable technologies (Skiba, 2013).

While the expanding role of technology is changing student learning, the more profound effect of technology is to be found in teaching. Many of the pedagogical shifts presented in the last section are enabled by digital technology. Interdisciplinary lessons, for instance, are enabled by the expansion of technology into the classroom to overcome transaction costs that previously prevented their deployment (21st Century Skills, 2007). For teachers, the Internet enables access to standards-based lessons and resources that can provide teachers with models, research-based strategies and useful materials while allowing them to devote more time to student learning than to preparatory activities (P21, 2007). Technology can also support teachers with professional development: online training, coaching, collaboration, and discussion forums are helping teachers implement research-based strategies and promising practices that can improve student achievement (C21, 2012). Educators now have the capability to learn and collaborate with peers, mentors, and experts, build ongoing professional relationships and, together, develop greater capacity in teaching 21st Century Skills.

Accordingly, many advocating 21st Century curricula also point out that it is important that educators and staff members master 21st Century teaching skills to be effective in their careers. Ongoing professional development is critical in ensuring that educators are kept abreast of emerging technologies and provided with suitable classroom applications for that technology (Kukulska-Hulme, 2011; Misra, 2010; Ryan & Fraser, 2010). Not only are students in need of becoming lifelong learners, but so too are instructors (Kukulska-Hulme, 2011). Teachers need to become "E-excellent teachers" who can adapt technologies to suit their specific educational objectives and acquire new teaching competencies with the perspective that online education is not a tool, but a 'new context for learning' (Misra, 2010, p. 24).

The technically competent teacher will have access to other powerful tools to facilitate the 21st century classroom. Effective assessment tools and techniques are required to ensure that students are developing and correctly applying 21st century skills (Pearlman, 2009). Computer-based testing and assessments can provide immediate, individualized, and customized results to facilitate student self-assessment and allow the educator to quickly adjust lesson plans when required. Teachers and administrators can use technology to facilitate relationships with parents and the broader school community, while education officials can more easily compare data between jurisdictions and administer adjusted curricula. In sum, technology is having a transformational influence not only on the skills taught in the classroom, but how those skills are taught.

It is important to note that our analyses revealed that, at present, not all schools have been able to use technology to support these new teaching paradigms. P21 (2007) research found two obstacles to capitalizing on technology in American schools: the belief that technology can only be leveraged to increase technical literacy, and a commonly held but incorrect assumption that American schools are already "well connected." In the Canadian context, Jenson, Fisher, and Taylor (2011) provided a comprehensive assessment of issues in the Ontario education system, and asserted that obstacles to the introduction of technology in the classroom include budgetary constraints, the antiquated belief that technology will encourage students to waste time, and that its introduction could encourage dangerous or improper use.[12] Chen, Gallagher-Mackay, and Kidder (2014) suggest Ontario educators are having a difficult time keeping up with the technologies and maintaining the devices that they currently have. Furthermore, great variance is reported in how technology is being used: in Ontario secondary schools, 43% of principals stated that the primary use of technology in classrooms at their schools was for videos with 33% reporting student access to external websites as the second major utility (Chen et al., 2014).

Nevertheless, the movement towards the digital classroom is well underway. In response to the growing literature on the new generation of learners, many American and Canadian schools are incorporating technology in the classroom. In the United States, efforts have been made to draw on both government funding and philanthropic contributions to provide digital access.[13] Chen et al. (2014) reported survey results that, in 2013–2014, 99% of Ontario schools studied provide students with access to computers and 80% of respondents report the incorporation of technology starting in kindergarten. The remaining students are reported to have access no later than grade 4; in fact, principals contend that students might have access from the beginning of their school career, but the technology is not fully utilized and integrated until a few years later. They also found that computer labs are no longer the focus of technology in Ontario schools: 96% of principals interviewed reported that classroom-based use of technology was the primary method of technological incorporation, while computer labs and libraries are now secondary options. As well, school boards and schools are increasingly encouraging students to 'bring your own device' (Alberta, 2012; Saskatchewan, 2013) with research demonstrating that students were able to shift from using these devices as sources of entertainment to channels for learning (Wideman, 2012).

The 21st Century classroom learning in the Post-Millennial context may not be focused entirely on gaining and internalizing information but, instead, may focus more on using creativity to re-interpret information. Whether this generation will be judicious in assessing the information they gather from the Internet remains to be seen. Our research suggest that they will need help in determining the reliability of

---

[12]See Rutherford's posts at: http://www.drcamillerutherford.ca/ and her presentation: "Challenges to Facilitating 21st Century Skills in the Classroom" at: https://www.youtube.com/watch?v=9mZtDqyVjtg.

[13]https://obamawhitehouse.archives.gov/the-press-office/2014/12/08/fact-sheet-new-commitments-support-computer-science-education.

the information at their fingertips and may be too trusting of the Internet as a resource for immediate information both in the classroom and at home (Pew Research Center, 2015). The research we examined suggests that many in this generation value sharing information and personal opinion, implying that they may be quite open to collaborative learning opportunities but may not have the wisdom to place new information in the right context, a skill identified in the P21 framework.

In assessing the potential of the 21st Century classroom to transform both what and how children learn, we acknowledge that some realities will persist that will serve to limit the impact on any one student. Some will be more focussed on extra-curricular activities such as sports, hobbies, social life, family or community, while others may not have the motivation, financial stability, family continuity or life conditions to concentrate on learning. Differences are likely to remain in educational outcomes (graduation rates, literacy levels, college entrance exam scores, etc.) based on well-known sub-group indicators such as gender, ethnicity/race, region and community income levels. However, high school graduation rates continue to rise in the US.[14] Researchers, however, suggest the newer pedagogy may reduce these gaps (Jenkins et al., 2006; Darling-Hammond, Zielezinski, & Goldman, 2014; Sharples, Slavin, Chambers, & Sharp, 2011). As one indicator of progress, US data reveals the previous gender differences for enrolment rate and academic performance between boys and girls for K-12 science and mathematics courses no longer exists although gaps persist based on ethnicity/race and income.[15] A promising development is 'bottom-up' knowledge transfer whereby children educate their parents about digital technologies thus transferring knowledge from the school to the home and from the youth to the parents (Correa, 2015). Benefits have been identified for lower income families in the US (Katz, Moran, & Gonzalez, 2017).

Our overall assessment is that the shifts in pedagogy and increased access to the digital environment will provide far greater opportunities for students, regardless of their circumstances, to achieve more than under the approaches that were in place in the 20th Century classroom. While teachers have always been able to identify the rare child prodigy or classroom genius, those with the aptitude, interest and determination can soar well beyond what was possible in previous years and others can learn about and learn from them far faster. While the bubbling volcano may still show up at science fairs, examples such as the 11 year old who invented a portable chemotherapy bag, 7th graders inventing new solar cells or receiving patents and teenagers creating new approaches to cancer treatments, supercapacitors, bandages that can detect bacteria or artificial intelligence for the visually impaired—and the fact that the world and business community knows of these amazing discoveries— are all attributable to new approaches to learning facilitated by the digital environment.[16]

---

[14]See annually updated data at: https://nces.ed.gov/fastfacts/display.asp?id=805.

[15]See the National Girls Collaborative Project data at: https://ngcproject.org/statistics.

[16]For some of the examples, see: http://www.edutopia.org/william-yuan-summa-options-science, http://inhabitat.com/13-year-old-makes-solar-power-breakthrough-by-harnessing-the-fibonacci-sequence/,   http://www.themarysue.com/17-year-old-girl-cancer-killer/,   http://www.oddee.com/

Tertiary Education

A university is just a group of buildings gathered around a library.—Shelby Foote

While our focus is on the primary and secondary levels of education that Post-Millennials receive, many youth will also undertake some form of tertiary education. Since the description of adult education is seen as "differing between country and country depending on historical circumstances" (Rubenson, 2010, p. 2), we define tertiary education as any formalized learning that occurs following secondary education, including university degrees, community college diplomas, vocational training, or certificate programs. In the last two decades, technology has influenced and changed the methods of delivering this form of education, both in distance formats and the traditional lecture hall. As illustrated with universities such as Phoenix and Walden in the US and Athabasca in Canada, some tertiary educational programs are now available completely online and are incorporating new approaches to andragogy (Bakia, 2010; Hiltz & Turoff, 2005; ICDE, 2009; Kanwar & Daniel, 2010; Means & Roschelle, 2010; Scott, 2010). In addition, students, parents, industries and, increasingly, governments that support post-secondary institutions are demanding that graduates obtain practical, transferrable skills to obtain the most value from their education. Thus, just as K-12 learning is evolving, important changes are also occurring in post-secondary contexts. Our analysis suggests that these changes will only accelerate when the pupils graduating from secondary schools equipped with 21st Century Skills move on to the next stage of their education.

Distance learning refers to programs delivered by tertiary institutions outside their physical campus. At one time, distance education was facilitated through traditional mail. Although distance learning created an opportunity for students to continue their learning without regard to their proximity to the educational institution (Abik, Ajhoun, & Ensias, 2012; Anderson & Dron, 2011), it suffered from little to no interaction amongst learners, making collaborative learning nearly impossible. The emergence of mass media and information technologies facilitated a second generation of distance learning: *electronic* learning or E-Learning (Abik et al., 2012; Anderson & Dron, 2011). Electronic learning has allowed more individuals to access tertiary education, increasing participation rates globally (Means & Roschelle, 2010; Millwood & Terrell, 2005). E-Learning builds on traditional distance education by facilitating collaborative and group learning through discussion boards and chat rooms, and provides more interactive tools for the learner, such as electronic readings, videos and e-quizzes.

More recently, the proliferation of smartphones and tablets has enabled *mobile* distance learning, where lessons can follow the student wherever they go. The increased use of wireless and mobile technologies was becoming the dominating trend in education over ten years ago (Kim, Mims, & Holmes, 2006). The integration of learning into social networks has led to *pervasive* distance learning that

---

item_99064.aspx, and http://blog.studentlifenetwork.com/2015/08/11/9-enormous-scientific-breakthroughs-and-the-young-canadian-students-behind-them/.

encourages the 'continuity of communication' and encourages students to share in the production and dissemination of knowledge (Abik et al., 2012). New technologies that permit this knowledge creation include blogs (Namwar & Rastgoo, 2008), wikis, instant messengers, social bookmarks, podcasts and vodcasts, allowing both instructors and learners to collaborate, create, publish, subscribe, and share information (Arnett, 2012; Saeed et al., 2009).

The increasing popularity of the massively open online course (MOOC) model of educational delivery, introduced in 2008, is noteworthy (Howard, 2014; Skiba, 2013; Wensveen, 2014). Based on connectivism and networking theories (Daniel, 2012) MOOCs offer large enrolment, are open for participation with little to no cost to the students, are offered online, and follow a course format with learning goals specific to an area of study (EDUCAUSE, 2013).[17] MOOCs are growing at an unprecedented rate as this model offers educational institutions the ability to present vast amounts of information and reduce common barriers to education.[18] MOOCs appeal to a variety of students, including: vocational learners, educators and researchers, higher education students, 'hobby' learners, and prospective students. MOOCs enable access to high quality academic content and the possibility to interact with multiple learners from different locations. This type of course is primarily offered through independent online platforms such as Coursera, edX, Futurelearn, and Udacity (Universities UK, 2013). Furthermore, many universities are now broadcasting videos and content from traditional brick-and-mortar lecture halls onto the Internet, allowing anyone with a connection to audit credit-based courses at no cost.

Despite being relatively new, MOOCs have already undergone variations in structure that have distinct pedagogical underpinnings. cMOOCs are structured around the traditional MOOC evolution that was based on networking and connectivism.[19] In a cMOOC environment, the learning experience is more communitarian: through technology, participants create and share knowledge, effectively becoming both student and teacher. xMOOCs align with a behaviourist pedagogical approach and follow more traditional learning formats (Daniel, 2012; Universities UK, 2013).[20] A student of an xMOOC can expect the same experience as they would in a classroom—grades, lectures, quizzes, homework—but all from the comfort of their computer. MOOCs enable life-long higher education and it is

---

[17]Connectivism assumes that the key characteristics of learning in connectivist learning environments, such as MOOCs, are openness, autonomy, diversity, and interactivity/connectedness (Downes, 2010).

[18]Yet another example of how the reduction in transactions costs due to digital advancements are creating disruptive changes to traditional models.

[19]McAuley et al. (2010) define cMOOCs as: An online course with the option of free and open registration, a publicly shared curriculum, and open-ended outcomes which integrates social networking, accessible online resources… and most significantly builds on the engagement of learners who self-organize their participation according to learning goals, prior knowledge and skills, and common interests. (p. 10).

[20]In his blog post, George Siemens states "cMOOCs focus on knowledge creation and generation, whereas xMOOCs focus on knowledge duplication", http://www.elearnspace.org/blog/2012/07/25/moocs-are-really-a-platform/.

predicted that they will remain a popular approach to delivering education for the foreseeable future (Howard, 2014).

As with our review of K-12 pedagogy, we recognized that, as technology continues to enter tertiary forms of education, changes will occur in traditional pedagogical approaches. Here too, digital evolutions influence not only content and delivery, but the assumptions behind learning. Abrami, Bernard, Bures, Borokhovski, and Tamim (2011) argue that as a result, "distance education and online learning have evolved beyond simple comparisons with classroom instruction" (p. 83). The new application of technologies counters the widely noted problem in distance learning of poor interaction between students, students and instructors, and between student and content. These researchers argue that emerging technologies have the power to create interactions that are "guided, focused, and purposeful" and extend the notion of being able to interact via technology in new, more complex ways such as through different forms of communication utilizing images, statements, and presentations (Abrami et al., 2011, p. 88). Furthermore, mobile learning can be viewed from a socio-cultural perspective arguing that learning is affected and modified by the tools used for learning that then influences the various ways the tools are used (Kearney, Schuck, Burden, & Aubusson, 2012). They state that "Central to our position here is the notion that learning is a situated, social endeavour, facilitated and developed through social interactions and conversations between people (Vygotsky, 1978), and mediated through tool use (Wertsch, 1991)." This notion is grounded in the understanding that learning does not occur in a vacuum, but rather in a geo-historically specific environment that is developed and facilitated through social interaction (Canning, 2010).

The concept of blended learning or hybrid learning refers to the combination of technology and direct, face-to-face contact (Singh, 2012). This concept is informed by the theory of social networking as a form of knowledge construction and the need for interactions in distance education. Common learning management platforms that encourage blended learning include Blackboard, Moodle, and Desire2Learn, that are becoming commonplace in Canadian universities. Blended learning takes the best elements and opportunities of the emerging technologies to enhance face-to-face learning. As with online learning, blended learning ultimately increases the likelihood of meaningful learning by considering pedagogical components (theory, instructional design, needs of the learners, etc.) that have been overlooked in the past when using technology for educational purposes (Hiltz & Turoff, 2005; Turney, Robinson, & Soutar, 2009). By adopting the pedagogy of blended learning, a balance is achieved between distance education and traditional face-to-face learning styles and they forecast that higher education institutions will have to adopt this approach to remain viable (Hiltz & Turoff, 2005).

Similar to the premises of blended learning, the notion of a 'flipped classroom' has emerged to indicate how aspects of blended learning are adopted from a classroom-based perspective. A 'flipped classroom' refers to the integration of online learning throughout the lesson and encourages social problem solving (EDUCAUSE, 2013; The Economist, 2011). In other words, technology is utilized to provide students an understanding of the core material prior to instruction, while classroom-based activity is focused on the application and exploration of the topic at hand. This approach can be used in distance and residential courses. Classroom learning is not eliminated, but rather time is spent on interactions via learning management systems, and digital resources between the instructor and students, students and students, and students and material. Resta and Laferrière (2007) highlight collaborative outcomes associated with technological developments such as higher-order thinking, deep understanding, and knowledge creation that differ significantly from traditional theories and approaches to education.

Since pedagogy is shifting toward transformative, meaningful learning experiences, some argue that traditional curricula may need to be customized to reflect the new modes of learning (Georgescu & Popescu, 2013). Further, Singh (2012) states that, "higher education institutions, faced with the massification of knowledge production and the increased use of communication information technologies, have struggled to come to terms with the current changes" (p. 5).

As with primary and secondary education, the changes demanded by new trends in education are creating problems for institutions of higher education as there is considerable variance in the ability of instructors to effectively incorporate emergent technology in the classroom (Carter & Graham, 2012). These implications have connections to institutional funding and influence from governing bodies and the organization must undergo a process of 'unlearning' to change habits, routines, and welcome the current pedagogy.

What does the future hold for technology and tertiary education? In their prediction of the future of distance education, Anderson and Dron (2011) highlight that they see a new paradigm emerging that is characterized by an increasing desire for privacy that will affect the networks in which we belong and the movement towards more object-based, contextual, or activity-based modes of learning. They also identify that new networks of learning are enhancing the ability of groups of individuals to act collectively and assist in guiding each other's education. The 21st century notion of life-long, self-guided learning as an outcome will remain a consideration for the evolution of new technologies in years to come (Parsons, 2010; Anderson, Boyles, & Rainie, 2012).

As a result, the continued presence of unlimited, free learning may indicate the changing role of tertiary educational institutions as the transmission of knowledge need not necessarily be linked with formal institutions. Although pedagogical foundations are changing as rapidly as the technology that interacts with them, the value of tertiary institutions in providing opportunities to develop 21st Century Skills will likely remain over time. We argue that at higher levels—much like the elementary and secondary experience—technology's most profound effect on education is in the changes to the methodology, tools and the assumptions that inform learning as process.

Life-Long Learning

The only thing that interferes with my learning is my education.—Albert Einstein

Our research led us to conclude that the pedagogical shifts that most Post-Millennials will be afforded will have implications for their approach to continued learning once they leave the classroom. Many Post-Millennials will seek continuous education as life-long learners with a strong preference for customized learning that takes place when they need it or as they need it rather than pre-planned career training or education (Daniel, 2012).

Strong connections have been shown between MOOCs and life-long learning and it is predicted that some form of open, distributed learning will remain a focus of educational approaches (Howard, 2014). Online learning is also an avenue for encouraging continued professional development by allowing individuals to manage their own learning (Bozalek et al., 2013; Cleveland-Innes & Emes, 2005; Lea & Jones, 2011; Rezaei-zadeh, O'Reilly, Cleary, & Murphy, 2011). To get each person to adopt the responsibility of designing and managing their own growth as a life-long learner, they must take on the role of an "independent, continuous, active learner" (Cleveland-Innes & Emes, 2005). By creating a learning experience that is authentic and transformative, the individual is able to make connections with knowledge that extend into multiple contexts and engages them in critical reflection (Bozalek et al., 2013; Cleveland-Innes & Emes, 2005; Lea & Jones, 2011; Rezaei-Zadeh et al., 2011; Schols, 2012; Wood & Bilsborow, 2013).[21] Ultimately, both higher education and any employee training or skill development programmes must focus on the student and strive for outcomes related to "knowledge and skill about learning and human development" (Cleveland-Innes & Emes, 2005, p. 87). We have highlighted collaborative outcomes associated with technological developments and underscored the importance of examining key outcomes of collaborative learning such as higher-order thinking, deep understanding, and knowledge creation.

In addition to life long learning being seen as an extension of formal education after graduation or a means to acquire valuable work skills, the digital environment has also facilitated significant changes in how individuals access practical skills for their everyday life. Youtube is the largest repository of do-it-yourself (DIY) videos with researchers demonstrating that the process of creating and accessing these clips is resulting in social and cultural changes (Gauntlett, 2011; Wolf, 2016). As highlighted in the initial portion of this chapter, this approach to DIY is fully consistent with the new ways that young people are learning to learn.

---

[21]A comprehensive presentation of the theory underlying authentic learning is presented in Herrington et al. (2010).

Conclusion

In sum, the changes in pedagogy and the expanding potential of the digital environment to support learning suggests that those entering the workforce in the future will have the potential to be far better equipped to deal with the dynamic, and potentially turbulent, demands of the new economy. We acknowledge 'potential to' does not automatically translate into 'will have' with full recognition of the many factors that can inhibit learning outcomes. It is clear, however, that today's youth are immersed in a digital culture, one that will continue into their working lives. Not only is this changing how these individuals interact with each other and society at large, it is also changing how they learn and, crucially, how they *learn to learn*. To this end, the digital age is changing the nature of education. Beyond the prevalence of the computer in the classroom, the engaged Post-Millennial student will be developing different skills than previous generations including the Millennials. We will explore the implications commencing with the introduction to the second section of this book and the following three chapters.

References

Abik, M., Ajhoun, R., & Ensias, L. (2012). Impact of technological advancement on pedagogy. *Turkish Online Journal of Distance Education, 13*(1), 224–237. Retrieved from http://eric.ed. gov/?id=EJ976961.

Abrami, P. C., Bernard, R. M., Bures, E. M., Borokhovski, E., & Tamim, R. M. (2011). Interaction in distance education and online learning: using evidence and theory to improve practice. *Journal of Computing in Higher Education, 23*(2), 82–103.

Alberta Ministry of Education. (2012). *Bring your own device: A guide for schools*. Edmonton, AB: Crown in the Right of the Province of Alberta. Retrieved from https://archive.education. alberta.ca/media/6749210/byod%20guide%20revised%202012-09-05.pdf.

Anderson, J. Q., Boyles, J. L., & Rainie, L. (2012). *The future impact of the internet on higher education: Experts expect more-efficient collaborative environments and new grading schemes; they worry about massive online courses, the shift away from on-campus life*. Washington, DC: Pew Research Center.

Anderson, T., & Dron, J. (2011). Three generations of distance education pedagogy. *The International Review of Research in Open and Distance Learning, 12*(3), 80–97. Retrieved from http://www.irrodl.org/index.php/irrodl/article/view/890/1663.

Arnett, A. A. (2012). There's an app for that. *Diverse Education, 29*(14), 14–15. Retrieved from http://eric.ed.gov/?id=EJ988561.

Bakia, M. (2010). Technology and learning—Global trends: Internet-based education. In *International encyclopedia of education* (3rd ed., pp. 102–108).

Bozalek, V., Gachago, D., Alexander, L., Watters, K., Wood, D., Ivala, E., et al. (2013). The use of emerging technologies for authentic learning: A South African study in higher education. *British Journal of Educational Technology, 44*(4), 629–638.

Canning, N. (2010). Playing with heutagogy: Exploring strategies to empower mature learners in higher education. *Journal of Further and Higher Education, 34*(1), 59–71.

C21: Canadians for 21st Century Skills and Innovation (2012). *Shifting minds: A 21st century vision for public education for Canada*. Accessed 11 January 2015 at http://www.c21canada. org/wp-content/uploads/2012/11/Shifting-Minds-Revised.pdf.

Carter, L., & Graham, R. D. (2012). The evolution of online education at a small northern Ontario university: Theory and practice. *The Journal of Distance Education, 26*(2). Retrieved from http://www.ijede.ca/index.php/jde/article/view/799/1433.

Chen, B., Gallagher-Mackay, K., & Kidder, A. (2014). *Digital learning in Ontario schools: The 'new normal'*. Toronto, ON: People for Education. Retrieved from http://www.peopleforeducation.ca/wp-content/uploads/2014/03/digital-learning-2014-WEB.pdf.

Cleveland-Innes, M., & Emes, C. (2005). Principles of learner-centered curriculum: Responding to the call for change in higher education. *The Canadian Journal of Higher Education, 35*(4), 85–110. Retrieved from http://journals.sfu.ca/cjhe/index.php/cjhe/article/viewFile/183522/184142.

Correa, T. (2015). The power of youth: How the bottom-up technology transmission from children to parents is related to digital (in)equality. *International Journal of Communication, 9,* 1163–1186.

Crumpacker, N. (2001). Faculty pedagogical approach, skill, and motivation in today's distance education milieu. *Online Journal of Distance Learning and Administration, 4*(4). Retrieved from http://www.westga.edu/~distance/ojdla/winter44/crumpacker44.html.

Daniel, J. (2012). Making sense of MOOCs: Musings in a maze of myth, paradox, and possibility. *Journal of Interactive Media in Education, 18*(3), 1–20.

Darling-Hammond, I., Zielezinski, M. B., & Goldman, S. (2014). *Using technology to support at-risk students*. CA: Learning Stanford. Stanford center for opportunity policy in education.

Dearn, J. M. (2010). Innovation in teaching and curriculum design. *International Encyclopedia of Education* (3rd ed., pp. 448–454).

Downes, S. (2010). What is democracy in education? Web log post. Accessible at http://halfanhour.blogspot.com/2010/10/what-is-democracy-in-education.html.

Economist Online (2011). Electronic education: Flipping the classroom. *The Economist*. London: The Economist Group.

Educause (2013). *7 things you should know about MOOCs II*. Retrieved from http://www.educause.edu/library/resources/7-things-you-should-know-about-moocs-ii.

Egbo, B. (2009). *Teaching for diversity in Canadian schools*. Toronto, ON: Pearson.

Fullen, M. A. (2012). *Stratosphere: Integrating technology, pedagogy and change knowledge*. Toronto: Pearson Canada.

Gauntlett, D. (2011). *Making is connecting: The social meaning of creativity from DIY and knitting to YouTube and Web 2.0*. Cambridge: Polity Press.

Georgescu, M., & Popescu, D. (2013). The different effects of e-learning technology in Romanian higher education. In *The International Scientific Conference eLearning and Software for Education*, (Vol. 1, pp. 492–498). Bucharest: "Carol I" National Defence University.

Herrington, J., Reeves, T. C., & Oliver, R. (2010). *A guide to authentic e-learning*. London: Routledge.

Hiltz, S. R., & Turoff, M. (2005). Education goes digital: The evolution of online learning and the revolution in higher education. *Communications of the ACM, 48*(10), 59–64.

Howard, K. (2014). *Massive open online courses (MOOCs): Implications and opportunities for the community college system in New Brunswick*. Department of Post-Secondary Education, Training and Labour. Fredericton, NB: Government of New Brunswick.

International Council for Open and Distance Education (ICDE). (2009). *Global trends in higher education, adult and distance learning*. Oslo: The International Council for Open and Distance Education.

Jenkins, H., Clinton, K., Purushotma, R., Robinson, A. J., & Weigel, M. (2006). *Confronting the challenges of participatory culture: Media education for the 21st century*. Chicago, IL: The MacArthur Foundation.

Jenson, J., Fisher, S., & Taylor, N. (2011). *Critical review and analysis of the issue of "skills, technology and learning": Final report*. Toronto: Ontario Ministry of Education.

Johansen, J. D., & Sondergaard, L. (2010). *Fact, fiction and faction*. Copenhagen: University Press of Southern Denmark.

Kanwar A., & Daniel, J. (2010). Higher education—teaching and learning in higher education: Distance education and open universities. In *International Encyclopedia of Education* (3rd ed., pp. 404–410).

Katz, V.S., Moran, M.B. & Gonzalez, C. (2017) Connecting with technology in lower-income US families. *New Media and Society*, published online at https://doi.org/10.1177/1461444817726319.

Kearney, M., Schuck, S., Burden, K., & Aubusson, P. (2012). Viewing mobile learning from a pedagogical perspective. *Research in Learning Technology, 20*, 1–17.

Kim, S. H., Mims, C., & Holmes, K. P. (2006). An introduction to current trends and benefits of mobile wireless technology use in higher education. *AACE Journal, 14*(1), 77–100. Retrieved from https://www.researchgate.net/publication/254387985_An_Introduction_to_Current_Trends_and_Benefits_of_Mobile_Wireless_Technology_Use_in_Higher_Education.

Kukulska-Hulme, A. (2011). How should the higher education workforce adapt to advancements in technology for teaching and learning? *Internet and Higher Education, 15*(4), 247–254. https://doi.org/10.1016/j.iheduc.2011.12.002.

Lea, M. R., & Jones, S. (2011). Digital literacies in higher education: Exploring textual and technological practice. *Studies in Higher Education, 36*(4), 377–393.

McAuley, A., Stewart, B., Siemens, G., & Cormier, D. (2010). *The MOOC model for digital practice*. Charlottetown: University of Prince Edward Island. Accessible at http://www.elearnspace.org/Articles/MOOC_Final.pdf.

Means, B., & Roschelle, J. (2010). Technology and learning: An overview of technology and learning. In E. Baker, B. McGaw, & P. Peterson (Eds.), *International encyclopedia of education* (3rd ed.). Oxford: Elsevier.

Millwood, R., & Terrell, I. (2005). Overview: New technology, learning and assessment in higher education. *Innovations in Education and Teaching International, 42*(3), 195–204. Retrieved from http://www.naec.org.uk/ultralab/ww3/publications/1%20Millwood%20and%20Terrell%20-%20Overview.pdf.

Misra, P. K. (2010). Preparing e-excellent teachers for the world of e-education: Potential strategies. *I-Managers Journal of Educational Technology, 7*(3), 21–29.

Namwar, Y., & Rastgoo, A. (2008). Weblog as a learning tool in higher education. *Turkish Online Journal of Distance Education, 9*(3), 176–185. Retrieved from http://tojde.anadolu.edu.tr/yonetim/icerik/makaleler/432-published.pdf.

Olson, H. A. (2002). *The power to name: Locating the limits of subject representation in libraries*. Dordrecht, The Netherlands: Kluwer Academic Publishers.

Organization for Economic Cooperation and Development. (2005). *The definition and selection of key competencies*. Paris, France: OECD.

Oser, R., Beck, E., Alvarado, J. L., & Pang, V. O. (2014). School and community wellness: Transforming achievement using a holistic orientation to learning. *Multicultural Perspectives, 16*(1), 26–34.

P 21: Partnership for 21st Century Skills. (2007). *The intellectual and policy foundations of the 21st century skills framework*. Washington: P21. Retrieved from http://www.p21.org/storage/documents/docs/Intellectual_and_Policy_Foundations.pdf.

Parsons, J. (2010). Envisioning education in the year 2050: By midcentury, what will education look like? *Alberta Teachers' Association Magazine, 90*(4), 30–35. Retrieved from http://www.teachers.ab.ca/Publications/ATA%20Magazine/Volume%2090/Number4/Pages/Envisioning-Education-in-the-Year-2050.aspx.

Pearlman, B. (2009). Designing new learning environments to support 21st century skills. In J. Bellanca & R. Brandt (Eds.), *21st century skills: Rethinking how students learn* (pp. 117–147). Bloomington, IN: Solution Tree Press.

Pellegrino, J. W., & Hilton, M. L. (2012). *Education for life and work: Developing transferable knowledge and skills in the 21st century.* Washington, DC: National Academies Press. (Report of the committee on defining deeper learning and 21st century skills; Center for education; National research council).

Pew Research Center. (2015). *Comparing Millennials to other generations.* Retrieved from http://www.pewsocialtrends.org/2010/02/24/interactive-graphic-demographic-portrait-of-four-generations/.

Resta, P., & Laferrière, T. (2007). Technology in support of collaborative learning. *Education Psychology Review, 19*(1), 65–83.

Rezaei-zadeh, M., O'Reilly, J., Cleary, B., & Murphy, E. (2011). A review of the bases and solutions to deficiency in the effective use of technology in the creation of lifelong learning in higher education. In *Conference proceedings of eLearning and Software for Education (eLSE)* (No. 02, pp. 575–586). Bucharest, Romania.

Rubenson, K. (2010). Adult education overview. In E. Baker, B. McGaw, & P. Peterson (Eds.), *International encyclopedia of education* (3rd ed.). Oxford: Elsevier.

Ryan, Y., & Fraser, K. (2010). Education development in higher education. In *International encyclopedia of education* (3rd ed., pp. 411–418).

Saeed, N., Yang, Y., & Sinnappan, S. (2009). Emerging web technologies in higher education: A case of incorporating blogs, podcasts and social bookmarks in a web programming course based on students' learning styles and technology preferences. *Educational Technology & Society, 12*(4), 98–109. Retrieved from http://www.ifets.info/journals/12_4/9.pdf.

Saskatchewan Ministry of Education. (2013). *Technology in education framework: Teaching and learning, administrative operations, provincial infrastructure.* Regina, SK: Saskatchewan Ministry of Education.

Schols, M. (2012). Examining and understanding transformative learning to foster technology professional development in higher education. *International Journal of Emerging technologies in Learning, 7*(1), 42–49. Retrieved from http://online-journals.org/i-jet/article/view/1764.

Scott, P. (2010). Higher education: An overview. In E. Baker, B. McGaw, & P. Peterson (Eds.), *International encyclopedia of education* (3rd ed.). Oxford: Elsevier.

Sharples, J., Slavin, R., Chambers, B., & Sharp, C. (2011). *Effective classroom strategies for closing the gap in educational achievement for children and young people living in poverty, including white working-class boys.* London, UK: Centre for Excellence and Outcomes in Children and Young People's Services.

Singh, R. J. (2012). Current trends in higher education learning and teaching. *South African Journal of Higher Education, 26*(1), 5–9.

Skiba, D. J. (2013). On the horizon: The year of the MOOCs. *Nursing Education Perspectives, 34* (2), 136–137. https://doi.org/10.5480/1536-5026-34.2.136.

Texley, J. (2007). Twenty-First-Century Skills for Tomorrow's Leaders. *Peer Review, 9*(1).

Turney, C. S. M., Robinson, D., & Soutar, A. (2009). Using technology to direct learning in higher education. *Active Learning in Higher Education, 10*(1), 71–83.

Vygotsky, L. S. (1978). *Mind in society.* Cambridge: MIT Press.

Watkins, C. S., & Howard, M. O. (2015). Educational success among elementary school children from low socioeconomic status families: A systematic review of research assessing parenting factors. *Journal of Children and Poverty, 21*(1), 17–46.

Wensveen, R. (2014). *MOOCS: The latest platform in e-learning.* Retrieved from http://www.careersandeducation.ca/online-education/moocs-the-latest-platform-in-e-learning.

Wertsch, J. V. (1991). *Voices of the mind: A socio-cultural approach to mediated action.* Cambridge: Harvard University Press.

Wideman, H. (2012). *Learning connections: Project year-end report 2011–2012*. Toronto, ON: Institute for Research on Learning Technologies, York University.

Wood, D. & Bilsborow, C. (2013). Enhancing creative problem solving in the higher education curriculum through the use of innovative e-learning technologies. In *Proceedings of the 8th International Conference on e-Learning*. Paper presented at ICEL-2013, Cape Town, South Africa, 27–28 June (pp. 416–423). London: Universities UK.

Wolf, C. T. (2016) DIY videos on YouTube: Identity and possibility in the age of algorithms. *First Monday 21* (6).

Part II
Here Come the Transformers

Our research examines the implications of the next youth cohort who having been immersed in the digital environment from a young age. In assessing the ideas offered in this volume, we again highlight that the intent is not to make accurate forecasts of specific events or the timing for when changes might occur but have endeavoured to integrate current research, theories and hypotheses to develop plausible suggestions for this cohort and the world of work that they may enter in the coming decade or two. We sought to identify potential shifts or even sharp breaks from the past based on our assumption that most organizations will be well prepared for continuities but would be best to anticipate plausible new contexts.

The first part presented our conclusions drawn from assessing three key domains. We presented our broad scan of evolutions in the digital environment and identified a number of ways in which the second and third order effects of *changes in the conditions of change* are likely to lead to significant disruptions to the socio-economic continuity of modern North America. A holistic approach is a key to assessing the plausible interactions among a range of factors that are or may soon be altered by disruptive change.

The second chapter provided our consideration of generational theory and cohort analyses: while we cannot predict key characteristics of the next generation, some trends emerge from those of a similar age with broadly shared similar experiences and where these experiences differ from antecedent cohorts. In addition, we recognized that a range of media are contributing to the creation of generally held assumptions or stereotypes concerning different age cohorts including the post-Millennials and, whether accurate or not, the stereotypes provided in our generational "portraits" will influence attitudes and expectations concerning this group as well as the self-image many in this cohort will share.

Drawing on the idea from cohort analyses that broadly shared experiences can lead to a degree of commonality, the third chapter examined transformations in the educational sector. We suggested that the enhanced collaborative teaching pedagogy will yield a more cooperative youth cohort than was previously generated by the more standardized education programs provided to older generations.

While acknowledging that there will be differences across American and Canadian schools in their capacity to develop twenty-first-century skills and to adopt emerging technologies, we suggest that the ubiquitous nature of the digital environment will influence both students and their teachers. Our primary conclusion offered is that the most important changes will not be in what students learn but how they will learn to learn.

While digital evolutions will have an effect across all age groups, this impact will vary by generational cohort. Thus, for older generations, the shift to a new digital age will represent a war of attrition as new ideas must first displace old values and ways of doing business. Current efforts in many cities to preserve the commercial taxi business in the face of Uber initiatives is but one good example. Post-Millennials, however, are being introduced to modern communications through technological interfaces and will therefore not have to "unlearn" the behaviours and expectations of former generations. As a result, they should be better able to surf the waves of changes to be produced as a result of the growing digital tsunami and adapt much more easily to a "new normal".

To translate post-Millennials' digital awareness into a productive skill set, teachers must stay abreast of pedagogical shifts emphasizing collaboration and efficiency in both the classroom and the workforce. Our examination of education and learning confirmed that there is a broad consensus among educators that changes in curricula and pedagogy must be a focus on developing twenty-first-century skills. While there are some variations in how these new skills are presented, it is clear that students in primary and secondary schooling today are being exposed to much more than the traditional curricula including topics such as: critical thinking; collaboration; communication; character; culture and ethical citizenship; and computer and digital technology/literacies.

Our analyses highlighted as the most critical factor not what students will learn but how they will learn how to learn. We see emphases being placed on activities that are exploratory, shared and creative with curricula designed to interconnect different subjects. This environment is likely to lead to more holistic approaches to problem-solving and the potential for young scholars to examine the information they encounter online as well as the confidence to generate new knowledge and new shared content at earlier ages than those before them. Our reviews of the next stages of learning extending through post-secondary education and into the workplace suggest that engaged post-Millennials will take even greater ownership and control of what they learn and how they learn. This, in turn, will cause further disruptions to traditional approaches to adult education and extend into changes to standard employee training programmes.

We expect post-Millennials who have benefited from new curricula to enter the workforce much better equipped to think their way through new ideas and harness the potential unleashed by the digital environment. Thus, the real product of having been raised from birth immersed in a digital environment will be their capacity to act as the "transformers" to move organizations from where they are to where they need to be to optimize the benefits offered by digital evolutions.

In sum, by the time the next generation comes of age, we believe that they will face different socio-economic and work conditions than we find ourselves in today. The digital age has already begun to alter how we "work" and the skill sets required for career success; we believe this revolution will both continue and accelerate into the coming years. As illustrated in descriptions of new jobs titles[1] and futurists' predictions that, by 2030, 2 billion current jobs won't exist[2] we see the potential for a digital tsunami that will alter the nature of work and jobs on a scale comparable to that during the Industrial Revolution—but likely to happen in about one-tenth of the time (Kurzweil, 2005).[3] A disruption of this magnitude underlines the need for new competencies, as well as for changing definitions for existing competencies that are important today.

Our conclusion is that the key to the success of any enterprise will be to shift from a workforce comprised of knowledge workers to one with expert thinkers: individuals able to apply the independence of thought and creativity required to not only identify a novel way to solve an emerging problem but to do so by analysing the context and by challenging assumptions to first understand what the problem is.[4] While all enterprises have expert thinkers, these have tended to be a small number of specialists; our assertion is that this capacity will need to be developed across the entire workforce. Thus, employers will not only have to identify the skills needed for future work requirements but to also create the types of work environment, organizational policies, managerial and leadership styles and reward systems needed to first, attract the best and the brightest, then, focus their efforts on the organization's goals and, finally, to retain the right mix of talent over time. As all of these will require a significant degree of rethinking and, in many cases, will present challenges to the workplace legacies the Boomers will have left behind. We argue that employers need to start now to examine how they will implement the required changes.

The three chapters in this second part of the book are intended to assist in these considerations by presenting what we have seen as the key characteristics that the post-Millennials are likely to bring to the workplace. While we presented a generalized portrait of this group earlier, in this part our analyses seek to parse the realities from the media-generated stereotypes. We represent two key caveats: first, we have focussed on plausible discontinuities—areas where we see important differences from what exists today—and second, while we present broad generalization, we recognize that individual differences will exist. Our descriptions are

---

[1]Illustrative new job titles include: robot counsellor, digital currency advisor, rewilder and gamification designer. See the Canadian Scholarship Trust Plan's "Jobs of 2030" project at: http://careers2030.cst.org/jobs/ as well as John Verdon's posts for the latest descriptions of new career fields.

[2]See Tom Frey's "Don't Get Blindsided by the Future" at: http://www.futuristspeaker.com/2014/03/162-future-jobs-preparing-for-jobs-that-dont-yet-exist/.

[3]Kurzweil (2005, p. 25) states: "… we'll see the equivalent of a century of progress *at today's rate* in only 25 calendar years".

[4]Thus, rather than coming up with new ways to make old mistakes, the key is reflected in the Einstein quote: If I had an hour to solve a problem I'd spend 55 min thinking about the problem and 5 min thinking about solutions.

intended to apply to many but not all of those in the current youth cohort. We start with a discussion of key competencies then shift to their identity and broad social values and then finish with consideration of their possible life and work goals. While we realize we cannot paint an accurate portrait of the next generation, we offer some preliminary sketches that bring a bit of definition.

Reference

Kurzweil, R. (2005). *The singularity is near*. New York: Viking

Cognitive Capacities and Competencies

4

We cannot solve our problems with the same thinking we used when we created them.

—Albert Einstein

Introduction

To build a robust workforce in preparation for what the digital age may bring, we highlighted changes being generated by evolutions in the digital environment and important shifts in education. As the first generation to have been raised from birth immersed in a digital environment and being given the benefits of a digital classroom, today's students should enter their adult life with the skills that employers will need for success in the future. "Should" does not mean "will"; for differing reasons some students will be able to develop their 21st Century Skills during schooling, others, however, will not. The focus of this chapter is on identifying those competencies that will matter in the future workforce. As employers will need to assess required competencies, our emphasis is on those that can be accurately measured and differentiated from strong to weak. We identified ten critical competencies that fit these criteria. They represent the key skills that the next generation of employers will require to succeed in the digital economy hence those the next generation of employees need to bring to the workplace. Most are linked to the P21 21st Century skills. However, our research identified an additional area of skill development that is occurring outside of the classroom. Ergo, our consideration of the critical 21st Century competencies will start with a brief discussion of the implications of what may be the most common characteristic used to describe young people today: their propensity for multi-tasking.

© Springer Nature Switzerland AG 2020
A. Okros, *Harnessing the Potential of Digital Post-Millennials in the Future Workplace*, Management for Professionals, https://doi.org/10.1007/978-3-030-25726-2_4

Multitasking as Lifestyle[1]

[Multitasking is], essentially, playing tennis with our cognitive energies—Blake Thorne

The previous chapter presented important new capacities that are being developed in the classroom, however young people are increasingly paying attention to multiple inputs and devices at the same time. While parents might bemoan the youngster sitting with earbuds on and thumbs flying on the smartphone keyboard and teachers may have concerns with short attention spans, our research concluded that the capacity to frequently shift focus or tasks is key to success in the modern workplace. Researchers report individuals switch tasks at work about every three minutes thus, whether self–induced (just checking my email) or imposed by others (just need a second of your time), constant task switching is a fact of working life (Adler & Benbunan-Fich, 2012; Mark, Gonzalez, & Harris, 2005; Thorne, 2015). To be clear on the workplace research, few are arguing that constant interruptions are beneficial as these usually erode productivity, increase stress, cause short term memory loss, can result in socio-emotional issues and, some argue, reduce cognitive functioning by 10 IQ points. It is, however, evident that the need to manage multiple tasks at the same time is a part of the reality across many fields of work and is becoming a part of everyday life in a rapidly evolving, technologically-driven world (Duggan, Johnson, & Sørli, 2013). Thus, as long as employers are going to create or enable distracted work environments, employees are going to have to learn how to cope with the demands.[2]

Multitasking is the rapid sequential management of multiple tasks. It occurs whenever someone divides their active attention to perform several independent tasks within a given period of time (Adler & Benbunan-Fich, 2012). The digital environment and a plethora of associated devices and platforms have given rise to the phenomenon of media multitasking: the process of multitasking that utilizes one or more digital devices. Media multitasking can lead to an individual managing multiple tasks across a number of mediums such as students sending text messages to friends while writing an essay on their laptop and concurrently listening to music on their headphones.

Multitasking across different mediums is a way of life for many in the digital generation. This is a direct result of the device-laden, digital environment that they are encountering. The ubiquity of media and constant technological progress seem to contribute to media multitasking behavior and, at times, can be performed without individuals even realizing it. A US national survey conducted in 2015[3] confirmed earlier research (Rideout, Foehr, & Robert, 2010) on multi-taking,

---

[1]This section draws on the series of reports generated for our project by Cherif and her colleagues.
[2]To link back to Chap. 2, this is an area where work on the quantified self and bio-feedback may be important as individual learn new strategies to cope. See the products currently available based on personal electroencephalogram devices at: https://emotiv.com/store/ and for brain sensing meditation at: http://www.choosemuse.com/.
[3]See *The Common Sense Census: Media Use by Tweens and Teens*; accessible at: https://www. commonsensemedia.org/research/the-common-sense-census-media-use-by-tweens-and-teens.

revealing that half do so while doing homework and up to 70% use multiple platforms when engaged in social activities. These data continue the trend of increased use over time with Rideout et al. (2010) showing substantial changes when compared to a survey conducted by the same authors five years earlier (Roberts, Foehr, & Rideout, 2005). Although some research indicates that boys and girls may engage in different types of multi-tasking activities (Cotton, Shank, & Anderson, 2014), our analyses did not suggest major gender differences in the prevalence or frequency of their multi-tasking (Strayer, Medeiros-Ward, & Watson, 2013; Common Sense Census, 2015).

The constant access to digital media will result in the Post-Millennials, and to a lesser extent, Millennials, developing a general predisposition towards multitasking and concomitant changes in how they process information. Research into neuroplasticity suggests that multitasking can become hardwired into the brain structures and cognitive functioning in both children and adults resulting in cognitive processes in young people that differ from previous generations (Granic, Lobel, & Engels, 2013; Minear, Brasher, McCurdy, Lewis, & Younggren, 2013). Further, while there is a body of research suggesting that those who spend excessive time playing video games can encounter negative results such as addiction, depression and violence, others have demonstrated positive outcomes in developing cognitive skills as well as improving emotional and social wellbeing (Granic et al., 2013).

Consequently, these differences in cognition translate into differences in competencies between generations. Anderon and Raine (2012) have suggested that Post-Millennials who have engaged in frequent multitasking over time will be more agile and efficient in the classroom and the workplace than their counterparts. Yet, since tasks compete for our attention, multitasking has been demonstrated to impair task performance and can lead to errors and a decrease in productivity (Hodgett & Jones, 2006a, b; Monsell, 2003; Strayer & Johnston, 2001).

We found evidence that suggests media multitasking negatively affects the recall of information delivered orally in the classroom, while multitasking in class, during study periods, or outside of class involving content unrelated to the course is negatively associated with academic success (Burak, 2012; Fried, 2008; Ravizza, Hambrick, & Fenn, 2014). The academic literature, however, has yet to establish the link between media multitasking and school performance. Several studies comparing the cognitive processing of heavy and light media multitaskers have led to inconclusive or contradictory results when considering their ability to filter environmental distractions, switch efficiently between multiple tasks, susceptibility to interference caused by irrelevant representations in memory, ability to sustain attention, or working memory capacity (Alzahabi & Becker, 2013; Baumgartner, Weeda, van der Heijden, & Huizinga, 2014; Cain & Mitroff, 2011; Minear et al., 2013; Ophir, Nass, & Wagner, 2009).

Multitasking may also influence Post-Millennials emotional and psychological traits. A number of studies point to a negative association between the propensity for media multitasking and emotional well-being, however, the directionality of this relationship is unclear (Anderson et al., 2010; Bushman & Anderson, 2002; Granic et al., 2013). Although a few studies could not establish a link between media multitasking frequency and extraversion, Wang and Tchernev (2012) found that those who engaged in more media multitasking scored higher on a neuroticism metric. In many studies, the frequency of self-reported media multitasking was positively correlated with the levels of self-reported impulsivity (Minear et al., 2013; Sanbonmatsu et al., 2013) and sensation seeking (Duff et al., 2014; Foehr, 2006; Jeong & Fishbein, 2007; Sanbonmatsu, Strayer, Medeiros-Ward, & Watson, 2013). Sanbonmatsu et al. (2013) suggest that these personality traits are associated with low concern for negative consequences possibly caused by the media multitasking behavior and a desire to experience the sensations of challenge and stimulation provided by running multiple tasks simultaneously. Such emotional duress will undoubtedly affect the Post-Millennial's ability to master and apply of 21st Century competencies as adults.

Our review suggests that there may be a difference in information processing style between individuals who are frequently engaged in media multitasking (heavy media multitaskers) and individuals who did not (light media multitaskers) with both positive and negative implications. Studies have shown that heavy media multitaskers tend to be breadth-biased in their cognitive control style, leading them to pay attention to a larger scope of information rather than focusing on a particular piece of information (Lin, 2009; Ophir et al., 2009). This breadth-bias in cognitive control is likely to cause detrimental effects on performance when heavy media multitaskers are asked to focus their attention on a particular task and to ignore environmental distractors. However, the ability to process information from different channels seems to be a good asset in situations where distractors convey important information about the task.

Some individuals do not appear to be adversely affected when they perform multiple tasks simultaneously: Watson and Strayer (2010) call these individuals "supertaskers"; defined as those able to perform in the upper quartile on each of several tasks performed in a multitasking condition (Strayer et al., 2011; Watson & Strayer, 2010). They found that supertaskers represented 2.5% of their study population (Strayer & Watson, 2012). A key finding in this research was that supertaskers showed less brain activity than the control group as multitasking difficulty increased. It would seem that supertaskers used their mental resources more efficiently, thus, achieving a performance equivalent to that of the control group with less brain activity.

We inferred that these individuals can engage in high cognitive load functions without the difficulties many encountered when multitasking. Additional research is required to interpret these results. Is this capacity innate or was it developed as a result of exposure to heavy multitasking activities? If this capacity was developed through an individual's frequent online and media interactions and multitasking, the 'constantly connected' youngster of today may be developing a crucial skill for success in the future (Anderson & Raine, 2012). At a minimum, as a result of their experiences with multitasking from young ages, we do anticipate that many Post-Millennials will be better prepared for the dynamics of a continuously interrupted workplace than most of their elders, including the Millennials.

21st Century Competencies

> Expert thinking [involves ...] metacognition, the set of skills used by the stumped expert to decide when to give up on one strategy and what to try next—Levy and Murnane (2004)

We concluded that, as a result of their education and personal lifestyle growing up in a wired world, many Post-Millennials should develop a generally shared set of competencies that they will take into their post-secondary and working careers. Broadly defined, competencies are the knowledge, skills, abilities, and other attributes that are observable, measurable, comparable, and that are critical for personal or career success (Campion et al., 2011; Catano et al., 2012). Strategies have been developed for identifying competencies with competency "libraries" produced that consolidate traits that have been identified by different organizations (Campion et al., 2011; Catano, Wiesner, & Hackett, 2012). Using self- and manager ratings of workplace performance, Bartram et al. (2002) and Kurz and Bartram (2002) have grouped most competencies into what they have called the "Great Eight." Bartram (2005) conducted meta-analyzes of 29 competency studies to map his eight competencies to other frameworks of measuring success in the workplace. Table 4.1 presents these eight generic competencies along with their definitions and hypothesized Big Five, motivation and ability relationships.

Table 4.2 presents the ten competencies we identified that the Post-Millennial should bring to the workplace. Many of these competencies mirror those emphasized by P21 in the previous chapter, however, our research also considered the nature of work and the types of competencies that have been identified as important on the job both for the current and future economy. In addition, we examined potential measures to assess these competencies to examine whether psychometrically sound instruments do or will soon exist.[4]

Communication and Collaboration

Communication can refer to written or oral skills such as persuading and influencing others. Written communication skills encompass the ability to write clearly and efficiently (Casner-Lotto & Barrington, 2006), while oral communication skills include articulating ideas clearly and efficiently, including public speaking and presentations (Casner-Lotto & Barrington, 2006). Collaboration is often used synonymously with teamwork and is defined broadly as managing relationships between colleagues, the ability to work with diverse teams, and the ability to negotiate and manage conflict (Casner-Lotto & Barrington, 2006). Finegold and Notabartolo (2008) expand on the concept of collaboration, noting that it requires effective communication skills and respect towards coworkers. P21 adds that collaboration also includes the ability to compromise and to share responsibility (P21, 2007; C21, 2012).

---

[4]See our reports by O'Keefe et al.

Table 4.1 Bartram's "Great Eight" and their predictors

Competency	Competency definition	Relationships
Leading and deciding	Takes control and exercises leadership Initiates action, gives direction, and takes responsibility	Need for power and control, extraversion
Supporting and cooperating	Supports others and shows respect and positive regard for them in social situations Puts people first, working effectively with individuals and teams, clients, and staff Behaves consistently with clear personal values that complement those of the organization	Agreeableness
Interacting and presenting	Communicates and networks effectively Successfully persuades and influences others Relates to others in a confident, relaxed manner	Extraversion, general mental ability
Analyzing and interpreting	Shows evidence of clear analytical thinking Gets to the heart of complex problems and issues Applies own expertise effectively Quickly takes on new technology Communicates well in writing	General mental ability, openness to new experiences
Creating and conceptualizing	Works well in situations requiring openness to new ideas and experiences Seeks out learning opportunities Handles situations and problems with innovation and creativity Thinks broadly and strategically Supports and drives organizational change	Openness to new experiences, general mental ability
Organizing and executing	Plans ahead and works in a systematic and organized way Follows directions and procedures Focuses on customer satisfaction and delivers a quality service or product to the agreed standards	Conscientiousness, general mental ability
Adapting and coping	Adapts and responds well to change Manages pressure effectively and copes well with setbacks	Emotional stability
Enterprising and performing	Focuses on results and achieving personal work objectives Works best when work is related closely to results and the impact of personal efforts is obvious Shows an understanding of business, commerce, and finance Seeks opportunities for self-development and career advancement	Need for achievement, negative agreeableness

Adapted from Bartram (2005). Copyright not required http://www.apa.org/about/contact/copyright/index.aspx

Table 4.2 10 Key 21st Century competencies

Competency	Description	Bartram eight	P21 competency
Communication	*Written, oral, and interpersonal skills, including articulating ideas clearly and efficiently*	Interacting and presenting	Learning and innovation, communication and collaboration; Life and career skills: leadership and responsibility
Collaboration	*Relationships between colleagues and customers, ability to work with diverse teams, as well as negotiate and manage conflict*	Supporting and cooperating	Learning and innovation, communication and collaboration, Life and career skills, leadership and responsibility
Critical thinking	*The capacity of active investigative thinking, analyzing arguments, making inferences using inductive and deductive reasoning, judging and evaluating*	Analyzing and interpreting	Learning and Innovation, critical thinking and Problem solving
Problem solving	*Goal-directed thinking and action in new situations where no routine solutions are in place*	Analyzing and interpreting	Learning and innovation, critical thinking and problem solving
Cognitive load management	*Discriminating and filtering important and data from multiple sources*	Analyzing and interpreting	
Adaptability and dealing with ambiguity	*Handling work stress, interpersonal and cultural adaptability, and dealing with uncertain situations*	Adapting and coping	Life and career skill: flexibility and adaptability
Innovation	*Building upon creativity, making it useful by drawing on real-world expertise, such as the dissemination of information*	Creating and conceptualizing	Learning and innovation, creativity and innovation
Creativity	*Freedom of thought and the ability to create new ideas and see new perspectives*	Creating and conceptualizing	Learning and innovation, creativity and innovation
Cross-cultural competency	*A multidimensional construct relating to functioning in culturally diverse settings*	Adapting and coping	Life and career skill, social and cross-cultural skills
Digital and media literacy	*Ability to perform tasks and think critically about information found in digital environments, to apply new knowledge proficiently, accessing and analyzing different media content, filter large amounts of information and data, to aid in decision-making*		Information, media, and technology skills

Communication and collaboration are both commonly cited as important 21st Century competencies (Casner-Lotto & Barrington, 2006; Cisco Systems, 2008; C21, 2012; Davies et al., 2011; Finegold & Notabartolo, 2008; P21, 2007; Trilling & Fadel, 2009). With regards to collaboration specifically, some estimates have shown that more than 80% of companies with more than 100 employees commonly perform work in teams (Cohen & Bailey, 1997). Moreover, advanced information technology has become pervasive, changing how team members communicate and interact as "virtual teams" (Avolio et al., 2000). Virtual collaboration was named one of the top ten skills for the future workforce (Davies et al., 2011). In a rapidly globalized environment (Chen et al, 2012; Davies et al., 2011; Early & Ang, 2003), virtual teams will also call upon cross-cultural competencies, which we explore later in this chapter.

Critical Thinking and Problem Solving

P21 defines critical thinking as "the capacity of active investigative thinking" (P21, 2007, p. 12). Other definitions commonly include analyzing arguments, making inferences using inductive and deductive reasoning, judging and evaluating, and making decisions and solving problems (Ennis, 1985; Facione, 1990; Lai, 2011). Problem solving encompasses goal-directed thinking and action in new situations in which no routine solutions are in place (Murray et al, 2005). It can be thought of as the "application of learning and innovation skills to a specific area of inquiry" (P21, 2007, p. 13) and may call on other skills, including critical thinking, self-direction, flexibility, patience, and the ability to deal with ambiguity, P21, 2007; C21, 2012). Some definitions include the process of applying scientific and engineering principles to finding solutions to problems. Critical thinking skills are increasingly in demand in the workforce (Finegold & Notabartolo, 2008). In a survey by the Society for Human Resource Management and Wall Street Journal Careers, employers reported that adaptability and critical thinking/problem solving were the most important skills compared with two years earlier (Finegold & Notabartolo, 2008). Further, this research shows that effective problem-solving skills are positively correlated to job retention, satisfaction, and performance in a survey of trainee truckers.

Cognitive Load Management

As already introduced in our discussion of multitasking, 21st Century workers will require the ability to evaluate the reliability and credibility of different information sources while filtering important information and data from multiple sources. This competency is defined by Davies et al. (2011) as "cognitive load management" and is new "core" competency. Due, in part, to the mass of information available on the Internet, the skills required to filter large amounts of information and data to aid in decision making is a contextual capability unique to the 21st Century worker (Dede,

2009). Along with critical thinking and problem solving, we found that these three competencies are the most in demand in the 21st century work environment (Casner-Lotto & Barrington, 2006; Davies et al., 2011; Finegold & Notabartolo, 2008; Gerber & Scott, 2007; Meier et al., 2000; Playfoot & Hall, 2010; P21, 2007).

Adaptability and Dealing with Ambiguity

Davies et al. (2011, p 9) discussed novel and adaptive thinking as one of the top ten future work skills and defined it as "thinking and finding solutions beyond those routine solutions and rules previously in place". Finegold and Notabartolo (2008) described adaptability as the capacity for change. Adaptability shares similarities and enables other competencies, such as critical thinking and problem solving (Cisco Systems, 2008; C21, 2012; P21, 2007). With new technologies constantly emerging, and the ways in which the technology and workforce are changing, employees must be adaptable to these changes to be successful (Pulakos et al., 2000). Being adaptable is also necessary for fostering creativity and innovation.

Creativity and Innovation

Creativity draws on freedom of thought, the ability to generate new ideas, a willingness to seek out learning opportunities, an ability to see new perspectives and the capability to think broadly and strategically (C21, 2012; P21, 2007). Innovation builds on creativity, translating the creative thought into something that is useful by drawing on real-world expertise such as the dissemination of information. It requires a degree of adaptability, along with effective communication and collaboration skills (P21, 2007). Several frameworks have suggested that creativity and innovation are important skills for the 21st Century worker (Cisco Systems, 2008; Dede, 2009) along with curiosity and risk-taking (Dede, 2009), while P21 (2007) expands creativity and innovation to include entrepreneurial thinking.

Cross-Cultural Competency and Cultural Intelligence

In an increasingly globalized world, the ability to work with those from different cultures is becoming increasingly important. Cross-cultural competency is described as the ability to work within and across different cultures (Davies et al., 2011). Owing to a globalized economy, workers may need different skill sets according to where and with whom they work. It is important that these workers be able to work and communicate effectively and appropriately as well as to perform as teams within diverse cultures. Accordingly, cross-cultural competency is related to both communication and collaboration (Davies et al., 2011).

The concept of cross-cultural competence is synonymous with Earley and Ang's (2003) conceptualization of cultural intelligence that is defined as a multidimensional construct relating to functioning in culturally diverse settings. Chen et al. (2012) found that workplace diversity can create positive outcomes including generating higher profits and an increased ability to meet the needs of their customers as well as negative outcomes related to miscommunication, mis-perception, increased tension and workplace conflict. Both the US P21 and Canadian C21 work includes social and cross-cultural skills in their frameworks. Global awareness, also termed multicultural literacy, is highlighted in many other studies and reviews that emphasize the need for 21st Century workers to have the capacity to learn from, and collaborate with individuals from different cultures (Dillon, 2006; Gabbard et al., 2011; Grady & Millett, 2007; Pacific Policy Research Center, 2010).

Digital and Media Literacy

There is wide consensus on the importance of including digital literacy as a 21st Century Skill (Cisco Systems, 2008; Davies et al., 2011; Dede, 2009; Dillon, 2006; European Commission, 2010; Pacific Policy Research Centre, 2010; Playfoot & Hall, 2010). Information, Media and Technology Skills also form one of the pillars of P21's framework for 21st Century learning. It extends beyond the ability to use ICT (Information, Communications and Technology) devices effectively; this skill includes information and media literacies. Literacy implies more than simply interpreting text; it includes understanding and making sense of the world around us (Dillon, 2006) and it focuses more on comprehension and thinking rather than simply reading and writing (Wittrock, 1991). As presented, Jenkins et al. (2006) have identified twelve different types of media literacy and our research revealed many more frameworks for understanding this domain. We see information and media literacy as a person's ability to perform tasks and think critically about the information found in digital environments and to apply that new knowledge in a proficient way (Jones-Kavalier & Flannigan, 2008). Qureshi (2014) argues that the digital divide has become less about economic and social well-being as predicted by many and more about digital literacy. In the coming years, the digital divide will separate those who have effectively developed the requisite intellectual skills and those who have not. Access to the digital environment is a pre-requisite but, by itself, will not guarantee skill acquisition.

Conclusion

Many of these 21st Century competencies are in demand by employers today and are expected to be even more important for the workforce of the future. As we highlighted, education is evolving to meet this new reality: many teachers are striving to not only address core subjects with the goal of ensuring understanding of the material but also to develop Post-Millennial students' ability to operationalize that knowledge with life and career skills, learning and innovation capacities and information, media and technology literacies. Those who can do so will be well positioned to master what the Institute for the Future and the Apollo Research Institute call 'transdisciplinary' skills (Davies et al., 2011, Nowotny et al., 2001). Since many contemporary and future global problems are complex and multifaceted in nature, knowledge workers will be required to be "T-shaped", which involves having a deep knowledge base in one field but an understanding of other broader disciplines (Davies et al., 2011). The same can be said about their competencies: the skills we have identified are for the most part complimentary, if not co-requisite. Those in the next generation should have the potential to enter the workforce bearing a portfolio of 'trans-competencies,' either taught in school, inherent to their upbringing or acquired through their independent exploration of the digital world in which they are immersed. Again, not all will achieve the maximum benefits from their studies thus, the key for employers will be to ensure that they are using reliable, accurate measures of these competencies to be able to match talent with tasks.

Neither our presentation of 21st Century competencies nor the initial discussion of multi-tasking suggested significant gender differences in these capacities. The extensive testing literature does reveal gender differences on many measures however draw on three perspectives. First, Willingham and Cole (1997) highlight that that individual women and men vary far more than do the two groups on virtually any measure that one might choose. Second, Wilder (1997) points out that performance differences are a product of multiple forces that interact over time and in complex fashion. Third, key aspects of these 'multiple forces' relate to how individuals are taught and how competencies are measured. Changes are being implemented in the ways in which students will acquire new knowledges and develop new competencies. When combined with the recognition that standardized measures for several of the new 21st Century competencies are still being developed, we have concluded that it is not possible nor justified to suggest that there will be significant differences on these new competencies when assessed for gender or, in the US context, race.

While each of these competencies is important, our research suggests several reasons why digital and media literacies are likely to be the most critical for employers into the future. First individuals are going to have to develop the capacity to navigate through the content clutter of the digital universe to not only identify relevant information but to make sense of the differing perspectives they encounter on what is seen as facts, knowledge, ideas and 'the truth'. The ability to do so will be aided by the new ways Post-Millennials should have *learned to learn* especially through their exposure to connected learning as exploratory, shared and creative. We return to Jenkins et al. (2006) notions of 'collective intelligence' (the ability to pool knowledge and compare notes with others toward a common goal) and 'media judgment' (the ability to evaluate the reliability and credibility of different information sources). We see these capacities as of increased importance given the growing marketplace populated by 'prosumers'; those who are both producing and consuming digital content—as well as goods and services acquired via digital media. The capacity of employees to monitor, understand and connect with these prosumers is going to be of increased importance in the future and, we argue, the Post-Millennials will be well suited to perform this function.

The next reason for the importance of digital and media literacies relates to life-long learning. Given the pace at which new ideas are generated (and contested), it is going to be the responsibility of each individual to update their workplace knowledge and skills. Those with digital and media literacy will be able to do so faster and smarter than others. Finally, a point we will return to in the last chapter, it should also be recognized that these 21st Century skills will also put pressure on organizations as individuals will also be using their capacity to find and create new ideas to push their employers to update or amend their policies, procedures and processes. Thus, those who enter with these skills will be able to move the organization forward but will also be able to use these to challenge the corporate status quo and, in doing so, become the 21st Century organizational transformers.

References

Adler, R. F., & Benbunan-Fich, R. (2012). Juggling on a high wire: Multitasking effects on performance. *International Journal of Human-Computer Interaction, 70,* 156–168.

Alzahabi, R., & Becker, M. W. (2013). The association between media multitasking, task-switching, and dual-task performance. *Journal of Experimental Psychology: Human Perception and Performance, 39,* 1485–1495.

Anderson, J., & Rainie, L. (2012). *Teens, technology, and human potential in 2020.* Washington, DC: Pew Research.

Anderson, C. A., Shibuya, A., Ihori, N., Swing, E. L., Bushman, B. J., Sakamoto, A., et al. (2010). Violent video game effects on aggression, empathy, and prosocial behavior in Eastern and Western countries: A meta-analytic review. *Psychological Bulletin, 136,* 151–173.

Bartram, D. (2005). The great eight competencies: A criterion-centric approach to validation. *Journal of Applied Psychology, 90*(6), 1185–1203.

Bartram, D., Roberton, I. T., & Callinan, M. (2002). Introduction: A framework for examining organisational effectiveness. In I. T. Robertson, M. Callinan, & D. Bartram (Eds.), *Organisational effectiveness: The role of psychology* (pp. 1–12). Chichester, UK: Wiley.

Baumgartner, S. E., Weeda, W. D., van der Heijden, L. L., & Huizinga, M. (2014). The relationship between media multitasking and executive function in early adolescents. *The Journal of Early Adolescence, 34,* 1120–1144.

Burak, L. J. (2012). Multitasking in the university classroom. *International Journal for the Scholarship of Teaching and Learning, 6*(2), 1–12.

Bushman, B. J., & Anderson, C. A. (2002). Violent video games and hostile expectations: A test of the general aggression model. *Personality and Social Psychology Bulletin, 28,* 1679–1686.

Cain, M. S., & Mitroff, S. R. (2011). Distractor filtering in media multitaskers. *Perception, 40,* 1183–1192.

Campion, M. A., Fink, A. A., Ruggeberg, B. J., Carr, L., Phillips, G. M., & Odman, R. B. (2011). Doing competencies well: Best practices in competency modeling. *Personnel Psychology, 64,* 225–262.

Casner-Lotto. J., & Barrington, L. (2006). *Are They Really Ready To Work? Employers' Perspectives on the Basic Knowledge and Applied Skills of New Entrants to the 21st Century U.S. Workforce.* New York: The Conference Board.

Catano, V. M., Wiesner, W. H., & Hackett, R. D. (2012). *Recruitment and selection in Canada* (5th ed.). Toronto: Nelson Canada.

Chen, X., Liu, D., & Portnoy, R. (2012). A multilevel investigation of motivational cultural intelligence, organizational diversity climate, and cultural sales: Evidence from U.S. real estate firms. *Journal of Applied Psychology, 97*(1), 93–106.

Cisco Systems, Inc. (2008). Equipping every learner for the 21st century: A white paper. San Jose, CA: Cisco Systems, Inc. http://newsroom.cisco.com/dlls/2008/ekits/Equipping_Every_Learner_for_21st_Century_White_Paper.pdf.

Cohen, S. G., & Bailey, D. E. (1997). What makes teams work: Group effectiveness research from the shop floor to the executive suite. *Journal of Management, 23*, 239–290.

Commission, European. (2010). *New skills for new jobs: Action now*. Luxembourg: Office for official publications of the European Communities.

Common Sense Census. *Media Use by Tweens and Teens*; accessible at: https://www.commonsensemedia.org/research/the-common-sense-census-media-use-by-tweens-and-teens.

Cotton, S. R., Shank, D. R., & Anderson, W. A. (2014). Gender, technology use and ownership, and media-based multitasking among middle school students. *Computers in Human Behavior, 35*, 99–106.

Davies, A., Fidler, D., & Gorbis, M. (2011). Future work skills 2020. Retrieved from http://apolloresearchinstitute.com/research-studies/workforce-preparedness/future-work-skills-2020.

Dede, C. (2009). Comparing frameworks for "21st century skills". In J. Bellanca & R. Brandt (Eds.), *21st Century Skills: Rethinking how students learn* (pp. 51–75). Bloomington, IN: Solution Tree Press.

Dillon, N. (2006). Skills for a new century. *American School Board Journal, 193*(3), 22–26.

Duff, B. R. L., Yoon, G., Wang, Z. G., & Anghelcev, G. (2014). Doing it all: An exploratory study of predictors of media multitasking. *Journal of Interactive Advertising, 14*(1), 11–23.

Duggan, G. B., Johnson, H., & Sørli, P. (2013). Interleaving tasks to improve performance: Users maximise the marginal rate of return. *International Journal of Human-Computer Studies, 71*(5), 533–550.

Earley, P. C., & Ang, S. (2003). *Cultural intelligence: Individual interactions across cultures*. Palo Alto, CA: Stanford University Press.

Ennis, R. H. (1985). A logical basis for measuring critical thinking skills. *Educational Leadership, 43*(2), 44–48. http://www.ascd.org/ASCD/pdf/journals/ed_lead/el_198510_ennis.pdf.

Facione, P. A. (1990). *Critical thinking: A statement of expert consensus for purposes of educational assessment and instruction*. Millbrae, CA: The California Academic Press.

Finegold, D., & Notabartolo, A. S. (2008). *21st century competencies and their impact: An interdisciplinary literature review*. Retrieved from the William and Flora Hewlett Foundation website: http://www.hewlett.org/library/grantee-publication/21st-century-competencies-and-their-impact-interdisciplinary-literature-review

Foehr, U. G. (2006). *Media multitasking among American youth: Prevalence, predictors and pairings*. Washington, DC: Henry J. Kaiser Family Foundation.

Fried, C. B. (2008). In-class laptop use and its effects on student learning. *Computers & Education, 50*, 906–914.

Gabbard, W., Starks, S. H., Jaggers, J., & Cappiccie, A. C. (2011). Effective strategies for teaching cultural competency to MSW students in a global society. *World Academy of Science, Engineering & Technology, 5*(8), 1389–1393. http://waset.org/publications/11311/effective-strategies-for-teaching-cultural-competency-to-msw-students-in-a-global-society.

Gerber, S., & Scott, L. (2007). Designing a learning curriculum and technology's role in it. *Educational Technology Research and Development, 55*(5), 461–478.

Grady, C. D., & Millett, S. M. (2007). *New research reveals top ten skills for 2020*. Ohio: EDGE subcommittee, Ohio Department of Education.

Granic, I., Lobel, A., & Engels, R. C. M. E. (2013). The benefits of playing video games. *American Psychologist, 69*(1), 66–78.

Hodgetts, H. M., & Jones, D. M. (2006a). Interruption of the Tower of London task: Support for a goal-activation approach. *Journal of Experimental Psychology: General, 135*, 103–115.

Hodgetts, H. M., & Jones, D. M. (2006b). Contextual cues aid recovery from interruption: the role of associative activation. *Journal of Experimental Psychology. Learning, Memory, and Cognition, 32,* 1120–1132.

Jenkins, H., Clinton, K., Purushotma, R., Robinson, A. J., & Weigel, M. (2006). *Confronting the challenges of participatory culture: Media education for the 21st century.* Chicago, IL: The MacArthur Foundation.

Jeong, S. H., & Fishbein, M. (2007). Predictors of multitasking with media: Media factors and audience factors. *Media Psychology, 10,* 364–384.

Jones-Kavalier, B. R., & Flannigan, S. L. (2008). *Connecting the digital dots: literacy of the 21st century.* Retrieved from: http://www.nmc.org/pdf/Connecting%20the%20Digital%20Dots.pdf

Kurz, R., & Bartram, D. (2002). Competency and individual performance: Modeling the world of work. In I. T. Robertson, M. Callinan, & D. Bartram (Eds.), *Organizational effectiveness: The role of psychology* (pp. 227–255). Chichester: Wiley.

Lai, E. R. (2011). *Critical thinking: A literature review.* Pearson Research Report.

Levy, F., & Murnane, R. (2004). *The new division of labor.* Princeton, NJ: Princeton University Press.

Lin, L. (2009). *Breadth-biased versus focused cognitive control in media multitasking behaviors Proceedings of the National Academies of Sciences, 106,* 15521–15522.

Mark, G., Gonzalez, V., & Harris, J. (2005, April) No task left behind? Examining the nature of fragmented work. In *Proceedings of ACM CHI'05.* Paper presented at ACM CHI'05, Portland, OR, pp: 113–120.

Meier, R. L., Williams, M. R., & Humphreys, M. A. (2000). Refocusing our efforts: Assessing non-technical competency gaps. *Journal of Engineering Education, 89*(3), 377–385.

Minear, M., Brasher, F., McCurdy, M., Lewis, J., & Younggren, A. (2013). Working memory, fluid intelligence, and impulsiveness in heavy media multitaskers. *Psychonomic Bulletin & Review, 20,* 1274–1281.

Monsell, S. (2003). Task switching. *Trends in Cognitive Sciences, 7,* 134–140.

Murray, T. S., Owen, E., & McGaw, B. (2005). *Learning a living: First results of the adult literacy and life skills survey.* Ottawa: Statistics Canada and the Organization for Cooperation and Development.

Nowotny, H., Scott, P. B., & Gibbons, M. T. (2001). *Re-thinking science: Knowledge and the public in an age of uncertainty.* Cambridge: Polity Press.

Ophir, E., Nass, C., & Wagner, A. D. (2009). Cognitive control in media multitaskers. *Proceedings of the National Academy of Sciences of the United States of America, 106,* 15583–15587.

P21: Partnership for 21st Century Skills. (2007). *The intellectual and policy foundations of the 21st century skills framework.* http://www.p21.org/storage/documents/docs/Intellectual_and_Policy_Foundations.pdf.

Pacific Policy Research Center. (2010). *21st century skills for students and teachers.* Honolulu: Kamehameha Schools, Research & Evaluation Division.

Playfoot, J., & Hall, R. (2010). Identifying knowledge, skills, competencies, values and ethics to meet 21st century challenges. Paper Presented at the Asia-Pacific Program of Educational Innovation for Development, Bangkok. http://www.whiteloop.com/publications/Identifyin20111129174126.pdf.

Pulakos, E. D., Arad, S., Donovan, M. A., & Plamondon, K. E. (2000). Adaptability in the workplace: Development of a taxonomy of adaptive performance. *Journal of Applied Psychology, 85*(4), 612–624.

Qureshi, S. (2014). Overcoming Technological Determinism in Understanding the Digital Divide: Where Do We Go From Here?. *Information Technology for Development 20*(3), 215–217.

Ravizza, S. M., Hambrick, D. Z., & Fenn, K. M. (2014). Non-academic internet use in the classroom is negatively related to classroom learning regardless of intellectual ability. *Computers & Education, 78,* 109–114.

Rideout, V., Foehr, U. G., & Robert, D. F. (2010). *Generation M²: Media in the lives of 8–18 year-olds*. Washington, DC: Henry J. Kaiser Family Foundation.

Roberts, D. F., Foehr, U. G., & Rideout, V. (2005). *Generation M: Media in the lives of 8–18 year-olds*. Washington, DC: Henry J. Kaiser Family Foundation.

Sanbonmatsu, D. M., Strayer, D. L., Medeiros-Ward, N., & Watson, J. M. (2013). Who multi-tasks and why? Multi-tasking ability, perceived multi-tasking ability, impulsivity, and sensation seeking. *PLoS ONE, 8,* e54402.

Strayer, D. L., & Johnston, W. A. (2001). Driven to distraction: Dual-task studies of simulated driving and conversing on a cellular telephone. *Psychological Science, 12,* 462–466.

Strayer, D. L., & Watson, J. M. (2012). Supertaskers and the multitasking brain. *Scientific American Mind, 23,* 22–29.

Strayer, D. L., Watson, J. M., & Drews, F. A. (2011). Cognitive distraction while multitasking in the automobile. In B. Ross (Ed.), *The psychology of learning and motivation* (Vol. 54, pp. 29–58). San Diego, CA: Academic Press.

Strayer, D. L., Medeiros-Ward, N., & Watson, J. M. (2013). Gender invariance in multitasking: A comment on Mäntylä. *Psychological Science, 24*(5), 809–810.

Thorne, B. (2015) *How distractions at work take up more time than you think.* http://blog.idonethis.com/distractions-at-work/.

Trilling, B., & Fadel, C. (2009). *21st Century skills: Learning for life in our times.* San Francisco, CA US: Jossey-Bass.

Wang, Z., & Tchernev, J. M. (2012). The "myth" of media multitasking: Reciprocal dynamics of media multitasking, personal needs, and gratifications. *Journal of Communication, 62,* 493–513.

Watson, J. M., & Strayer, D. L. (2010). Supertaskers: Profiles in extraordinary multitasking ability. *Psychonomic Bulletin & Review, 17,* 479–485.

Wilder, G.Z. (1997). *Antecedents of Gender Differences* (Report commissioned by Educational Testing Service). Mahwah, NJ: Lawrence Erlbaum Associates.

Willingham, W. W. & Cole, N. S. (1997). *Gender and fair assessment* (Report commissioned by Educational Testing Service). Mahwah, NJ: Lawrence Erlbaum Associates.

Wittrock, M.C. (1991). Educational Psychology, Literacy, and Reading Comprehension. *Educational Psychologist 26*(2), 109–116.

Identity and Social Skills

5

> *People resist a census but give them a profile page and they'll spend all day telling you who they are.*
> —Max Barry, Lexicon

Introduction

In the previous chapter we identified the key 21st Century competencies that young people will have the potential to bring to the workplace. Our analyses drew on the evolutions in K-12 pedagogy that allow us to make some fairly specific predications regarding the types of skills young people should acquire in the near future. This chapter provides an overview of the identity and social skills that members of the Post-Millennial cohort are likely to have when they enter the labour market. As with the chapter to follow on our conclusions regarding their life and work expectations, the information we present is slightly more speculative. We have, however, identified certain areas of continuity and key differences between many of the Millennials currently in the workforce and the digital Post-Millennials who will follow them. Hence, we are prepared to provide some ideas on aspects members of these two cohorts may share and others in which they are likely to diverge.

In developing our ideas, we acknowledge the Yogi Berra wisdom that "it's tough to make predications, especially about the future" thus, our assessments are based on three key concepts we have highlighted previously. First these personal characteristics will be strongly influenced by the environment in which today's youth are growing up with significant variability in key factors such as family and community circumstances but stronger similarities in their exposure to newer curriculum and teaching approaches in schools as well as their immersion in the omnipresent digital environment since being toddlers. Second some may have had, or might yet encounter, experiences in their future that will serve as Massey's

© Springer Nature Switzerland AG 2020
A. Okros, *Harnessing the Potential of Digital Post-Millennials in the Future Workplace*, Management for Professionals,
https://doi.org/10.1007/978-3-030-25726-2_5

(1979) 'significant emotional events'. We recognize that such events could serve to alter the attitudes, views and expectations of individuals, shared sub-groups or, if of sufficient magnitude, the cohort as a whole. Third, we extend our observation that the P21/C21 initiatives are changing how the Post-Millennials are learning to learn. Compared to the majority of the Millennials, we posit those who benefit from this education as developing different perspectives on their world.

As identified in our initial 'portraits' of both groups, although we cannot predict key characteristics for each person or even sub-groups within the Post-Millennial cohort, this will not prevent their elders from forming clear impressions and developing broadly shared stereotypes as to who these young people are. We argue that the digital environment will serve to both help create and to communicate this image in ways that did not exist even when the Millennials were in their youth. Whether accurate or not, the 'labels' that get 'stuck' onto young people will have an impact as these will influence how others see them. However, unlike the Millennials before them, many Post-Millennials (and their parents) are more likely to be monitoring the impressions others have of them and to use this to their advantage. Thus, they will probably be much more adept at being 'mirrors' and 'chameleons'; reflecting to others what they believe the other wishes to see or blending into their social and work surroundings. Employers will need to learn that the Post-Millennials may live by the motto: *I'm not who you think I am*. To appreciate our analyses, we shall consider how Post-Millennials are going to develop an understanding of their world, which involves a brief detour through the concepts related to social construction.

Social Construction

> Social order is a human product, or more precisely, an ongoing human production—Berger and Luckman[1]

Social construction holds that the manner in which we understand the world—our reality—is developed through social processes that serve to create broadly shared views, definitions, ideas and connotations that are assigned to objects or events. More specifically, it is the "tradition of scholarship that traces the origin of knowledge and meaning and the nature of reality to processes generated within human relationships" (Gergen & Gergen, 2008). As these authors identify, cognizance that this depends on our social relationships and is premised in language and symbols is key to developing shared understandings. These perceptions become accepted as "fact" hence 'reality' and often become so deeply embedded in our way of seeing the world that we spend little, if any, time actually thinking about them. This is not to say that a tangible object or a shared event only exists on the basis of a

---

[1]Noting that there are vast literatures in philosophy, anthropology and theology on this subject, this section is informed by the works that followed from Berger and Luckman's (1969) sociological perspectives presented in *The Social Construction of Reality*.

social norm; it is that their meaning is derived from how we collectively have made sense of them through our interactions with one another (Edwards, Ashmore, & Potter, 1995). This leads to generally held ideas as to what is correct, true (the truth) or inevitable (it just is and has to be) and, particularly when related to human endeavours, often to what is valued as good, right or proper. The challenge is that this broadly shared world view is actually dependent on the social circumstances in which it was created; in other words, it is an artifice or invention of the specific society that created it. Thus, what is considered as natural or inevitable can, in fact, be recognized as an understanding that has been created through social processes and, hence, can be redefined or interpreted in a different manner. It is possible to observe significant differences in how certain concepts are understood or defined when comparing across different societies or the same social setting over time. The concepts of marriage and gender are good illustrations of differences that exist across cultural contexts and, within countries, over time.

While most individuals come to the realization that many of the ideas we accept as "fact" are actually contestable, children are generally raised with parents, teachers and others of influence communicating a simplified understanding of the world with an emphasis on facts, truth, rules and little room for children to explore alternate meanings or interpretations.[2] We see the Millennial cohort as having started to change these circumstances and anticipate that the Post-Millennials will take these evolutions further. Since communication forms the basis of social construction, the ongoing changes in how individuals (and especially youth) interact with one another owing to the digital age are likely to affect aspects of the construction of Post-Millennial understandings, values and attitudes regarding society and the world (Gündüz, 2017).

We have already seen the significant influence the connected, digital world has had on Millennial values. In a study of how Millennials interact, it has been noted that their use of social media accelerates the dissemination of information and the discussion of ideas; the end result of which can be a rapid cascading of social norms and cultural memes (Edwards et al., 1995). Engaged Millennials seem to be more interconnected globally and are able to share information more widely and rapidly than ever before. Accordingly, social norms can be promoted through digital media and resulting "normal" behaviour seems to be a broadly consensual group process. Further, many have become concerned about the persona they project to the world and try on many identities, something much more easily facilitated through the Internet (Pew Research Center, 2015).

We suggest that the Post-Millennial cohort will be seen to push these evolutions further. To return to two of our key findings, we anticipate that the combination of open, exploratory learning in the classroom and greater access to the content of the Internet while expose children to a wider range of views and perspectives as well as the skills (or, at least, the potential) to assess the 'knowledge' and the received

---

[2]Again, there are extensive literatures across several disciplines and across different cultures as to how children are encouraged or discouraged from dealing with contestable knowledge; our presentation is informed by the works of Kegan (1982) and Kohlberg (1972) on stages of moral development.

world view that they are encountering.[3] Research continues to demonstrate that children are being allowed unsupervised use of digital technologies at earlier ages; a 2013 survey conducted for Microsoft found parents allowed unsupervised use of computers at age 8, apps at age 9, mobile phones at 11 and social media sites at 12.[4] A 2015 small sample study of children up to age four revealed that almost all (96.6%) used mobile devices and most 3-and 4-year old's did so unsupervised (Kabali et al., 2015). As we will develop further, unsupervised does not mean un-informed; research suggests that many parents have spent some time to educate their children on appropriate usage, something that did not occur as frequently for the Millennials as they first encountered the on-line world (Grunwald Associates, 2000). While most Millennials used the Internet and especially social media to connect with each other, many Post-Millennials will (and already are) using these capacities to analyse the world around them more critically.

Similarly, the Post-Millennials as a whole will be more aware of the image others have of them and will be engaging at earlier ages in trying on different identities. To return to the Jenson et al. (2011) types of media literacy, some will have learned how to 'play' to different audiences and will be much more intentional in choosing how they will present themselves in different contexts. While others may not do so, they are likely to notice those who do (Herring & Kapidzic, 2015). This capacity to engage in social construction and to use social media to try out new identities combined with the fact that they will have learned to do so at an earlier age, has us suggest that they will enter the workplace as effective 'mirrors' and 'chameleons'. In this regard, research suggests that there are gender differences: girls and young women are reported to be more active and more intentional in presenting different images to others (Carrasco, 2016; Carmon, 2010; Lenhart, 2015; Schoenberg, Modi, & Salmond, 2013). To understand the implications of young peoples' use of the digital environment for social construction, we will now turn to the identity others may have created for them and the identities and values they may choose to adopt. Throughout this discussion we will highlight the ways in which we expect the Millennial and Post-Millennial groups to be similar and to differ.

---

[3]We recognize parental concerns in this area, however, there is a recognition that more children are encountering a wide range of information at an earlier age. Examples of recent media coverage, include Canada: http://www.theglobeandmail.com/news/toronto/polarized-debates-over-ontario-sex-education-curriculum-continue/article24915342/, the US: http://bigstory.ap.org/article/f365ce6b31104450bd821ff502824717/omaha-and-much-us-debate-over-sex-education-rages, and the UK: http://www.telegraph.co.uk/education/educationopinion/11434500/Who-should-deliver-sex-education.html.

[4]The comScore survey "How Old Is Too Young?" is accessible at: https://www.microsoft.com/about/philanthropies/youthspark/youthsparkhub/programs/onlinesafety/resources/.

Continuity and Change: Millennial and Post-Millennial Identity

> The children now love luxury; they have bad manners, contempt for authority; they show disrespect for elders and love chatter in place of exercise. Children are now tyrants, not the servants of their households.—paraphrase of a quote from Aristophanes

Driven in part by media coverage—and also the habits of many of their parents; the Millennials have been subject to significant attention, analyses and descriptions leading to a fairly widely shared image of this generation. We see several areas of continuity from the Millennials to the next age group particularly regarding perceptions by others of their: constant access to digital devices; use of social media; and, for a sizable number, similarities in how they are being raised. As these defining characteristics in how the world has perceived the Millennial cohort will remain visible for many youngsters, we have concluded that the first wave of Post-Millennials entering the workforce will likely be assumed by others to be just "junior Millennials". It will be important, however, for employers to anticipate specific ways in which the Post-Millennials as a group or as individuals may differ from the Millennials.

As they have now entered adulthood and the workforce, we have a clearer picture of many of the traits and individual attributes of members of the Millennial generation. Many researchers and media echoes/memes emphasize aspects of the seven distinguishing traits of the Millennial persona that were initially presented by Howe and Strauss in their initial projections in *Millennials Rising*. They depicted this generation as: sheltered, special, confident, pressured, achieving, team-oriented, and conventional. We will explore some of the key factors that are influencing who young people are and who they are assumed to be and, in each of the areas examined, we will start by presenting information on the Millennials and then turn to considerations of how the Post-Millennials are likely to be similar and where we anticipate they will differ.

Parenting

Several of the Howe and Strauss traits are strongly related to descriptions of the Millennial generation's experiences as children. Many were raised by "helicopter" parents who were active in their lives and are often depicted as hovering over their child to safeguard against injury, whether it be physical or emotional, enrolling them in numerous activities and negotiating with teachers, coaches, professors, and even employers on their child's behalf to ensure success (Strauss and Howe, 2000; Rainer & Rainer, 2011; Raines, 2002).[5] Parents rallied for safety in schools, playgrounds, cars and homes often achieving changes in government legislation

---

[5]For a recent extension of this phenomenon, see Elwood Watson's article "Overbearing, Snowplough Parents Have Replaced Helicopter Parents" accessible at: http://www.huffingtonpost.com/elwood-d-watson/overbearing-snowplough-pa_b_5720354.html.

(Strauss and Howe, 2000). Millennials who experienced this parenting, in turn, feel that they are the primary focus of their parents' attention and are vital to their families as well as to their state. Many not only welcome the involvement of their parents, they seek it (Strauss and Howe, 2000; Rainer & Rainer, 2011). This added parental attention and strong parent/child relationship has been noted to give many Millennials a boost of confidence. Zemke et al. (1999) mention that "[b]y and large, their parents, two-thirds of them anyway—planned to have these kids, and these kids experience the confidence that comes from knowing you are wanted" (p. 130).

While feeling special and having confidence are both positive characteristics, the literature suggests that the Millennials with strong parental attachments have, at times, felt pressured to succeed (Rainer & Rainer, 2011). Researchers reveal that parents have stressed the importance of their children taking advantage of oppor- tunities that are offered to them. This has often resulted in an overscheduled life filled with activities and a focus on academics, especially math and science. In turn, this led to a less time for unstructured activities or to spend outdoors than previous generations enjoyed (Howe, 2007; Strauss and Howe, 2000; Raines, 2002; Zemke et al., 1999). The net result is that many Millennials' expectations mirror their parents' desire to achieve academically and this generation may be on their way to becoming the most well-educated to date (Hyler, 2013; Pew Research Centre, 2015).

Research also suggests that—due in part to their upbringing—many Millennials have a "sense of entitlement" (Ng, Schweitzer, & Lyons, 2010); although McGlynn (2010) counters that this may only be a stereotype created by elders who don't fully understand them. It could also come from a perception of Millennials having a lack of respect for authority (Stein, Time Magazine, May 20, 2013, p. 31). Ng et al. (2010) set out to validate some of these work and employment related traits, characteristics, and assumptions with a view to having a clearer picture of exactly who Millennials are. Their report suggests that many of the stated characteristics of Millennials are accurate. Consequently, as they come of age and depart the shelter of their parents, some Millennials experience shock when they discover they no longer occupy the prime focal point of their new authority figures and can be disheartened when they realize that their expectations of individual help and attention do not extend to the workplace (McGlynn, 2010).

Our research suggests that many of today's youth are also being raised by parents who are heavily involved in their children's lives and seek to provide similar benefits during their upbringing. This has always been the focus of par- enting. However, we suggest that factors such as smaller family size, the increased age (and life experience) of parents when raising children and parental level of education are having an impact on the nature of parental activities. Thus, many Post-Millennials are likely to share some similar characteristics with the Millennials and will be assumed to do so by those who will help define this next generation.

We noted, however, a small but significant call for more balance in how children are being raised. The actions of helicopter parents and 'tiger moms'[6] have resulted in their children acquiring a poor reputation (Pew Research Center, 2015; Rainer & Rainer, 2011; Taylor, 2016; Twenge, 2006). At the extreme, it has led to the counter-argument of 'free range' parenting with some opting for what they see as the more carefree and less structured approach that children experienced in previous generations.[7] At a minimum, we see the next generation of children being raised by parents who will generally be more aware of the image they are creating of their offspring and the consequences that may result. As Post-Millennials will most likely also be aware of these ramifications, to return to the concept of social construction and how this can influence identity, our general conclusion is that many of today's parents and their children will be conscious of, and likely engaged in, defining how this cohort may be characterized by the larger world. On the surface, we will probably see continuity through similar parenting behaviours, but we also see anticipate differences due to subtle shifts as parental influence is likely to be conducted in a more socially aware manner.

Social Media and Social Skills

The area that has probably received the greatest amount of attention for the youth cohort is their use of social media and related social and interpersonal skills. Both Millennials and Post-Millennials are characterized by the constant use of devices to connect via social media and the data suggest that this is becoming more wide-spread and is occurring sooner in life. Across a range of countries, research continues to show children owning or using mobile devices at earlier ages with a 2014 US report revealing that 53% of six year olds have a cell phone,[8] 2012 UK data indicating that 75% have one by age 10,[9] and a 2013 US study that 38% of children under two years old have used a mobile device to access online media.[10] They are being accused of having poor interpersonal skills because of how much Millennials' use digital media to socialize online through texting and social media rather than in person or face-to-face. As Post-Millennials will be seen to be engaging in the same behaviours, they will likely be assumed to have the same weakness.

---

[6]See Chua (2011) and associated media coverage regarding what are seen as over-controlling parents who place strong pressures on their children to succeed. In Japanese culture, referred to as Kyoiku mama.
[7]See Lenore Skenazy's (2009) *Free-Range Kids* and the related media coverage of this parenting style.
[8]http://wric.com/2015/04/07/survey-discovers-6-years-old-is-the-average-age-of-kids-when-they-first-receive-a-cell-phone/.
[9]http://www.dailymail.co.uk/news/article-2198450/Three-quarters-British-children-aged-10-mobile-phone-twice-overseas.html.
[10]https://www.commonsensemedia.org/research/zero-to-eight-childrens-media-use-in-america-2013/key-finding-2%3A-kids%27-time-on-mobile-devices-triples.

We found considerable academic literature, media articles and on-line discussion/posts reflecting on the Post-Millennials' use of social media and related social skills. This generation is seen as using technology as a means to an end; their devices are useful tools to enrich social interaction but do not define the individual as it appears to have for many of the Millennial generation (Pew Research Center, 2015; American Press Institute, 2015). For the vast majority with access, technology integrates seamlessly into their lives but is not the end in and of itself. Although the Post-Millennials are often described as emotionally attached to their technology, research suggests that, for those who have access to them, their smartphones represent a social hub that provides them with inspiration, interactivity and a creative outlet as well as increasingly serving as a parental substitute to help organize their lives (Pew Research Center, 2015).

To return to the discussion of social construction, our assessment is that engaged Post-Millennials (and their parents) will be navigating through the online world with a different set of skills and greater social awareness when compared to the Millennials or their parents. The new curriculum being introduced in schools focussed on enhancing digital literacy includes developing a greater appreciation of the consequences of having an online presence and the capacity to exercise better judgment on what content to share with others. Recent research is showing that the Millennials are, rather belatedly, paying attention to their online image particularly when employers are asking for access to their social media accounts.[11] Our assessment is that Post-Millennials will be growing up with a much better understanding of the implications of how others view their actions and, especially, their 'digital footprint' of online posts and perceived communications skills, hence, will be a bit more attentive to the longer term consequences of their decisions.[12] Additionally, as one component of digital literacy, research is revealing that many teenagers use multiple different social media platforms with a nuanced understanding of which one to use for what purpose (Colleoni, Rozza, & Arvidsson, 2014; Del Vicario et al., 2016; Lenhart, 2015).

We are also seeing initial indications that some of the Post-Millennials have recognized the problems the Millennials are having in the workplace due to poor communications skills and difficulties with interpersonal interactions. A recent study highlighted that a majority of Post-Millennials identified 'soft skills' as likely to be of more importance in landing their first job than 'hard' skills (personal characteristics versus job-specific knowledges).[13] In this context, we also noted that the new 21st Century Skills curriculum is placing greater emphasis on developing communications skills appropriate to the digital environment.

---

[11]For a recent discussion of how Millennials view their online reputation, see: https://www. reputationmanagement.com/blog/2016/1/22/do-millennials-care-about-their-reputation.

[12]We acknowledge that teens, in particular, will continue to engage in degrees of socially inappropriate or risky behaviours including sexting however that they will be developing greater self-awareness hence self-control over time.

[13]See the Adecco 2015 Way to Work Survey accessible at:
  http://www.taprootfoundation.org/about-probono/blog/generation-z-entering-workforce-your-company-ready.

Together, these developments are likely to result in different consequences for the 'digital in their DNA' Post-Millennials as compared to the older 'digital native' Millennials. Youngsters now have the capacity for unprecedented global social interaction and connection to global discourses as well as an awareness of, and, for some, control over, the power of social media. Unlike the Millennial cohort who generally adopted digital technologies at a mid-point in their youth, the Post-Millennials have been living within social media from birth (or more accurately, their parents started passing on digital media skills to their children from the time they decided whether to post the sonogram on Facebook). Whether at home, in school or connecting with each other, today's children have the opportunity to develop the awareness and skills needed to navigate through growing up online. This generation will have the potential to enter the workforce more skilled at social interactions and more media savvy than the Millennials. While the socially incompetent will continue to exist, the Post-Millennials will contain a far greater number with digital media literacy and strong social skills. The challenges for employers will be to differentiate the truly skilled from the carefully packaged—and then to learn to live with the ideas and worldviews that these individuals will bring to the workplace.

Diversity

An important reason behind our suggestion that the Post-Millennials will likely possess increased abilities for effective social interactions will come from their broader and deeper exposure to diversity. Again, a better appreciation of diversity has been observed with many in the Millennial cohort, however, our assessment is that this may be further advanced with today's youth. The digital environment has enabled Millennials to experience many aspects of diversity including awareness of ethnicities, languages, religious perspectives, sexual orientations, gendered identities and a host of other individual or sub-group factors that make "them" different from "us" or "me". Thus, even if not present in their local geographical community, Millennials were introduced to diversity in their virtual lives (Brinckerhoff, 2007; Erickson, 2008; Rainer & Rainer, 2011). For young people, their exposure to, and often acceptance of, diversity extends beyond race or ethnicity, or the African-American-Caucasian divide that defined so much of the 20th century (Strauss & Howe 218, 2000): Millennials are more likely to embody or appreciate other viewpoints, gender equality, differences in sexual orientation, non-traditional living arrangements, and interracial relationships than previous generations (Greenberg & Weber, 2008; Pew Research Center, 2010; Zemke et al., 1999). Often Millennials have been a driving force behind movements for greater female empowerment, gay marriage and increased interracial dating/marriage (Pew Research Center, 2012; Statistics Canada, 2015; Tanner, 2010).

In the US and Canada in particular, exposure to diversity online is being met with increasing diversity within communities. The Millennial generation is the most diverse to date and population projections especially related to immigration indicate that this trend will continue. We will comment on the indicators of attitudes below, however, will note that, at a minimum, contact and awareness is increasing. In 2011, visible minorities made up 41% of the American population and approximately 23% of the Canadian population. This marks a significant increase from 2001 when visible minorities made up 26% of the population in the United States and 17% in Canada (Pew Research Center, 2011; Statistics Canada, 2011). Statistics Canada data reveal that the proportion of Canadians who identify as visible minorities rose rapidly as members of the Millennial generation were born. Urbanization in both the US and Canada plays a role as larger cities tend to have more diversity and continue to serve as a magnet for young adults.

A specific aspect of evolving understandings amongst the youth cohort pertains to gender and gendered identities. Assessments of the attitudes of US Millennials and Post-Millennial teens illustrate the shifts in perspectives. A 2015 poll of 1000 US Millennials by Benson Strategy Group revealed that half of respondents viewed gender as a spectrum rather than a dichotomous male vs female categorization with important sub-group differences with those endorsing the spectrum response higher for females (57% vs. 44% for males); White (55% vs. 32% for African Americans and an even split for Hispanic) and Ideologically Liberal (75% followed by Moderates at 52% and Conservatives at 30%).[14]

As 2016 poll of 600 US Millennials (aged 21–30) and Gen Z/Post-Millennials (13–20) revealed highly levels of awareness and acceptance by both groups with the younger cohort reporting greater variations in personal identity.[15] Both group strongly or somewhat agreed that 'gender does not define a person as much as it used to' (74% for Millennials and 78% for Gen Z); that 'people are exploring their sexuality more than in the past' (90% and 91%); and large proportions reported being familiar with terms such as transgender (90% and 84%), queer (76% and 72%) and asexual (72% and 69%). An interesting difference was that 65% of Millennials described themselves as 'completely heterosexual' while only 48% of the younger cohort did so with the differentiation explained by the younger respondents selecting a degree of bisexual identity (6% in both groups identified as 'completely homosexual'). Canadian media coverage has conveyed similar messages although no recent formal polling or academic research was identified that addresses these issues amongst teens.

Socially, Millennials also demonstrate tendencies towards both platonic and amorous socialization in groups rather than hanging out in small cliques or one-on-one dating (Tanner, 2010). Perhaps as a result of electronic social networking, many Millennials are described as comfortable relying on peers and parents for support, and preferring to work in groups, sharing goals and failures (Drago, 2006; Fritzon et al., 2008; Pinder-Grover & Groscurth, 2009; Stafford & Griffis, 2008; Tanner, 2010). As a result of the aforementioned ethno-cultural

---

[14]The poll results are accessible at: https://fusiondotnet.files.wordpress.com/2015/02/fusion-poll-gender-spectrum.pdf.

[15]The news release for this poll is accessible at: https://www.jwtintelligence.com/2016/03/gen-z-goes-beyond-gender-binaries-in-new-innovation-group-data/.

diversity in which Millennials were raised, many are also more comfortable navigating diversity within these groups.[16]

Migration and Multiculturalism

However, when considering attitudes regarding diversity, awareness does not always translate to acceptance and accepting diversity in society does not always lead to embracing it in one's daily life. In line with Howe and Strauss' characterization of the Millennials as conservative and Adams' description of the different Canadian Millennial 'value tribes', the data show that, at a minimum, there is diversity in young peoples' attitudes regarding diversity particularly with regards to issues related to immigration and social integration. We found attitudinal research covering the US, UK and Canada that suggested it is, in fact, a minority of Millennials who personally embrace diversity in their life with differences in the areas of race, migration and social integration.

As reflected in Apollon's (2011) report title *Don't Call Them "Post-Racial": Millennials' Attitudes on Race, Racism, and Key Systems in Our Society*, the US Applied Research Center found a wide range of attitudes regarding race, immigration and other aspects of diversity with their conclusion that the Millennials are not monolithic. We also noted that identity politics have been a factor in public discourse in the US for many years with narratives emerging from the actions of police and the run up to the November 2016 Presidential election serving to create what the Southern Poverty Law Center called "a year awash in deadly extremist violence and hateful rhetoric from mainstream political figures".[17]

Similarly, while 2012 UK research indicated Millennials in that country are more accepting of diversity related to sexual orientation and same sex marriage when compared to their elders, there were few generational differences across the UK regarding immigration with a strong majority in all age groups indicating that numbers of newcomers were too high and that immigration presented more problems than opportunities.[18] Against the backdrop of high youth unemployment, the combination of ongoing refugee crises and political rhetoric have resulted in polarizing perspectives on migration and social integration across a range of

---

[16]See the Institute for Public Relations Dec 2016 report accessible at: http://www.instituteforpr. org/millennialswork-perspectives-diversity-inclusion/.

[17]See the SPLC Spring 2016 Intelligence Report accessible at: https://www.splcenter.org/news/ 2016/02/17/splcs-intelligence-report-amid-year-lethal-violence-extremist-groups-expanded-ranks-2015.

[18]Noting that attitudes across Europe regarding immigration continue to shift, this 2011 report indicated that attitudes in the UK were the most negative when compared to France, Germany, Italy, Spain or the US. See, Blinder (2012).

European nations. Data from May 2015 indicated that, at that time, only Sweden held a positive attitude regarding non-European Union migration.[19]

Conversely, according to a 2015 survey by the Environics Institute, Canadian attitudes on immigration and multiculturalism have remained steady or grown more positive in the last few years.[20] As one indicator, the policies on Syrian refugees became a ballot issue in the October 2015 Federal election with the majority of the electorate supporting a more open and proactive approach. In December 2015, Environic's Michael Adams provided a comparison of US and Canadian attitudes revealing 68% support for the Canadian government intent to bring in 25,000 refugees against only 28% of Americans endorsing the US President's plan to accept 10,000.[21] As an extension, a 2012 survey conducted for the Mosaic Institute and the Association for Canadian Studies reported that "eighty-two per cent of respondents aged 18 to 24 said they believed multiculturalism should be exported to other countries to help them address ethnic, religious or linguistic conflicts," whereas only 57% of people aged 65 or older said the same. The study notes that multiculturalism's strongest support comes from those "who have grown up knowing nothing else." More young Canadians agreed that newcomers to Canada are accepting of "different cultures, races and religions," and have a positive social effect on Canada. Young Canadians also believed much more strongly that "it is easy for people from different racial, religious and cultural communities to form close relationships with each other." Only 46% of those 65 or older agreed, whereas 80% of young people did.[22]

We offer three conclusions regarding the likely attitudes regarding various forms of diversity amongst the Post-Millennials as they enter the future workforce. First, they will probably mirror today's adults with a range of personal preferences regarding a number of aspects of their chosen lifestyle, friends and interests. Thus, while all are likely to have a good understanding of the identities related to members of the LBGT+ communities, some who are not part of these communities will have close friends from these groups while others will opt not to. Similarly, organized religion will be a central aspect in the lives of some; personal spirituality will matter to others while neither will be of relevance for yet others.

Second, despite these ranges in personal choices, the Post-Millennials will be generally supportive of policies and programs that are designed to remove the barriers that prevent individuals or groups from expressing their identity in the

---

[19]Accessible   at: http://www.voxeurop.eu/en/content/news-brief/4932007-map-showing-eu-countries-attitude-towards-foreign-immigration.

[20]Accessible   at: http://www.environicsinstitute.org/uploads/institute-projects/environics%20institute%20-%20focus%20canada%20spring%202015%20survey%20on%20immigration-multiculturalism%20-%20final%20report%20-%20june%2030-2015.pdf.

[21]His 9 Dec 2015 OpEd in the *Globe and Mail* titled: "Why Canada, U.S., diverge on Syrian refugees" is accessible at: http://www.theglobeandmail.com/opinion/distinct-societies-why-canada-us-diverge-on-syrian-refugees/article27652245/.

[22]See the report at: https://acs-aec.ca/en/.

manner they choose. Again, their broader exposure to different worldviews and better ability to understand social construction is likely to lead them to endorsing principles of equity and inclusion regardless of whether they personally embrace the life styles or views being endorsed.[23]

Finally, events on the national and international stage and the responses of those in positions of influence may yet become a key factor in how they come to understand the world around them.[24] To return to our earlier caution regarding the dangers of virtual echo chambers, those who are exposed to only a narrow range of reinforcing opinions may develop different views from those who seek to see issues from multiple perspectives.

Collaboration and Teamwork

The digital world and its ability to connect an entire cohort has also created a generally shared sense of togetherness for both the Millennials and, we believe, is extending to the Post-Millennials (Cone Inc. & AMP Insights, 2006; Greenberg & Weber, 2008; McGlynn, 2010). To return to the descriptions of their over-scheduled lives, many have been placed into groups or teams for daycare activities, summer camps, projects, Girl Guides and Boy Scouts, sports and much more. While these activities served to keep children entertained and engaged, this early introduction to teamwork continued throughout their lives and was further enhanced by their ability to communicate instantaneously with each other and to engage in collaborative problem solving (Howe, 2007). As a result, research shows that, on the job, Millennials enjoy working in inclusive teams that ensure no one is left behind (Deloitte, 2005; Elmore, 2010; Greenberg & Weber, 2008; Martin & Tulgan, 2006; Raines, 2003; Wilcox, 2001).

Particularly in Canada and to a lesser extent the US and other nations, the Millennials were also subject to major shifts in education policies that were intended to address a number of issues including early drop outs (Jenson et al., 2011). These changes, however, were perceived to result in an environment where students did not receive failing grades or accurate teachers' assessments of their scholastics standing and where parents received reports cards containing little constructive criticism or any concrete identification of pupil weaknesses.[25] When combined with the push for non-competitive team sports (generically known in Canada as 'timbits hockey'), a component of the 'sheltered' and 'special' identity presented by Strauss and Howe (2000) and perpetuated in general discourse is that

---

[23]To paraphrase from the original attributed to Oliver Wendell Holmes, Jr. "Your right to swing your cultural fist ends where my cultural nose begins": live your life as you wish but don't impose your values on me.

[24]As stated earlier, in part of her analyses, Agati (2011) demonstrated that the events of 9/11 had differing impacts depending on how closely these affected the lives of the participants.

[25]We acknowledge that the curriculum updates of the late 80s through 1990s were more extensive than we have summarized; see Anderson and Jaafar (2003) for a comprehensive presentation in the Ontario school system.

the Millennials had not faced competition or honest assessments of their actual worth. The perspective has been that they believe everybody should get a trophy just for showing up and has led to a plethora of high school and university commencement speeches intended to warn the graduates that they were in for a rude awakening (Sykes, 1995).

Noting that there is some debate on the degree to which Millennials really have been sheltered from honest feedback, our assessment of the Post-Millennials is that they are continuing to value teamwork and that inclusion/togetherness is going to remain an important part of the Post-Millennial philosophy. These, however, do not mean that youngsters are not still competitive particularly in sports or scholastics and it is probable to assume these attitudes will extend to careers when they enter the workforce.[26]

We do see this focus on teamwork and collaboration as an area of increased insights and openness amongst the Post-Millennials. Strauss and Howe (2000) assert that Millennials have adapted, and will continue to adapt, to the increasing emphasis on community rather than individualism within North American society. Thus, our conclusion on teamwork is that the Post-Millennials will strongly value group and team efforts with the nuanced differentiation between a recognition that each is still going to be assessed and rewarded on their individual talent and accomplishments but an expectation that all will be acknowledged for their contribution.

Global Citizenship and Civil Engagement

Another main aspect of the Millennials' image that has been created due to their use of social media pertains to their interest in global issues. Some have argued that previous generations' lives were more focused on their geographic location while these digital natives were able to explore a wider world while in their teens. Researchers have suggested that the Millennials, to a great extent, perceive themselves as global citizens connected with peers from every walk of life who are accessible by a tap on a smartphone (Elmore, 2010; Erickson, 2008; Lancaster & Stillman, 2002). Further, instant access to media and worldwide events has created a generation with more shared experiences than ever before. They are said to be experiencing defining moments of their lives globally "together" (Strauss and Howe, 2000; Raines, 2002; Martin & Tulgan, 2006) and thus are more likely to approach their environment from a global perspective (Tanner, 2010).

Strauss and Howe labelled the Millennials as fitting the civic-minded 'hero' archetype. Part of their argument is that their shared global experiences have led to the Millennial being more civic-minded and wanting to make a difference in their

---

[26]For illustrations in the mass media, see Kathryn Blaze Carlson "No winners: Children still keeping score despite move to end sports competition" National Post 22 September 2012 and Sarah Boesveld "Many parents see competitive activities as not just important, but essential for their children's success" National Post, 16 August 2013.

own community. Raines (2002) indicated that "serve your community" was one of the main messages for this generation. A 2017 poll of 790 US teens revealed almost 90% had engaged in a civic action such as volunteering for a cause they care about or raising money for such a cause.[27] Echoing the Strauss and Howe findings, Statistics Canada data from 2010 revealed that 15 to 24 year old's have the highest volunteer rate in Canada at 58%, amplified perhaps by volunteer hours required by many Canadian high schools to graduate (Vézina & Crompton, 2012). Many have suggested that this desire to serve a greater good extends into the broader community and global issues (Cone Inc. & AMP Insights, 2006; Martin & Tulgan, 2006; Raines, 2002). The view is that, through their exposure to global discourses, Millennials have a desire to connect to, and be a part of, the global picture rather than simply be influenced by their local surroundings and shared cohort. As reflected in their 2008 book "Generation We", Eric Greenberg and Karl Weber argued that American Millennials were highly politically engaged with Norris and Krook (2009) emphasizing that this can be through non-traditional forms as illustrated by the Occupy Wall Street Movement (Levitin, 2015).

Other researchers, however, have challenged these assertions particularly with regards to Millennials in the US. Some such as Trzesniewski and Donnellan (2010) have reported data suggesting there have been no real changes in attitudes concluding that young American adults in the 2000s are similar to those of the same age in the 1970s. Twenge (2006) reported that comparisons of data going back as far as the 1920s showed a clear shift towards self-centered individualism accompanied by increases self-importance and narcissism. Twenge et al. (2012) followed up this study with more detailed analyses to conclude that civic engagement declined from the Boomers to Gen X and yet again from Gen X to the Millennials with some of the largest declines related to environmentalism—which has been an aspect touted by Strauss and Howe (2000) as of high importance for this cohort. As we highlighted in our earlier presentation of Generational Theory, our own analyses of the Quebec student protests suggested that a main factor for this movement was preservation of their own privileges (particularly stopping planned increases in tuition fees) and not a desire to make the world better for others. Again, in the Canadian context, Adam's research also reveals that the majority of Millennials are more focussed on themselves than on others.

Our conclusion in this area for both the Millennials and the Post-Millennials is: 'it depends'. As reflected in the differing sub-groups on Michael Adam's analyses or the conflicting data from research, we suggest that the variations amongst either of these age groups are probably too large to make any meaningful generalization possible. Both across each generation and over time, the degree to which individuals or sub-groups are focussed on themselves and their families versus the larger world will likely vary including by the issue under consideration; the tenor of the larger national and international debates on the topic; and, their personal

---

[27]The poll conducted by the Associated Press- NORC at the University of Chicago is accessible at: http://www.apnorc.org/projects/Pages/american-teens-are-politically-engaged-but-pessimistic-about-countrys-direction.aspx.

circumstances. In this regard, we noted: "Millennials have an acute nose for authenticity" (Stuart & Lyons, 2008, p. 3). As illustrated in cases such as the student protests in Quebec that we studied, the Occupy Movement or the Arab Spring, social media can serve a powerful role in mobilizing local and international attention and action when a cause gains currency. The most important finding from our consideration of global citizenship and civic engagement is that the Post-Millennials will enter adulthood with the latent potential to become active, quickly. Only time will tell what the triggers might be for such actions but, when viewed against the general forecasts of marginal economic growth, climbing health care costs especially with aging Boomers and the "balloon mortgage" payments coming due on items such as infrastructure, environmental degradation, coastal flooding, drought and changing energy dynamics, we make two forecasts. First, many Post-Millennials will enter the workforce with an age-old focus on trying to make ends meet—and keeping an eye open for an unprecedented wealth transfer when the Boomers wills are finally read. Second, however, they may quickly mobilize around an issue that becomes salient and will demand political action and societal changes to be implemented as soon as possible.

The Dark Side of Social Attitudes: Trolls, Cyberbullying and Sextortion

While our research has highlighted positive aspects of the impacts of the digital environment on the values and attitudes of both the Millennials and Post-Millennials, it is important to note that there are definitely concerns raised in certain areas with social media holding a central role in some cases. The main issue arising here is the juxtaposition between online anonymity and loss of personal privacy. On the one hand, the Internet allows for individuals to be provide comments, make posts and share content without anybody else knowing who they are but, on the other hand, once an individual's personal identity is attached to any content (a post, picture, comment, etc.), it is widely and broadly available to the multitudes.[28] As with our earlier comments that Millennials are only now starting to pay attention to their online image and reputation, society as a whole is just coming to terms with the ways in which the combination of individual anonymity and loss of personal privacy are enabling some to engage in anti-social practices and for others to be harmed as a result.[29]

Internet trolls are seen as those who (generally anonymously) provide comments that appear to be designed primarily to upset others and stir up controversial follow on posts or tweets (Roberts, 2011) . Although research is limited, Buckels et al.

---

[28]As an illustration, see Paecher (2013) for an examination of on collaborative online constructions of identity amongst young women.

[29]Amongst our research team, John Verdon argues that both social and technological changes will lead to the end of privacy as we have known it for over 500 years; others were not swayed and especially did not see this happening in the next decade or so thus we have assumed that anonymity will remain for the near future.

(2014) concluded that cyber-trolling appears to be "a manifestation of everyday sadism with trolling related to sadism, psychopathy and Machiavellianism". We also noted that the frequency of online yelling matches that erupt in newspaper comments sections have resulted in many mainstream papers removing this option. In addition, while moderators of online chat fora have been struggling for some time now in determining which comments should be tolerated versus deleted, Google has sponsored work to create algorithms to identify and, presumably, block those engaging in anti-social trolling; an indicator of the magnitude of the problem (Cheng, Danescu-Niculescu-Mizily, & Leskovec, 2015). At its worst, trolling behaviour can result in personally targeted attacks on a publicly named individual that, in some cases, has resulted in dire consequences. In sum, we recognize that the capacity for individuals to share comments anonymously does result in instances of anti-social commentary and, depending on the jurisdiction, illegal actions that constitute libel or even hate crimes.

As an extension, cyberbullying refers to repeated direct contact with a malicious individual who can harm the person. In contrast to trolling, cyberbullies are generally identified as aggressive and manipulating with research linking this behaviour to low self-esteem, anger, frustration, and suicidal tendencies amongst other emotional or psychological issues (Brighi et al., 2012; Kowalski & Limber, 2013; Wang, Nansel, & Iannotti, 2011). The increasing incidents of cyberbullying for teens had been noted to be rising in many countries although some recent reports suggest this has leveled off. A comprehensive 2013 US study revealed that 21% of females and 8.5% of males in Grade 9–12 reported being victim with rates higher in the more junior grades (Kann et al., 2014). Further, some data is suggesting that teen females bully more often than boys (Patchin & Hinduja, 2013). Unfortunately, cyberbullying has been associated with a number of teen suicides that have garnered significant media attention, including some teens who had approached police or medical professionals but did not receive the assistance they were seeking.[30] We also noted that those who engage in, or are victims of, cyberbullying are often also engaged in physical bullying and that face-to-face antagonism is still more prevalent than online bullying (Craig & McCuaig Edge, 2008). We also recognize that the central behaviours are not new (Koss, 1988) but the opportunities to do so anonymously have increased.

Sextortion generally refers to the use of power to extort sexual favours either in the form of online pictures or images (nudity or sex acts) or leading to in-person meetings that lead to the same. Colloquially known as cappers, the individuals who engage in these behaviours are using blackmail and other forms of social control to achieve either personal gratification or, what has become for some, to engage in a warped game of wining 'caps'. Reports in Canada, the US and elsewhere have identified a significant increase in cases especially involving younger teenage girls.[31] To date, there is no rigorous research examining the perpetrators of sextortion.

---

[30]In the US, see the Carla Jamerson case, in Canada: Rehtaeh Parsons, in the UK: Brodie Panlock.
[31]See http://www.usatoday.com/story/news/nation/2014/07/01/sextortion-teens-online/11580633/ and http://www.cbc.ca/news/canada/manitoba/sextortion-canadian-teens-1.3240470.

Together, these three types of anti-social, and often criminal, behaviours illustrate some of the issues that have arisen from the extensive use of the Internet; the challenges of younger teens or adolescents being online; and, in some cases, youth lack of either the preparatory skills to protect themselves or the adult supervision needed to do so. A review of online websites suggests awareness of this issue. Concerned community groups, law enforcement and health practitioners are seeking to provide this information to both teens and their parents and educational programmes are being incorporated in school activities across a range of locations.

While, at one level, these responses can be seen as the 21st Century equivalent of teaching children to look both ways before crossing the street, we see a deeper issue and, to extend, one where the Post-Millennials may learn valuable life lessons that the Millennials did not. The core issue is linked to Robert Putnam's argument that societies function better when citizens from a range of communities with differing perspectives find ways to engage with each other in meaningful exchanges (Putnam, 1995; Putnam, 2000) . Reflected in his 1995 essay title *Bowling Alone: The Collapse and Revival of American Community*, a central idea drawn from his work is that those who engage in activities in isolation (bowling alone) avoid having to acknowledge or respect the views of others while those who do so in groups (members of bowling leagues) recognize they have to 'own' their personal opinions and have to, at a minimum, listen to those who express their views. The acceptance of personal responsibility for one's words and deeds is considered to be a component of the maturation from adolescence to adulthood. This review of the dark side of social media highlights ways in which those who have not successfully made this transition are using and abusing social media while others are still learning the skills to protect themselves from harm. As yet another facet of events that were not effectively foreseen at the time, many Millennials are now learning some important life lessons regarding both individual responsibility and vulnerability when one is sharing personal information (TMI: too much information). Our conclusion is that the Post-Millennials and their parents are watching and learning hence are likely to be developing better social skills to navigate around the shoals and sharks. At a minimum, they will probably be less naïve as to the dark side of social media.

Conclusion

This chapter has provided an overview of our conclusions regarding the identity and social skills that the Post-Millennials are likely to bring to the workplace. Only time will tell exactly how those in this age group will enter adulthood. Still, there will be considerable variability amongst different sub-groups; so, employers should consider two important factors. First, others will try to categorize the Post-Millennials and, in doing so, are likely to see them as 'junior Millennials'. Certainly, some of the contributing factors such as involved parents and constant use of devices will make them appear similar however we have identified ways in which these two groups will, in fact, differ. Second, Post-Millennials will be far more aware of the reputation they will be earning than were the Millennials when they were adolescents. Due to their increased use of the digital environment to understand the world, the new learning skills they are developing today in school and slight shifts in parenting styles, we have concluded that it would be best to assume today's children will grow up a little faster and a little smarter. They and their parents are often aware of the generalized stereotypes of Millennials as basement dwelling gamers or social Neanderthals who cannot form a coherent sentence and will be seeking to ensure that they are seen in a more positive light.

Not only will many pay more attention to the image others have of them, but they have the potential to be much better equipped and more experienced at influencing this image by actively engaging in the construction and representation of their cohort. Many of the Post-Millennials will be much more comfortable with seeing issues, definitions, social norms and institutions as socially embedded hence either contestable or fluid. An implication here is that many will recognize that the 'truth' comes with an expiry date. Further, in areas of individual diversity, they will be more aware of alternate worldviews, lifestyles and value sets and, we believe, more likely to stand on principle to ensure that others can live their lives based on these alternate cultural systems—as long as these do not infringe on the ability of others to live by their own values. We do recognize that current socio-political issues and discourses are resulting in many of today's children being exposed to narratives of intolerance and xenophobia and it will be of value to track how this climate is going to influence their attitudes and perspectives. How do Post-Millennials understand citizenship and, in particular, how do they navigate contrasts between constructed national identities versus global perspectives with the resulting tensions amongst individual, group and collective identities, rights and obligations? While some researchers had predicted that the Millennials would become the torchbearers demanding important social changes, the data suggests that they are more focussed on fitting in and getting ahead; we suggest that the Post-Millennials will probably have similar goals but with the latent potential to shift focus.

We also see most Post-Millennials continuing the trend of a strong preference for collaboration and teamwork; especially with their peers. This is not seen, however, to be at the expense of either individualism or competition nor with naïve assumptions of universal egalitarianism: regardless of the pursuit, they are likely to be fully aware that some will be seen to have succeeded and others will have failed. The preference for working in groups will mean that they will value inclusion and openness with a desire to reach out to others and to bring their talent and ideas forward with the expectation that all who do so will be acknowledged for their contributions.

Our review of the environment in which the Post-Millennials are living also revealed several concerns regarding anti-social behaviours with trolls, cyberbullies and cappers taking advantage of the anonymity that they can adopt and the vulnerabilities of young people who share too much personal information. We see parents, teachers, community groups and governments paying increased attention to these issues with efforts to strengthen awareness, prevention and enforcement of laws to minimize what can be hurtful, if not deadly, outcomes of these activities. While the focus will remain on controlling these specific activities, we do see these efforts as having the potential to introduce teens, in particular, to the idea of taking ownership and accepting personal responsibility for one's words and deeds, thus, helping create more mature and informed adults.

In sum, we see the Post-Millennials having the potential to enter the workforce better equipped to make sense of, and succeed in, their careers. Significant differences will exist in the degree to which any one individual has benefited from opportunities to develop requisite skills and in the value frameworks each will use in their own life. Nonetheless, when compared to the descriptors for the Millennials, we expect most to be much more aware of their image and actively engaged in both defining who they are and in presenting to others the image that is required to fit in and get ahead. For this reason, we suggest that they will be effective in mirroring back to their boss the image, attitudes and behaviours that is expected and in changing their language, actions and presentation to blend into their organizational surroundings. We do anticipate, however, that they will extend *caveat emptor* to not only being aware of the products or services they are buying but also more aware of the employment opportunities and careers that organizations will be selling them. As we will extend in the final chapter, our conclusion is that employers will need to consider the consequences of the current approach of ensuring new employees adapt to the organizational culture. To the degree that the Post-Millennials are prepared to present one image in the workplace while refraining from presenting who they really are, employers are at risk of missing out on the views, perspectives, competencies and creative ideas that these new workers will possess hence will not be prepared to surf the coming digital tsunami that we see as going to sweep over the economy.

References

Agati, H. A. (2011). *The millennial generation: Howe and Strauss disputed.* (Doctoral dissertation). Retrieved from ProQuest Dissertations and Theses. (Accession Order No. ATT 3492308).

American Press Institute. (2015). How Millennials Get News: Inside the Habits of America's First Digital Generation accessible at: http://www.americanpressinstitute.org/wp-content/uploads/2015/08/Media-Insight-Millennials-Report-March-2015.pdf.

Anderson, S. E., & Jaafar, S. B. (2003). *Policy trends in Ontario education—1990–2003.* Toronto: International Centre for Educational Change.

Apollon, D. (2011). *Don't call them "post-racial": Millennials' attitudes on race, racism, and key systems in our society.* New York: Applied Research Center.

Berger, P. L., & Luckmann, T. A. (1969). *The social construction of reality: A treatise in the sociology of knowledge.* New York: Penguin.

Blinder, S. (2012). *UK public Opinion towards immigration: Overall attitudes and levels of concern.* Oxford: The Migration Observatory, University of Oxford.

Brighi, A., Melotti, G., Guarini, A., Genta, M. L., Ortega, R., Mora-Merchán, J., et al. (2012). Self-esteem and loneliness in relation to cyberbullying in three European countries. In Q. Li, D.

Cross, & P. K. Smith (Eds.), *Cyberbullying in the global playground: Research from international perspectives*. Oxford: Wiley-Blackwell.

Brinckerhoff, P. (2007). *Generations: The challenge of a lifetime for your nonprofit*. Saint Paul, MN: Fieldstone Alliance.

Buckels, E. E., Trapnell, P. D., & Paulhus, D. L. (2014). Trolls just want to have fun. *Personality and Individual Differences, 67,* 97–102.

Carmon, I. (2010). *What Facebook does to teenage girls*. Jezebel, November 5. http://jezebel.com/5682488/what-does-facebook-do-to-teenage-girls.

Carrasco, M. M. (2016). *The ideal Millennial working woman: A thematic analysis of how female professional identity and community are constructed online*. Paper presented at the Kent University Research Symposium.

Cheng, J., Danescu-Niculescu-Mizily, D., & Leskovec, J. (2015). *Antisocial behavior in online discussion communities*. Paper presented at the 15th International Conference on Weblogs and Social Media (ICWSM), Oxford, UK. Retrieved from http://arxiv.org/pdf/1504.00680v1.pdf.

Chua, A. (2011). *Battle hymn of the tiger mother*. New York: Penguin.

Colleoni, E., Rozza, A., & Arvidsson, A. (2014). Echo chamber or public sphere? predicting political orientation and measuring political homophily in twitter using big data. *Journal of Communication, 64*(2), 317–332.

Cone Inc. & AMP Insights. (2006). *Millennial cause study—The Millennial generation: Pro-social and empowered to change the world*. Retrieved from http://blogthinkbig.com/wp-content/uploads/Cone-Millennial-Cause-Study-La-hora-de-cambiar-el-mundo.pdf.

Craig, W. M., & McCuaig Edge, H. (2008). Bullying and fighting. In W. Boyce, M. King, & J. Roche (Eds.), *Healthy settings for young people in Canada*. Ottawa, Ontario: The Public Health Agency of Canada.

Del Vicario, M., Bessi, A., Zollo, F., Petroni, F., Scalaa, A., Caldarellia, G., et al. (2016). The spreading of misinformation online. *Proceedings of the National Academy of Sciences of the United States of America, 113*(3), 554–559.

Deloitte. (2005). *Who are the Millennials? A.k.a. Generation Y*. Oakland, CA: Deloitte Development LLC. Retrieved from http://www.mcosa.net/SPF-SIG%20TRAINING%20Folder/us_consulting_millennialfactsheet_080606.pdf

Drago, J. P. (2006). *Generational Theory: Implications for Recruiting the Millennials*. Carlisle, PA: U.S. Army War College.

Edwards, D., Ashmore, M., & Potter, J. (1995). Death and furniture: The rhetoric, politics and theology of bottom line arguments against relativism. *History of the Human Sciences, 8*(2), 25–29.

Elmore, T. (2010). *Generation iY: Our last chance to save their future*. Atlanta, Georgia: Poet Gardner.

Erickson, T. (2008) *Plugged In: The Generation Y Guide to Thriving at Work*. Boston: Harvard Business Press.

Fritzon, A., Howell, L, & Zakheim, D. (2008). *Military of Millennials*. Toronto: Booz & Company. Retrieved from http://www.strategy-business.com/media/file/resilience-03-10-08.pdf.

Gergen, K. J., & Gergen, M. (2008). Social constructionism. In L. M. Givens (Ed.), *The SAGE Encyclopedia of Qualitative Research Methods*. (Vol. 2, p. 816). Thousand Oaks, CA: SAGE.

Greenberg, E., & Weber, K. (2008). *Generation we: How millennial youth are taking over America and changing our world forever*. Emeryville, CA: Pachatusan.

Grunwald Associates. (2000). *Children, families, and the internet*. Retrieved from http://www.grunwald.com/pdfs/CHILDREN-FAMILIES-AND-INTERNET-2000.pdf.

Gündüz, U. (2017). The effect of social media on identity construction. *Mediterranean Journal of Social Sciences, 8*(5), 85–92.

Herring, S. C., & Kapidzic, S. (2015). Teens, gender, and self-presentation in social media. In J. D. Wright (Ed.), *International encyclopedia of social and behavioral sciences* (2nd ed.). Oxford: Elsevier.

Hyler, J. N. (2013). *Millennial generation opinions of the military: A case study* (Master thesis). Retrieved from http://www.dtic.mil/dtic/tr/fulltext/u2/a580427.pdf.

Jenson, J., Fisher, S., & Taylor, N. (2011). *Critical review and analysis of the issue of "skills, technology and learning": Final Report.* Toronto: Ontario Ministry of Education.

Kabali, H. K., Irigoyen, M. M., Nunez-Davis, R., Budacki, J. G., Mohanty, S. H., Leister, K. P., et al. (2015). Exposure and use of mobile media devices by young children. *Pediatrics, 136*(6), 1044–1051.

Kann, L., Kinchen, S.. Shanklin, S. L., Flint, K. H., Hawkins, J., Harris, W. A., Lowry, R., Olsen, E., McManus, T., Chyen, D., Whittle, L., Taylor, E., Demissie, Z., Brener, N., Thornton, J., Moore, J., & Zaza, S. (2014). Youth risk behavior surveillance—United States, 2013. *Morbidity and Mortality Weekly Report, 63*(4), 1–168. Retrieved from http://www.cdc.gov/mmwr/pdf/ss/ss6304.pdf.

Kegan, R. (1982). *The evolving self: Problem and process in human development.* Cambridge, MA: Harvard University Press.

Kohlberg, L. (1972). *Collected papers on moral development and moral education.* Cambridge, MA: Center for Moral Education.

Koss, M. P. (1988). Hidden rape: Sexual aggression and victimization in the national sample of students in higher education. In M. A. Pirog-Good & J. E. Stets (Eds.), *Violence in dating relationships: Emerging social issues* (pp. 145–168). New York, NY: Praeger.

Kowalski, R. M., & Limber, S. P. (2013). Psychological, physical, and academic correlates of cyberbullying and traditional bullying. *Journal of Adolescent Health, 53*(1 Supplement), S13–S20.

Lancaster, L. C. and Stillman, D. (2002). *When Generations Collide. Who They Are. Why They Clash. How to Solve the Generational Puzzle at Work.* New York: Collins.

Lenhart, A. (2015). *Teen, social media and technology overview 2015.* Washington: Pew Research Center.

Levitin, M. (2015) The triumph of occupy wall street. *The Atlantic,* 10 Jun 2015.

Martin, C., & Tulgan, B. (2006). *Managing the generation mix: From urgency to opportunity* (2nd ed.). Amherst, MA: HRD Press.

Massey, M. E. (1979). *The People Puzzle: Understanding yourself and others.* Reston, VA: Reston.

McGlynn, A. P. (2010). Millennials—the "always connected" generation. *The Hispanic Outlook in Higher Education, 20*(22), 14–16.

Ng, E., Schweitzer, L., & Lyons, S. T. (2010). New generation, great expectations: A field study of the millennial generation. *Journal of Business and Psychology, 25*(2), 281–292.

Norris, P., & Krook, M. L. (2009). *One of Us: Multilevel models examining the impact of descriptive representation on civic engagement.* HKS Faculty Research Working Paper Series RWP09-030, John F. Kennedy School of Government, Harvard University.

Paecher, C. (2013). Young women online: collaboratively constructing identities. *Pedagogy, Culture & Society, 21*(1), 111–117.

Patchin, J. W., & Hinduja, S. (2013). Cyberbullying among adolescents: Implications for empirical research. *Journal of Adolescent Health, 53*(4), 431–432.

Pew Research Center. (2012). *The rise of intermarriage: Rates, characteristics vary by race and gender.* Retrieved from http://www.pewsocialtrends.org/2012/02/16/the-rise-of-intermarriage/.

Pew Research Center. (2015). *Comparing Millennials to other generations.* Retrieved from http://www.pewsocialtrends.org/2010/02/24/interactive-graphic-demographic-portrait-of-four-generations/.

Pinder-Grover, T. & Groscurth, C. R. (2009). *Principles for teaching the millennial generation: Innovative practices of U-M faculty* (CRLT Occasional Paper No. 26). Ann Arbor, MI: Center for Research on Learning and Teaching.

Putnam, R. D. (1995). Bowling alone: America's declining social capital. *Journal of Democracy, 6*(1), 65–78.

Putnam, R. D. (2000). *Bowling alone: The collapse and revival of American community*. New York: Simon & Schuster.

Rainer, T., & Rainer, J. (2011). *The Millennials: Connecting to the largest generation*. Nashville, TN: B&H Publishing Group.

Raines, C. (2002). *Managing Millennials*. Retrieved from http://www.generationsatwork.com/articles_millenials.php.

Roberts, J. W. (2011). *Little brother is watching and recording you: Social control in a deviant group*. (Doctoral Dissertation). Retrieved from ProQuest Dissertations and Theses. (Accession Order No. ATT 1497185).

Schoenberg, J., Modi, K., & Salmond, K. (2013). *The State of girls: Unfinished business*. New York: Girl Scouts Research Institute.

Skenazy, L. (2009). *Free-range kids: Giving our children the freedom we had without going nuts with worry*. San Francisco: Jossey-Bass.

Stafford, D. & Griffis, H. (2008). *A Review of Millennial Generation Characteristics and Military Workforce Implications*. Arlington, VA: Center for Naval Analysis.

Statistics Canada. (2015). *Mixed unions in Canada*. Ottawa: Statistics Canada. Retrieved from https://www12.statcan.gc.ca/nhs-enm/2011/as-sa/99-010-x/99-010-x2011003_3-eng.cfm.

Strauss, W., & Howe, N. (2000). *Millennials rising: The next great generation* (3rd ed.). New York: Vintage Books.

Stuart, A., & Lyons, D. S. (2008). *Millennials in the workplace*. Halifax, NS: Knightsbridge Robertson Surrette. Retrieved from http://www.kbrs.ca/insights/millennials-workplace.

Sykes, C. J. (1995). *Dumbing down our kids: Why American children feel good about themselves but can't read, write, or add*. New York: St Martin's.

Tanner, L. (2010). *Who are the Millennials?* DRDC CORA Technical Memorandum 2010-284. Ottawa, ON: Defence R&D Canada—Centre for Operational Research and Analysis.

Taylor, P. (2016). *The next America: Boomers, Millennials, and the looming generational showdown*. Washington, D.C.: Pew Research Center.

Trzesniewski, K. H., & Donnellan, M. B. (2010). Rethinking "generation me": A study of cohort effects from 1976–2006. *Perspectives on Psychological Science, 5*(1), 58–75.

Twenge, J. M. (2006). *Generation me: Why today's young Americans are more confident, assertive, entitled–and more miserable than ever before*. New York: Atria Books.

Twenge, J. M., Campbell, W. K., & Freeman, E. C. (2012). Generational differences in young adults' life goals, concern for others, and civic orientation, 1966–2009. *Journal of Personality and Social Psychology, 102*(5), 1045–1062.

Vézina, M., & Crompton, S. (2012). *Volunteering in Canada*. (Component of Statistics Canada Catalogue no. 11-008-X, Canadian Social Trends). Ottawa: Statistics Canada. Retrieved from http://www.statcan.gc.ca/pub/11-008-x/2012001/article/11638-eng.pdf.

Wang, J., Nansel, T. R., & Iannotti, R. J. (2011). Cyber bullying and traditional bullying: Differential association with depression. *Journal of Adolescent Health, 48*(4), 415–417. https://doi.org/10.1016/j.jadohealth.2010.07.012.

Wilcox, A. (2001). *Recruiting the next generation: A study of attitudes, values, and beliefs* (Master thesis). Retrived from http://calhoun.nps.edu/handle/10945/10862.

Zemke, R., Raines, C., & Filipczak, B. (1999). *Generations at work: Managing the clash of veterans, Boomers, Xers, and Nexters in your workplace*. New York: AMA Publications.

Work and Life Goals

6

No headstone reads: I wish I spent more time at the office

—Anon

Introduction

Expectations that the Post-Millennials are likely to have regarding work and life goals are offered as ideas for consideration and review as these young people actually enter the workforce. To be sure, the dreams and aspirations of adolescents often undergo adjustments when they encounter the realities of adulthood and, especially, the economic conditions at play when they seek to launch their careers. As with the previous chapter, we have, however, identified certain areas of likely continuity and differences between the Millennials currently in the workforce and the Post-Millennials who will follow them. Thus, we are prepared to provide some ideas on aspects that these two groups may share and others in which they may diverge. We have placed our findings in the future context of the Boomers making their exit from the workforce but leaving a legacy of organizational structures, workplace practices and implicit career expectations that we assess will increasingly not meet the expectations of younger workers nor the corporate flexibilities needed to survive the coming new world order in business affairs. We, therefore, anticipate significant differences of views and expectations across hierarchical levels and age groups within organizations with the likelihood of 'culture clashes' either flaring up or become outright conflicts for which the C suite[1] may not be fully prepared.

---

[1]Referring to the most senior corporate level occupied by the "Chiefs" including, commonly, Chief Executive Officer, Operating/Operations Officer, Financial Officer, Information Officer, Human Resources Officer, etc.

© Springer Nature Switzerland AG 2020
A. Okros, *Harnessing the Potential of Digital Post-Millennials in the Future Workplace*, Management for Professionals, https://doi.org/10.1007/978-3-030-25726-2_6

Post-Millennials Coming of Age

> Maturity is a bitter disappointment for which no remedy exists, unless laughter could be said to remedy anything.—Kurt Vonnegut

As the eldest of the Post-Millennial cohort are just starting to get their drivers licences and the youngest are yet to be born, it will be some time before we have a good understanding of this age cohort—or even if using 2000–2020 as the appropriate birth years makes sense to suggest that those in this age group can be meaningfully described. Drawing on our earlier assessments of the probable impact on the economy and future employment due to evolutions in the digital environment, we are suggesting that a narrative that these young people will be aware of as they grow up and, in particular, as they prepare for their future careers, will revolve around the changes and, in some cases, radical rearrangements of existing industries, types of jobs and future employment prospects.[2] As an important background to the foreseeable work expectations of the Post-Millennials, we see significant continuity in life experiences and lifestyle trends that are currently evident with the Millennials including important differentiations due to their life circumstances and individual interests. We also expect some areas of similarity with regards to their employment goals although forecast differences in certain work expectations. We start with some of the key factors and life events that will be important for this cohort then turn to an assessment of the work context they will enter before than considering some of the critical dynamics that are likely to emerge within the workplace.

Education

> It is the mark of an educated mind to be able to entertain a thought without accepting it.—Aristotle

The most obvious intermediate step between the current status of the Post-Millennials and their entry into the workforce will be completion of their formal education. As stated previously, the Post-Millennials are on track to be the most educated cohort ever. For Millennials, the 2015 annual OECD assessment of educational attainment reflects that, in the United States and most European nations, approximately 45% of those aged 25–34 have attended post-secondary schooling, Canada stands at just under 60% (Schleicher, 2015). The forecasts for the Post-Millennials are for continued increases with the OCED report projecting that 50% of young people will graduate from some form of tertiary education.[3] In the

---

[2]Noting that some of this narrative is already emerging in the news media and policy spaces such as the 2016 World Economic Forum: http://www.weforum.org/events/world-economic-forum-annual-meeting-2016.

[3]There are a range of criteria for post-secondary or tertiary education with differences across countries as to the associated number of years of education and levels of learning. Most do not include technical or vocational training programmes, language training or certificates that require less than one year of study. The nomenclature in use continues to evolve in many countries particularly related to associate degrees.

US, the Department of Education has projected that the number of students enrolling in post-secondary degree programmes will continue to increase each year through to 2021 (US Department of Education, 2014) .[4] Although slightly dated, in Canada, a study in 2004 reported that two-thirds of 15-year-olds intend to go on to university after completing their secondary studies, with almost 40% aspiring to more than one degree (Human Resources and Skills Development Canada, 2004). More recently, a 2011 study forecast an average 9% increase in student enrolment during 2010 to 2020[5] and Fallis (2013) concluded that 75% of students in Ontario would undertake post-secondary education and confirmed that a growing number are either continuing on to graduate school or taking a second university or college programme.

A central question for the Post-Millennials is whether the gender differences in post-secondary participation will persist or if men will start to close the gap. In Canada, women account for 60% of undergraduate degree enrollees and outnumber men in professional programmes such as law and medicine and across all graduate degree programmes (Ferguson & Wang, 2014). The rates for undergraduate and graduate degree programmes are generally similar in the US (Lui, 2011). In fact, with the exception of Japan, women outnumber men in undertaking post-secondary education in all nations reported in the 2015 OECD survey.

A higher rate of graduate studies by women reflects their aspirations for successful careers and meaningful work (Accenture, 2008; Espinosa, 2012; Peter & Horn, 2005; Wang, Parker, & Taylor, 2013). While the link between advanced education and better jobs has been a mantra passed down from the Boomers on, it is only recently that there has been alignment in the expectations of students, employers, educators and policy makers. The rates of recent graduate unemployment or, more often, underemployment is resulting in students increasingly opting for programmes that will provide them with the skills needed to land a good job.[6] Employers have welcomed this emphasis as they have been seeking a better match of job-ready skills (Ehlert, Senn, Kling, & Beers, 2013). As an extension of our previous discussion of the priorities associated with the US P21 and Canadian C21 initiatives, it is what political leaders have promised.[7] The government's emphasis on ensuring that post-secondary education leads to meaningful (and well paid) employment is relatively recent and not something that had been highlighted by politicians when the Millennials were making their choices regarding university or college. Noting the continuity that not all university students place scholastic

---

[4]Noting that US President Obama has made it a goal that the US would have the highest college graduate rate in the world by 2020.

[5]See *Trends in Higher Education: Volume 1—Enrolment* published by The Association of Universities and Colleges of Canada; accessible at: https://www.univcan.ca/wp-content/uploads/2015/11/trends-vol1-enrolment-june-2011.pdf.

[6]https://www.insidehighered.com/views/2013/10/04/job-skills-increasing-focus-many-colleges-essay and http://www.theglobeandmail.com/news/national/education/the-expectation-gap-students-and-universities-roles-in-preparing-for-life-after-grad/article21187004/?page=all.

[7]See President Obama's expectations at: https://www.whitehouse.gov/issues/education/higher-education, Prime Minister Trudeau's at: http://pm.gc.ca/eng/minister-employment-workforce-development-and-labour-mandate-letter and Ontario Premier Wynn's at: https://www.ontario.ca/page/2014-mandate-letter-training-colleges-and-universities.

excellence at the top of their priority list, we, nonetheless, anticipate two consequences for the Post-Millennials who have now been given this assurance. First, in
comparison to the Millennials, more will be expecting to get real value out of their
education hence may take greater ownership of their course of study. Second, they
are also likely to have increased expectations to be able to apply their knowledge
when they enter the workforce thus, as we will develop further, will assume that
employers will give them challenging and meaningful work on day one.

Major Life Decisions

> There is an expiry date on blaming your parents for steering you in the wrong direction
> —J.K. Rowling

An obvious corollary to the higher percentages of young people taking tertiary
education is them delaying major decisions related to adulthood: securing full-time
employment, getting married, having children and purchasing a home (and leaving
the parental basement) are key 'rites of passage'. Some of the Millennials are also
changing the order in which they achieve these milestones (when they do). One
trend is more Millennials having children before getting married.[8] For those who do
marry, another trend is that the average age for first marriage continues to climb.[9]
Further, marriage rates are forecast to continue to drop from around 91% for
Boomers through the 82% rate for Gen Xers to less than 70% for Millennials
(Wang & Parker, 2014). Twenty-one percent of US Millennials are currently
married as compared to 42% for Boomers at the same age. Finally, there are some
differences between the US and Canada with regards to both fertility rates 1.77
(US) versus 1.61 (Canada) and especially the average mother's age for first birth at
26 in the US versus 29 in Canada.[10]

Millennials may not only be changing the order and timing of major life events
but redefining some of these for themselves particularly the meaning and status of
'marriage' and 'parent'. To date, little scholarly work has been published examining
the extent or implications of these redefinitions however, it would appear that, as
with gender identity, the Millennials are moving away from the binary categorization of being either single or married and also differentiating the understanding
of parent from that of husband, wife or married partner. Similarly, gender roles in
families are shifting with more women assuming to (or having to) provide for the

---

[8]For Canadian coverage see: http://globalnews.ca/news/2194724/millennials-shaking-up-
traditional-order-of-love-marriage-then-kids/ and in the US: http://www.npr.org/2014/10/16/
354625221/for-more-millennials-its-kids-first-marriage-maybe.

[9]Government statistics from 2014–2015 show the median age for first marriage in the US at 27 for
women and 29 for men and, in Canada, 28 and 31 respectively.

[10]Noting that the gaps between the two nations have been closing with the US fertility rate
dropping and age at first birth rising; for updated US statistics see: the Center for Disease Control
and Prevention data at https://www.cdc.gov/nchs/fastats/births.htm.

financial needs of themselves and their children and more couples are reporting being comfortable with the idea of the woman in the household as the principal income earner. 2013 US data reveals that women are the sole or primary income earner in 40% of all families with children including 15% of all families with children where the woman has a higher income than her husband/partner (Wang et al., 2013) and there are similar trends in Canada (Clark, 2013).

To revisit our earlier discussion of social construction, our research indicates that the Post-Millennials are growing up in a context in which the definitions and expectations associated with many aspects of social roles and personal identity are shifting and, in particular, are being seen by younger adults as much more fluid. The understanding and definition of many of these concepts are used to provide social structure including establishing role behaviours and personal obligations. When combined with our conclusions of the exploratory nature of learning they are now encountering in schools and the capacities to access multiple world views, we suggest that it is quite likely that the Post-Millennials will push the boundaries even further resulting in them redefining, hence living their lives based on, alternate interpretations that may extend to the meaning of career, work or citizenship. Organizations would be wise to monitor how Post-Millennials are understanding concepts related to employment as this will influence work expectations and behaviours.

Financial Status

> Today, there are three kinds of people: the have's, the have-not's, and the have-not-paid-for-what-they-have's.—Earl Wilson

A second factor arising from post-secondary education is the increasing numbers of young adults who have already accumulated sizable debts prior to entering the fulltime workforce. Student loans as the most significant factor. The current data is slightly contradictory and differs between the Canadian and American context. Further, we noted different narratives being conveyed in the news media when compared to reports by financial institutions. As highlighted in the title "Four ways student debt is wreaking havoc on Millennials" in a 2015 Bloomberg article, the news media are presenting the issue of student debt as a crisis and a major contributing factor to two of the issues already discussed: delays in starting families and purchasing the first home.[11] Conversely, 2015 analyses in both countries revealed that the Millennials are actually in good financial health, fiscally informed, satisfied with their current status and generally optimistic regarding their financial future (Caranci & Petramala, 2015; Navient, 2015).

---

[11]Among recent articles, see http://www.bloomberg.com/news/articles/2015-12-10/four-ways-student-debt-is-wreaking-havoc-on-millennials; http://time.com/money/4168510/why-student-loan-crisis-is-worse-than-people-think/; http://www.huffingtonpost.ca/news/student-debt-canada/ and http://www.newswire.ca/news-releases/canadas-post-secondary-students-head-back-to-school-worried-over-money-debt-and-job-prospects-cibc-poll-522022061.html.

In several areas, the data on Millennials finances shows a marked difference between the US and Canada. 2014 numbers show 27% of Millennials held student debt in the US versus 16% in Canada with the average amounts owning at $35,000 vs $27,000.[12] A key difference between countries has been financial support from parents with 75% of US students receiving assistance from family during college and 40% receiving support even after graduating.[13] Conversely, a 2012 Canadian study revealed that only about 11% of pre-retirement parents are providing financial support to their adult children (HSBC, 2013). Our assessment of these reports suggests the difference may be due to the fact that Canadian respondents were only reporting cases of ongoing payments to their adult children and not the practice of providing one-time 'gifts' to support major expenditures particularly homeowner-ship. This may help explain the even greater contrast of data that show that 50% of Canadian Millennials own their home and the average age of first home purchase is the youngest ever while only 36% of US Millennials are home owners with a slight delay in first purchase from historical norms (Caranci & Petramala, 2015). Two contributing factors were noted in explaining these differences. First, in comparison to Americans, Canadian homeowners (particularly the Millennials' parents) did not experience declines in house prices post- 2008 and, when combined with continued low interest rates, have been able to provide more support for the critical house down payment than their US peers. Second, the 2001 extension of paid parental leave from 10 to 35 weeks has allowed Canadian Millennials to start families without suffering a significant drop in income during the first year after birth that is often linked to first home purchase.

An issue in this consideration of Millennial and, eventually, Post-Millennial financial affairs pertains to where they are choosing to life. We see a continued trend towards young adults gravitating to large cities and, particularly in Canada, seeking to live in the downtown core with ready access to the leisure activities of major urban centres. Both Canadian and American research is demonstrating this pattern which has been summarized as the Millennials' preference for cities not suburbs and subways not driveways (Nielsen, 2014). In relation to homeownership, while two-thirds of American Millennials are buying detached houses, the largest number of purchases made by their Canadian peers were condos, followed by townhouses and lastly detached housing.[14] The general assumption in much of the news media is that those who purchase urban condos will follow the previous pattern of fleeing to the suburbs when they have children.[15] Research, however, is showing that the Millennials are in the process of redefining this aspect of their lives

---

[12]The percentages are for all people in this age group; 69% of US students graduate with student debt.

[13]See   http://www.advfn.com/news_Are-Young-Millennials-Getting-It-Together-Less-Th_ 69373419.html   and   http://www.moneytalksnews.com/report-millennials-relying-heavily-the-bank-mom-and-dad/ respectively.

[14]See   http://www.nahb.org/en/news-and-publications/Press-Releases/2015/january/millennials-seek-smaller-houses-but-wont-sacrifice-details-panelists-say.aspx and http://homeownership.ca/ dreaming-of-homeownership/benefits-for-first-time-home-buyers/our–first-home/.

[15]http://globalnews.ca/news/1854709/home-ownership-for-millennials-are-they-dreaming/.

as well with many seeking to stay closer to the urban core and, in particular, many are not prepared to pay the price of lengthy commutes to work each way in exchange for the four bedroom detached house when raising their family.[16] This is one of the main reasons for the increased emphasis on 'walkability' scores in real estate values.[17]

In addition to identifying some divergence in the fiscal status of US and Canadian Millennials at present, this review suggests areas of continuity and change. Many are taking on early debt to acquire advanced education. With the expectation that this investment will pay off in the long run and, particularly for Canadians who have managed to do so with less overall debt, the evidence is that they have been able to take the important step of purchasing their first home and building net equity. While only time and relevant economic factors will determine how the Post-Millennials experience this facet of adulthood, two factors stand out. First (yet again), the Millennials are redefining social expectations with regards to housing. While the suburban detached home may still be part of the 'dream', realties are causing Millennials to adopt a style of living much closer to that of major European cities. As the cohort to follow these trail blazers, many Post-Millennials may adopt this 'new normal' that could have significant consequences for other aspects of urban functioning including transportation, energy requirements and the use of public spaces including the three-way tussle amongst cars, bikes and pedestrians and the realization that not all parks have to look like Capability Brown's landscaped British gardens. Particularly in the American context, recent analyses have suggested that the preference is likely for "mixed-use" neighbourhoods with housing, stores and workplaces integrated in the same area.[18] An implication for employers will be the likely increased desire for Post-Millennials to work near their home with the expectations that they will be able to pop back and forth between work and home during the day.

Second, marginally hidden in the data is the role of Millennial women in leading many of the changes that are occurring. As already mentioned, women make up the majority of students in both undergraduate and graduate degree programmes and there is evidence that they pay down debt faster. Further, the percentage who become the primary wage earner is increasing and, while the decision to start a family is usually shared between the couple, the decision not to is most often the woman's. When combined with the Michael Adam's Millennial data showing women over-represented in some key sub-groups and the recognition that the Millennials as a whole are redefining many social norms including gendered roles, it is plausible to suggest that tracking the evolutions of social expectations and

---

[16]http://www.pewtrusts.org/en/research-and-analysis/blogs/stateline/2015/07/23/millennials-living-on-the-edge-of-the-big-city.

[17]https://www.biggerpockets.com/renewsblog/2015/02/19/housing-data-revealsmillennials-flock-markets-high-density-walkability/.

[18]See the April 2016 article by Alissa Walker at http://gizmodo.com/millennials-will-live-in-cities-unlike-anything-weve-se-1716074100 and the June 2015 article by Ben Cummins posted at: https://www.planetizen.com/node/86755/what-millennials-want-and-why-it-doesnt-matter.

lifestyle decisions amongst Post-Millennial women will be particularly important, especially those who have acquired marketable skills.

Work Experience and Job Vacancies

The best preparation for good work tomorrow is to do good work today—Elbert Hubbard

The following section will address the plausible work expectations of the Post-Millennials when they start their career however, because of the large numbers continuing on to post-secondary education,[19] Post-Millennials are not only likely be the most educated to enter the fulltime workforce, they will probably be the oldest. In Canada, the age to reach the maximum fulltime employment rate has risen from age 25 in 1976 to 31 in 2012 and is forecast to continue to rise (Galarneau, Morissette, & Usalcas, 2013). Many, however, will have already gained work experience as the majority of post-secondary students hold a part time job. A central challenge is that a 2010 Canadian report revealed that 96% of these positions were in the service sector (Marshall, 2010). The reality is that most will have about 10 years of part time experience prior to seeking full time employment but not necessarily in the most rewarding of jobs.

In assessing the work expectations that Post-Millennials are likely to develop, we evaluated the messages that they are already hearing and the ones that will probably emerge as the disruptions due to the evolutions in the digital environment take hold. The first factor will be the high likelihood that the current reference to a jobless economic recovery will be recognized as a fundamental restructuring of the economy.[20] As we highlighted earlier and as illustrated during the 2016 World Economic Forum, the coming "Fourth Industrial Revolution" is forecast to lead to significant changes in the labour market and, at a minimum, continued discourse in the public domain (Schwab, 2016). A factor that has been identified is the trend of increased use of robotics that is forecast by some to replace 5 million jobs by 2020.[21] An interesting nuance in the analyses conducted is that robotics will replace far more jobs currently held by men than by women.[22]

A second message, and one that will be significantly different than received by the Millennials, who have been told it is a tough job market, is that there should be a lot of job openings with, as we noted in the introduction to this volume, gaps between the size of the labour force and the number of jobs needed for growing

---

[19]And especially the increasing percentage who are taking more than the minimum time to graduate.

[20]As illustrated in https://www.washingtonpost.com/business/economy/jobless-recoveries-are-here-to-stay-economists-say-but-its-a-mystery-why/2013/09/19/6034bcb4-20c7-11e3-966c-9c4293c47ebe_story.html.

[21]http://www.nbcnews.com/id/42183592/ns/business-careers/t/nine-jobs-humans-may-lose-robots/#.VtyaI4fSnj0; http://bgr.com/2015/11/16/robots-replacing-human-jobs/ and http://www.smh.com.au/technology/innovation/davos-2016-robots-will-steal-5-million-jobs-by-2020-20160120-gma2yi.html.

[22]http://www.theneweconomy.com/business/male-not-female-jobs-will-be-taken-by-robots.

economies.[23] Current Canadian forecasts are for 400,000 retirements per year and a total of one-third of the entire workforce is about to retire.[24]

We have, therefore, concluded that a number of Post-Millennials will approach their transition from education to fulltime careers with a degree of optimism. Many will be aware that there will be significant shifts in both workforce demographics due to retirements and forecasts that entire sectors of employment will be swept away but to be replaced by new digital-dependent jobs. Those who have focussed on their studies will be graduating from P21 secondary education programmes and, for many, from post-secondary courses that universities and colleges will have promised will provide them with job-ready skill sets. While they may realize employers may not layout the red carpet, the Post-Millennials will be anticipating at least a welcome mat at the door.

Applying acquired digital literacy and increased social awareness, they will likely also have put more effort than their Millennial elders in doing their homework researching different organizations and projected career fields. With increased digital connectivity and transparency, the current 'rate my employer' web sites will have morphed into more detailed 'rate my boss' fora.[25] One of the conclusions we have reached is that applicants will often be interviewing and assessing the employer just as much as the other way around. Further, to extend our comments that the Millennials are redefining socially constructed concepts such as marriage, parenting and the normal markers of adulthood, we anticipate that the Post-Millennials will have the potential to use the shifts in the global economy and local job markets to redefine the related concepts of work, job and career. The experiences of many who will start their employment navigating the 'gig economy' will contribute to these redefinitions.[26]

Particularly for those with the right skillsets to match the jobs of the coming Fourth Industrial Revolution, we assess that the competition over these entrants will provide them with a different sense of importance and options than the Millennials and, in particular, Gen Xrs enjoyed. As an illustration, Dobbs et al. (2012) reported that the demand for high-skill labour in advanced economics is growing faster than supply with a forecast 13% shortage by 2020. In considering which sub-groups of the Post-Millennial cohort employers will be seeking to hire, we offer two key conclusions. First, a current trend will continue: women will be leading the way in seeking advanced education, redefining social roles, reordering major life decisions and developing the 21st Century job skills in greatest demand. While they will have

---

[23]Noting that this is likely to occur in Canada and several European countries before taking place in the US.

[24]See http://www.thespec.com/news-story/2258356-third-of-canada-s-work-force-will-retire-in-next-five-years/ and http://www.theglobeandmail.com/globe-investor/retirement/the-boomer-shift-how-canadas-economy-is-headed-for-majorchange/article27159892/.

[25]http://www.ratemyemployer.ca/Home.

[26]For a short presentation on the benefits and drawbacks of the gig economy; see: Why The Gig Economy Is The Best And Worst Development For Workers Under 30 at: https://www.forbes.com/sites/larryalton/2018/01/24/why-the-gig-economy-is-the-best-and-worst-development-for-workers-under-30/2/#701cac575b96.

male colleagues who are also in this category, the second is that prototypical ideal new hire that many employers will be seeking will be the Post-Millennials who are closest to Michael Adam's Diverse Strivers: those most interested in success in their careers and willing to put in the effort to earn it (again, this group is majority women). The challenge is that 100% of employers can't all draw from the 10% who are currently classified as Diverse Strivers. It will, therefore, be important for employers to identify the ways in which Post-Millennial sub-groups will differ to understand who they are hiring and to tailor their marketing strategies to attract the right talent accordingly.

Weisure Time

The traditional Boomer workplace is characterized by the "9-to-5, clock-in-clock-out" organization with an integrated philosophy that hard work and sacrifice (often measures as 'time at the desk') are the key to career success (Glass, 2007). Technology provides opportunities to challenge this paradigm as it permits: the capacities to telecommute; the connectivity to conduct work via mobile devices; the ability to cater to unconventional hours for international connections; and, the potential for successful careers as freelance contractors working for multiple employers at the same time.

The breakdown of this paradigm began with Generation X calling for 'work-life balance' in response to the Boomers' unrelenting dedication to their work (Jenkins, 2007; Karp, Fuller, & Sirias, 2002). Work-life balance ranks as one of the most important workplace attributes for Millennials (Crampton & Hodge, 2006). Millennials are described as having less preference for a traditional office work environment than their elders; the Post-Millennials may be even more allergic to the cubicle (Ozkana & Solmaz, 2015). For digital generations, the quest for a work-life balance means that the division between labour and leisure will increasingly blur. Already, Millennials expect there to be no boundary between the workplace and their personal lives (Meister & Willyerd, 2010; Moss, 2011; Rainer & Rainer, 2011; Wiggins, 2012). Meister and Willyerd (2010) explain that "Millennials live in 'weisure' time, the next step in work life, where work and leisure are one and the same" (p. 57). Researchers suggest that the constant state of 'being busy' that comes with multitasking will lead to the Post-Millennials placing high importance on having the flexibility to come and go as need be and, in particular, to shift from a work commitment to a personal activity when they wish to fulfill all of their life commitments (Deloitte, 2005; Elmore, 2010; Lowe et al., 2008; Martin & Tulgan, 2006; Meister & Willyerd, 2010; Moss, 2011). As accomplished serial multitaskers, many Post- Millennials are likely to see work and their career as just another ball in their juggling act. When necessary, they will put in overtime but they expect to be able to leave early or come in late and to be paid based on task completion, not for time that they put in at the workplace (Elmore, 2010; NAS Insights, 2007).

In considering the evolutions toward the demand to blend work and life, employers are already contributing to this shift. Employees have reported an increased expectation by bosses that they can be contacted about work issues outside of normal hours. A 2015 Harris Poll of US white- collar workers revealed that 63% believe the idea of a 9–5 job is outdated with 40% reporting that they kept working outside of these traditional hours and while away from the office.[27] By the time the Post-Millennials arrive in the workplace, we suggest there will likely be a well-established *quid-pro-quo*: you can contact me about work at home but I can connect with others about personal issues when at work.

Social Justice and Workplace Fairness

The combination of younger generations sharing perspectives across borders and the experiences of a 21st Century education will result in many Post-Millennials developing an interest in social justice (Fox, 2011; Gaudet, 2016). This will inform their desire to make a difference, not just 'get a job' (Shandler, 2009). Millennials are known for the intent of many to have an impact on the world and this has been shown to be an influential factor when deciding on their career path and workplace (Deloitte, 2005; Elmore, 2010; Lancaster & Stillman, 2002; Rainer & Rainer, 2011). Within an organization, this sense of justice can manifest itself in the importance younger workers place on being treated fairly (Zemke et al., 1999, Ng & Gossett, 2013). They value organizations that are honest and clear about the job conditions and provide meaningful work (Zemke et al., 1999; Pew Research Center, 2015).

We expect that many Post-Millennials will place an emphasis on fairness in the workplace. The Ng and Gossett (2013) research involving younger Canadian Millennials attending university, revealed that the public sector is a preferred choice for many due, in large part, to their perceptions of higher ethical standards, more inclusive workplaces and greater social responsibility (along with secure employment) as compared to the private sector. When the expectations of fairness and flexibility are combined with the importance placed on working in inclusive teams and their 'acute nose for authenticity' (Stuart & Lyons, 2008), a facet of those seeking a participatory culture will be exercising the capacity to speak up (and speak out) on issues of ethics and social responsibility (Gaudet, 2016). We expect Post-Millennials will continue the trend of the Millennials and be more likely to draw attention to issues of discrimination, nepotism, harassment and ethical shortcuts than most older workers. Further, if they do not see the violation being addressed in an appropriate manner, will then make their concerns known in public fora through their ubiquitous social media platforms.[28] We concluded that, as with the observation that the desire of younger people to be consulted on work issues

---

[27]See the summary at: http://www.careerbuilder.com/share/aboutus/pressreleasesdetail.aspx?sd=7/23/2015&id=pr905&ed=12/31/2015.
[28]As one illustration, see the 2015 results of the American Civil Liberties Union poll of Millennials in 18 nations indicating support for the actions of Eric Snowden in releasing classified documents. ACLU reported that: "In each country, a majority of Millennials familiar with Snowden have a positive opinion of him." Accessible at: https://www.aclu.org/snowden-poll-results.

that affect them can be seen as reflecting a sense of entitlement, their willingness to point out what they see as unethical behaviour could be interpreted as a lack of respect or a challenging of authority especially when managers view the issues as common practice or just the cost of business.

Conclusion

This chapter has provided our analyses of the important events and decisions that many Post-Millennials will be encountering prior to entering the work force on a fulltime basis. The most important factors will arise from the initial decisions taken with regards to post-secondary education. Choices made at this stage will influence not only the advanced knowledge that these graduates will bring to their job but their financial status and, for many, will affect how they address other major life decisions including marriage, children, homeownership and preferred geographical location. While not necessarily applying to all, we expect that social commentary will reflect that the Post-Millennials will be seen to extend the approach of the Millennials in not only choosing to break the existing norms surrounding the order in which these rites of passage are enacted but to redefine the social meaning attached to these. Researchers and media commentaries have already noted that many young people are becoming comfortable with reframing gender from a binary male-female to an understanding that this is better seen as a fluid construct with degrees of masculinity and femininity as well as the recognition that some may choose to present themselves one way at a certain time or in a certain context and yet another way in a different setting.[29] Similarly we anticipate that younger generations will choose to engage in critical social construction to develop alternate understanding of concepts related to marriage and parenting. While most of the focus for the Millennials is on defining aspects of their personal life, we anticipate that the Post-Millennials will be the first to do so for aspects of their work life. While there will certainly be traditionalists in both age groups, we see cohorts within these generations as being much more comfortable with alternate interpretations of how one approaches their personal or work life—with the traditionalists tolerating but not opting to embrace these alternatives.

An implication of our analysis is that the Post-Millennials to contain a sizeable cohort who will not only be the most educated when they start their careers but the oldest. This means that they will be bringing more life experiences and life lessons with them when they enter the full-time work force hence will also arrive with a better sense of who they are, what matters and what they expect from employment —and employers. We have highlighted that they will probably see themselves as ready to make a meaningful contribution on day one with the potential to provide critical new competencies that will be key to business success as organizations

---

[29]The reference here is to the concept of liminality. For more of our perspectives on this issue, see the report by Scott and Okros.

grapple with the dislocations created by the coming wave of the digital tsunami. In exchange for being the catalyst for significant corporate change, they will be expecting to be able to integrate their personal and work lives much more than the Millennials have been able to do to date. As another of the evolutions from binary views of the world, they will not be approaching their career with the stark differentiation between work and leisure but seeking to blend these in the more fluid approach of *weisure* time. Similarly, they will be applying their personal views on social justice and fairness to assess potential employers. Thus, their perceptions of how organizations differ in the approaches to *weisure* time and workplace fairness may be important factors that will influence whether the skilled Post-Millennials will consider a firm for employment. In the following section we will turn to considerations of the implications once the Post-Millennials are actually on the job, however, our conclusion from this chapter is that employers need to recognize: if they do not apply, you cannot hire them thus branding is going to be as important to attract talent as it is to attract customers.

References

Accenture. (2008). *Millennials at the gates: Results from Accenture's high performance IT research*. New York: Accenture Research.

Caranci, B., & Petramala, D. (2015). *Canadian and U.S. Millennials: One of these is not like the other*. Toronto: Toronto Dominion Bank. Retrieved from https://www.td.com/document/PDF/economics/special/Canadian_US_Millennials.pdf.

Clark, W. (2013). *Delayed transitions of young adults*. Statistics Canada 11-008-XWE. Ottawa: Statistics Canada.

Crampton, S. M., & Hodge, J. W. (2006). The supervisor and generational differences. In *Proceedings of the Academy of Organizational Culture, Communications and Conflict* (Vol. 11, pp. 19–22).

Deloitte. (2005). *Who are the Millennials?* A.k.a. Generation Y. Oakland, CA: Deloitte Development LLC. Retrieved from http://www.mcosa.net/SPFSIG%20TRAINING%20Folder/us_consulting_millennialfactsheet_080606.pdf.

Dobbs, R., Madgavkar, A., Barton, D., Labaye, E., Manyika, J., Roxburgh, C., Lund, S., & Madhav, S. (2012). *The world at work: Jobs, pay, and skills for 3.5 billion people*. McKinsey Global Institute. Accessible at http://www.mckinsey.com/global-themes/employment-and-growth/the-world-at-work.

Ehlert, R., Senn, K., Kling, C., & Beers, R. (2013). It takes more than a major: Employer priorities for college learning and student success. *Liberal Education, 99*(2). Retrieved from https://www.aacu.org/publications-research/periodicals/it-takes-more-major-employer-priorities-college-learning-and.

Elmore, T. (2010). *Generation iY: Our last chance to save their future*. Atlanta, GA: Poet Gardner.

Espinoza, C. (2012). *Millennial integration: Challenges millennials face in the workplace and what they can do about them*. Unpublished Ph.D. thesis, Antioch University. Retrieved from: https://etd.ohiolink.edu/rws_etd/document/get/antioch1354553875/inline.

Fallis, G. (2013). *Rethinking higher education: Participation, research, and differentiation*. Montreal: McGill-Queen's University Press.

Ferguson, S.J., & Wang, S. (2014). *Graduating in Canada: Profile, labour market outcomes and student debt of the class of 2009–2010—Revised*. Statistics Canada 81-595-M. Ottawa: Statistics Canada. Retrieved from http://www.statcan.gc.ca/pub/81-595-m/81-595-m2014101-eng.htm.

Fox, H. (2011). *Their highest vocation: Social justice and the millennial generation.* New York: Peter Lang.

Galarneau, D., Morissette, R., & Usalcas, J. (2013). *What has changed for young people in Canada?* Statistics Canada 75-006-X. Ottawa: Statistics Canada. Retrieved from http://www.statcan.gc.ca/pub/75-006-x/2013001/article/11847-eng.pdf.

Gaudet, R. (2016). *Whistleblowing: How Millennials' desire for transparency affects national security.* Baker Scholar Projects. Accessible at http://trace.tennessee.edu/utk_bakerschol/35.

Glass, A. (2007). Understanding generational differences for competitive success. *Industrial and Commercial Training, 39,* 98–103.

HSBC. (2013). *Future of retirement: A new reality.* London: HSBC Insurance Holdings. Retrieved from https://www.hsbc.ca/1/PA_ES_Content_Mgmt/content/canada4/assets/pdf/FoR_Report_Canada.pdf.

Human Resources and Skills Development Canada. (2004). *Aspirations of Canadian youth for higher education—Final report.* Learning Policy Directorate, Strategic Policy and Planning. Catalogue SP-600-05-04E. Ottawa: Human Resources and Skills Development Canada.

Jenkins, J. (2007). *Leading the four generations at work.* Accessible at http://www.amanet.org/movingahead/editorial.cfm?Ed=452.

Karp, H., Fuller, C., & Sirias, D. (2002). *Bridging the boomer Xer gap. Creating authentic teams for high performance at work.* Palo Alto, CA: DaviesBlack.

Lancaster, L. C., & Stillman, D. (2002). *When generations collide: Who they are. Why they clash. How to solve the generational puzzle at work.* New York, NY: Harper Collins.

Lowe, D., Levitt, K. J., & Wilson, T. (2008). Solutions for retaining Generation Y employees in the workplace. *The Business Renaissance Quarterly, 3*(3): 43–58.

Lui, O. L. (2011). *Examining American post-secondary education.* ERS RR-11-22. Princeton, NJ: Educational Testing Service.

Marshall, K. (2010). Employment patterns of post-secondary students. *Statistics Canada September 2010 perspectives.* Catalogue no. 75-001-X. Ottawa: Statistics Canada. Retrieved from http://www5.statcan.gc.ca/olc-cel/olc.action?objId=81-595-M&objType=2&lang=en&limit=0.

Martin, C., & Tulgan, B. (2006). Managing the generation mix: From urgency to opportunity (Expanded 2nd ed.). Amherst, MA: HRD Press.

Meister, J. C., & Willyerd, K. (2010). *The 2020 workplace: How innovative companies attract, develop and keep tomorrow's employees today.* New York, NY: Harper Collins.

Moss, A. (2011). *Generation Y: An exploratory study of worker experiences, values, and attitudes in the Federal Government* (Unpublished doctoral dissertation). Cleveland State University, Cleveland, OH.

NAS Insights. (2007). Recruiting & managing the generations. Cleveland, OH: NAS Recruitment Communications. Retrieved from www.nasrecruitment.com/TalentTips/NASinsights/GenerationY.pdf.

Navient. (2015). *Money under 35.* Wilkes-Barre, PA: Navient. Retrieved from https://www.navient.com/assets/about/who-we-are/Money-Under-35-Study.pdf.

Nielsen. (2014). *Millennials: Breaking the myths.* New York: Nielson Holdings.

Ng, E. S. W., & Gossett, C. W. (2013). Career choice in Canadian public service: An exploration of fit with the Millennial generation. *Public Personnel Management, 42*(3), 337–358.

Ozkan, M. & Solmaz, B. (2015). Mobile addiction of Generation Z and its effects on their social lifes. *Procedia—Social and Behavioral Sciences, 205,* 92–98.

Peter, K., & Horn, L. (2005). *Gender differences in participation and completion of undergraduate education and how they have changed over time.* NCES 2005-169. Washington, D.C.: National Center for Education Statistics. Retrieved from http://nces.ed.gov/das/epubs/2005169/.

Pew Research Center (2015). *Comparing Millennials to other generations.* Retrieved from http://www.pewsocialtrends.org/2010/02/24/interactive-graphic-demographic-portrait-of-four-generations/.

Rainer, T., & Rainer, J. (2011). *The Millennials: Connecting to the largest generation.* Nashville, TN: B&H Publishing Group.

Schleicher, A. (2015). *Education at a glance 2015.* Paris: Organisation for Economic Co-operation and Development. Retrieved from http://www.keepeek.com/Digital-Asset-Management/oecd/education/education-at-a-glance-2015_eag-2015-en.

Schwab, K. (2016). *The fourth industrial revolution.* Geneva: World Economic Forum.

Shandler, D. (2009). *Motivating the Millennial knowledge worker: Help today's workforce succeed in today's economy.* United States: Axzo Press.

Stuart, A., & Lyons, D. S. (2008). *Millennials in the workplace.* Halifax, NS: Knightsbridge Robertson Surrette. Retrieved from http://www.kbrs.ca/insights/millennials-workplace.

US Department of Education. (2014). *Projection of education statistics to 2021.* National Center for Education Statistics. https://nces.ed.gov/fastfacts/#.

Wang, W., & Parker, K. (2014). *Record share of Americans have never married: As values, economics and gender patterns change.* Washington, D.C.: Pew Research Center. Retrieved from http://www.pewsocialtrends.org/2014/09/24/record-share-of-americans-have-never-married/#will-todays-never-married-adults-eventually-marry.

Wang, W., Parker, K., & Taylor, P. (2013). *Breadwinner moms.* Washington, D.C.: Pew Research Center. Retrieved from http://www.pewsocialtrends.org/2013/05/29/breadwinner-moms/.

Wiggins, G. L. (2012). *A descriptive analysis of generation Y employees working in Georgia State Government: Implications for workforce planning.* (Doctoral dissertation). Retrieved from ProQuest Dissertations and Theses. (Accession Order No. ATT 3544061).

Zemke, R., Raines, C., & Filipczak, B. (1999). *Generations at work: Managing the clash of veterans, Boomers, Xers, and Nexters in your workplace.* New York: AMA Publications.

Part III
Mirrors and Chameleons

Our first part identified major changes that are developing from the emerging digital environment; reviewed generational theory and cohort analyses; and addressed the evolutions in education designed to impart twenty-first century learning. Our second part then presented the characteristics that members of the youth cohort are likely to bring into their adult lives. Although our conclusions are inherently speculative generalizations, the skills, values, and traits we identified are logical consequences of a digital upbringing. Accordingly, many of the traits expressed by Millennials—having grown up during the digital revolution of the late twentieth and early twenty-first century—will be similar in many respects for their post-Millennial successors. The greater lessons for employers, however, pertain to how these two generations will differ.

In Chap. 4, we extended our conclusions on changing pedagogy to consider the cognitive skills and competencies that will be important in the workplace and that post-Millennials will be encouraged and trained to master. We find that the skills these young people can develop should position them well for the twenty-first-century knowledge economy, including apparent strengths in traditional competencies such as critical thinking, problem solving, adaptability, and creativity. While many hold the view that Millennials struggle with interactions at work, post-Millennials have the potential to be recognized as stronger communicators throughout their careers.

The effective twenty-first-century worker should also excel with the skills that will be required of continuously networked knowledge workers: cultural sensitivity in an increasingly globalized economy, cognitive load management abilities to filter the massive amounts of information accessible by technology, and media and digital literacies to enable the application of comprehension and critical thinking to the material at hand. These skills will be the most important for future employers: knowledge workers will have to pick through both a large quantity of content to discern and evaluate the information—much of it from different sources and created in many different ways—to achieve corporate objectives. Further, those with digital and media skills will find the greatest success in upgrading their skills as their careers progress. In sum, the competent post-Millennial worker will be one with considerable soft skills and an ability to sift through immense amounts of information to deliver results, and holders of competencies that should only strengthen during their careers through their capacity for lifelong learning.

Beyond these "taught" capabilities is the preference of many post-Millennials toward multitasking. The product of a digital upbringing—both in terms of information bombardment and the use of multiple devices—multitaskers, especially "supertaskers," may be fundamentally altering the development of their cognitive capacities. These post-Millennials should be more adept at succeeding within the dynamic, continuously interrupted workplace that is becoming pervasive.

We then considered the sense of identity and social skills that the post-Millennial cohort will carry into adulthood. In Chap. 4, we concluded that the most critical factor arising from a twenty-first-century education is not what students will learn, but how they will learn to learn. For post-Millennials, the power of the digital tsunami is not in its ability as a tool—as Millennials see it—but as the means for socialization and the establishment of social norms; the processes of social construction mediated through digital media. Certainly, parenting, external environments, and socioeconomic conditions will factor into a child's socialization. For instance, we expect post-Millennials to be exposed to childrearing similar to that of their predecessors: Parents will still be active participants in their children's lives, albeit with some of the "parenting" left to the next generation of digital personal assistants. Nevertheless, the Internet and social media, in particular, will play a significant role in the construction of the "self," as the medium represents an ongoing, global conversation that can serve to establish social norms by consensus (Turner, 2015). Digital access will also facilitate a more thorough exploration of what an individual could be by allowing for the adoption of a number of personas through their various social media accounts. This exposure to the digital "testing ground" should strengthen their ability to effectively communicate with others. Yet, despite the role of groups and collaborative learning in collectively socializing this generation, we conclude most will emerge with a keen sense of individualism.

The relative anonymity of the Internet, along with the presence of social media platforms that allows for such "self-testing" has also enabled several disturbing developments, including cyber-trolling, online bullying, and sexual extortion. This exposure to the dark side of the Internet, however, can serve to promote a greater understanding of the consequences of the digital self. Both parent and child should be much more aware of the creation of their "image" to their outside world, with many of today's youth likely having a greater understanding than Millennials on how the digital self may reflect on the physical self and personal reputation. post-Millennials should be much more attuned to the consequences of what they post on the Internet.

Finally, we considered the expectations that the post-Millennials may have regarding work and life as they enter adulthood. The continued emphasis on advanced schooling is forecast to produce the most educated cohort in history. Additionally, post-Millennials will be exposed to the twenty-first-century curriculum that emphasizes the skills employers will be seeking. With the emerging mantra from political leaders and educators that equates a post-secondary education with meaningful careers, we expect many post-Millennials to take their studies seriously and more easily transition into meaningful job opportunities.

This generation will be aware of the economic realities they are likely to face, such as a projected period of slow economic growth in the coming decades and the reality of fundamental shifts in the industry that are quickly making some vocations obsolete. They know that, for those with more years in school, their careers will undergo a staggered start: many years of part-time work and uncertainty in preparation for their career. They will also be aware of the pending demographic challenges and need for twenty-first-century skills in the workforce, thus should accordingly approach the workforce with reasonable hopes.

We expect their focus on education should fundamentally alter both the timing and definitions of many of their major life events. The social construction of their reality that started in their childhoods will extend into their adult years and will serve to challenge traditional social roles and "benchmarks." Post-Millennials will build on the Millennials' construction of alternate understandings of concepts related to marriage, parenting, and home to do the same for work, employment, and career. Along with the propensity to multitask, post-Millennials will extend the current Millennials' pattern of blurring the differentiation between work and leisure into a daily juggling act, unconstrained by the time clock. Many of these changes are gendered in nature: women—now in the majority in post-secondary institutions; more accepting of evolving identities; and facing fewer barriers to fulfilling careers —may be strong drivers of the new "adulthood," "career," or "workday".

Notwithstanding the variability in socioeconomic environments, unforeseen significant emotional events, and the presence of sub-cohorts and value tribes; a picture nevertheless emerges of the potential post-Millennials when they arrive at work for day one. Employers should be able to select individuals with a greater understanding of self, gifted in the twenty-first-century hard and soft skills, holders of more life experience, a strong understanding of economic conditions and pending shifts, and an awareness of what they expect from their careers. Even before that first day, their ability to communicate, propensity to "do their home-work" on an employer, and their understanding of their image in the eyes of others —particularly in response to stereotypes older generations may hold of them—will allow those who have benefited from their education and digital connections to mold their persona to what is expected by their employer: a "chameleon" using "mirrors" to succeed. These skills may serve the post-Millennial as they encounter possible workplace culture clashes we will present in Chap. 7. Here, post-Millennials have the potential to be out front, demanding changes to how "work" is conducted. In particular, as Boomers retire, the structures and processes this group will have left behind will likely be seen as antithetical to the values and worldviews that digital generations will bring. Employers will be challenged to alter the structures and assumptions behind the "Boomer workplace" to attract and retain a competent team. These expectations and potential culture clashes will be presented in the first chapter recommendations on how to build the optimum workplace for the twenty-first-century expert workers will form the basis of the following chapter.

Reference

Turner, A. (2015). Generation Z: Technology and social interest. *Journal of Individual Psychology, 71*(2), 103–113.

Post-Millennials in The Workplace

7

> *The millennial generation, now entering into employment, will reshape the world of work. Are you ready?*
> —PWC Study of Millennials Impact

Introduction

As summarized from the previous sections, the Post-Millennials are currently developing a host of competencies, perceptions, understandings and expectations regarding their personal lives, community and family relationships, central personal values and beliefs, and, most critically for this volume, their goals for employment and their career. Our consideration of the likely status and expectations of those in this age group as they enter the full-time workforce suggest several factors that employers should consider as they anticipate how this cohort will be approaching major life events, embarking on their career and, of critical importance, seeking to achieve some degree of work-life balance.

Once these young people are hired, they will bring with them a range of work-related capabilities and also a host of expectations. Again, we offer the caveat that only time will tell as to exactly how the Post-Millennials will affect workplace dynamics and who amongst this group will possess which attitudes, skills and expectations, hence the acknowledgement that our generalizations do not apply to each individual. We do, however, present factors that employers should consider once the Post-Millennials are on the job. Our central conclusion is that their arrival just as the last of the Boomers are retiring will set up several areas of potential cultural conflict. We see GenXers and Millennials having to oversee a significant shift from the employment philosophy and practices that will constitute the Boomers legacy to the corporate environment. New approaches will be needed not only to accommodate the Post-Millennials but also to evolve the organization for

© Springer Nature Switzerland AG 2020
A. Okros, *Harnessing the Potential of Digital Post-Millennials in the Future Workplace*, Management for Professionals,
https://doi.org/10.1007/978-3-030-25726-2_7

the emerging digital economies. We will commence with an overview of this legacy and the implicit expectations and norms that will probably dominate many established organizations and use these to examine the tensions that we see arising when the Post-Millennials make their presence felt.

The Clash of Generations (and the Remaking of the World Business Order)

> Got my dream job by responding to a classified ad—Old Economy Steve meme

While we have focussed our attention on what the Post-Millennials will be looking for in their workplace, we fully recognize that the brunt of the digital revolution in the workplace will take place with the presence of four cohorts in the workplace: Late Boomers and some Generation X occupying the C-level suites; passed over GenX and Millennials in the middle management levels and late starter Millennials and the Post-Millennials working up the career levels. We noted that some authors and bloggers are providing observations on generational issues within the workplace; however, our assessment is that the analyses provided tend to focus on only one or two characteristics and do not provide any frameworks for assessing why these clashes may occur. We deduced that the four cohorts will initially be operating in a corporate culture that is a legacy of Boomer values, assumptions, structures, and rules. We see friction points and culture clashes are quite likely to occur as digital DNA is transferred into the traditional, hierarchical work environment. Three factors reflect the implicit set of assumptions regarding work and careers that the Boomers have imprinted on organizations hence will survive their exit: organization structures, career models, and organizational culture.[1]

Organizational Structures

A key point in any consideration of the common hierarchical organization is that individuals are provided with significant amounts of structure or, more specifically, certain limits on the amount of discretion, initiative or creativity that they can use in getting the job done. We argue that organizations have two components: structural systems (rules, regulations, work descriptions, reporting relationships, managerial or governance systems, etc.) and social systems (culture, workplace environment, core values and principles, style of supervision, reward systems, method of motivation, etc.).[2]

Simplistically, the structural components are regulated using rules-based bureaucratic processes that ensure that the right work gets done using allocated resources while the personal aspects are influenced by principle-based social

---

[1]For more on different corporate models see the original work by Mintzberg (1979).

[2]See Okros et al. (2011) for additional presentation of the theories and concepts we have drawn on.

processes that ensure that the work gets done the right way and for the right reason. The normal functions of management (planning, organizing, delegating, controlling) along with common human resource activities (job analysis, job descriptions, performance appraisal, succession management, etc.) are all premised on a taken-for-granted assumption that those appointed to higher positions in the hierarchy have greater power and authority to make decisions concerning the work and work environment of those who work for them. Even the use of participative decision-making styles or workplace teams are embedded within structures (rules, regulations, reward systems, etc.) and cultures (the taken for granted assumptions and dominant norms of expected behaviours) that serve to constrain what any one individual or any one team may or can do: others (the ubiquitous 'they') have already set the conditions within which the individual or team is then allowed to exercise a degree of independence. We acknowledge that the typical entrepreneurial start up does not initially share the characteristics we are presenting however note that most management texts suggest that, at some stage, they need to transform from the 'two geeks in a garage' approach to the dominant model presented here. The key is that, to survive and thrive as an organization becomes established and, especially, if it has reached a threshold in terms of size, internal complexities or differentiated business lines,[3] there is usually a need to impose increased structure and common culture hence the organization gradually adopts most of the characteristics we have presented.[4]

This approach to structuring organizations occurred with the shift from a predominantly blue-collar workforce, engaged in harvesting resources and manufacturing goods, to a mainly white-collar workforce, engaged in information management and the provisions of services. This shift was well embedded by the time the Boomers commenced their career in the 1960s so has been seen as the status quo ever since.

The Career Employment Model

While the primary purpose of organizational structures is to ensure that the right work gets done the right way, these also inform how individuals progress through their career. The typical organizational chart reflects a pyramid comprised of a large number of employees at the bottom with multiple layers of increasingly smaller numbers of individuals in supervisory and middle management functions and ultimately a small cadre of executives with a single person at the apex of the organization. Not only do each of the successive layers represent increased responsibilities, power and compensation but, when combined with information conveyed through the structural and social systems, provides the path for the individual to rise in their career.

---

[3]Creating some of the key transaction costs and attractors of efficiency identified earlier.
[4]Again, for the original conceptualizations, see Mintzberg (1979).

An important aspect in this progression is the use of career 'ladders' representing the sequential employment 'steps' that enable individuals to advance through their career. Again, coincidental with the entry of the Boomers was the establishment of merit-based career promotion (rather than seniority based) as the primary model. While most companies have adopted competency frameworks as central to assessing individuals for external hiring or internal promotion, as reflected in the refrain that Millennials can't get their first fulltime job unless they have had a fulltime job, employers continue to place a high value on work experience.[5] The preference for work experience is an implicit part of the philosophy of career success that the Boomers have integrated into corporate culture. The 'Old Economy Steve' meme is an illustration of the Millennial's frustration with the way in which Boomers achieved career success versus what they are now encountering.[6]

Organizational Culture

The third critical aspect in understanding pending generational clashes pertains to organizational culture.[7] While many firms have engaged in the exercise of creating mission, vision and value statements as a method to articulate their desired corporate identity and dominant culture, it is actually of greater importance to understand the informal operant or lived culture rather than the ideal that is formally espoused in corporate value statements. As the key component of the social systems referred to earlier, organizational culture provides the series of informal cues that influence how elements of the structural systems (rules, regulations, supervisor directions, etc.) are actually implemented. As such, workplace culture is a powerful mediator. We concluded that the crux of the tension will come from the contrast between what is referred to as 'tight' versus 'loose' culture with the key differences summarized in Table 7.1.[8]

As reflected by the efforts of organizations to create or impose a commonly shared culture, tight cultures emphasize consistency, conformity and similarities in language, dress and behaviours with clear workplace norms, well established role requirements, an emphasis on self-sacrifice for the common good and reliance on a narrative or corporate history to ensure current employees views are grounded on an understanding of the organization's story of success. In contrast, a loose culture allows for acceptance of ambiguities, alternate language and freedom to adopt different behaviours, flexible norms, few status differentiations, voluntary contributions to benefit others and a focus on building a better tomorrow rather than preserving a successful past.

---

[5]In a 2015 international survey, 58% of employers valued work experience as the most important for new employees http://universumglobal.com/2020outlook/.

[6]For more on this meme, see Jordan Weissmann' "Old Economy Steve: The Official Meme for Embittered Millennials" *The Atlantic* 28 May 2013.

[7]We generally ascribe to the conceptualizations presented by Edgar Schein.

[8]For the original conceptualizations of tight vs loose cultures, see Pelto (1968); for application in the organizational context, see Hofstede (1998).

Table 7.1 Characteristics of tight versus loose cultures

	Tight culture	Loose culture
Identity	Homogeneity with clear boundaries as to who is a member of the culture (and who is excluded) and a strong single identity for all members	Heterogeneity with a philosophy that it is the individual who determines whether they are part of the larger group and acceptance that individuals may have multiple identities
Norms	Explicit social norms and associated standards of appropriate behaviour with severe sanctions applied to those who deviate from these norms	Flexible social norms and standards of behaviour shaped by the idea that one does not impose their own norms, values or standards on others
Roles	Clearly differentiated and stratified role requirements (manager vs. supervisor vs labourer) with a requirement to fulfill role requirements in a way that is consistent with the social norms	A lack of emphasis on roles and role requirements with few status distinctions or role-specific obligations
Obligations	An emphasis on the subordination of one's own interests (or view) to the good of the overall group incorporated in the prototype of the 'good citizen' as one who makes personal sacrifices to contribute to an overarching goal	An emphasis in citizenship and ones' obligations to others on maximizing the benefits to all hence the concept of 'good citizen' as one who voluntarily makes a contribution to other's wellbeing, quality of life or community initiatives
Clarity	A concern for clarity in language, rules and social regulation with limits on the articulation of contrary viewpoints or acts of disobedience	Acceptance of ambiguity and the likelihood of miscommunication and misunderstanding with the obligation of each to understand the other's perspective
References	A reliance on history, customs and traditions to reinforce key themes and to ensure cultural continuity and stability over time	An expectation that societies and social norms will evolve hence an orientation towards the future as something to be created rather than a past to be preserved

The remainder of this chapter will turn to a consideration of the factors that many Post-Millennials will consider to matter when they enter the workplace. Our analyses will draw on these considerations of the implicit models and assumptions related to organizational structures, careers and cultures that have become deeply embedded in corporate practice throughout the tenure of the Boomers in the workplace. We offer that the different taken-for-granted assumptions surrounding the world of work and, to return to the concept of social construction, the view that these represent the 'natural order of things' in corporate affairs will result in significant generational clashes as the Post-Millennials enter the workplace.

Technology and Social Media

> We understand that in order to be truly digital, organisations must be digital from the inside out—Michael Keegan

The Post-Millennials will bring values and assumptions to the workplace formed during their youth and young adulthood. As the first completely digital generation, they have the capacity to join the tech-savvy Millennials to bring the full force of technology into the workplace. When the 21st Century graduate becomes the 21st Century worker, high among their expectations will be the expansive use of technology in the workplace (Lowe, Levitt, & Wilson, 2008; Meister & Willyerd, 2010; NAS Insights, 2007). Technology and connectivity are already of great importance to Millennials; they are known to use their own devices in the absence of sufficient technology provided by their employers (Meister & Willyerd, 2010). Many Post-Millennials will push harder for ready access to cutting-edge technology at work as well as for the ability to use social media platforms.

While Millennials see the comprehensive use of technology as a means to increase productivity and efficiency, Post-Millennials are more likely to see technology as enabling creative ways to advance corporate goals. For the truly digital cohort in this generation, these technologies do not represent new tools but will serve as the central facilitator of new ways of thinking and working. For instance, Post-Millennials will meet the workplace need for efficiency by using technology to create an environment that compliments their inclination towards multitasking. The expectation that Post-Millennials will use social media in the workplace as a means of facilitating collaboration will also represent a creative departure from the norms of workplace communication. Further, when combined with their capacity to explore issues in different ways, push boundaries and challenge taken-for-granted assumptions, engaged Post-Millennials will be at the forefront of developing new approaches to business practices. Some organizations are seeing these effects already with the Millennials in the workplace but, to return to our example of Uber ride sharing, the Millennials are just illustrating the transition approaches; the Post-Millennials will create the new ways of doing business—for those organizations able to harness this potential.

The emphasis on technology in the workplace has already advanced with Millennials using digital devices more than their older colleagues (Chowdhury, 2013; Kunins, 2010). Most of this generation share a philosophy that the device is complementary to the workplace: they are less likely than Generation X and the Boomers to see the use of digital devices as detrimental to workplace etiquette or a faux pas in the meeting room (Meister & Willyerd, 2010). Millennials are even willingly breaking corporate policies on technology, partially in response to what they perceive as an outdated work environment and because they believe that they better understand how technologies can meet the needs of the organization. Although Boomers and Gen X are competent in the use of technology, they hold different views on their appropriate use. In the Proskauer's 2014 International survey of business practices, 70% of employers reported taking disciplinary action against employees for violating company policies on social media use in the office and 36% said they actively block access to social media at work.[9]

The increasing presence of "digital DNA" in the office will generate a requirement for significant shifts in corporate practices, processes and structures. These will be a challenge for those comfortable with the current status quo, particularly the remaining representatives of the Boomer generation who will assume that the employer has the right to control the use of technology and access to social media. As Post-Millennials engage in behaviours that may be seen as breaking company policies or violating social norms, the use of technology and the value systems that come with it have the potential to form the basis of significant intergenerational conflict.

Teams and Collaboration

None of us is as smart as all of us.—Ken Blanchard

We already live in a globalized economy, with world-wide supply chains, transnational corporations, and extensive international trade. The interconnections created by these economic realities have already begun to change how we work: for the current workforce—from Boomers to Millennials—working in teams has become a widespread practice. The nature of teams and teamwork is, however, changing due to the capacities of digital technologies such as teleconference and videoconference. MacDonnell et al. (2009) argue that virtual teams have become a norm in the workplace however Gilson et al. (2015) caution that there are generational differences in approaching virtual teams. To return to *weisure* time, not all members of the team need to be at the office to participate in the collective effort nor, to link to multi-tasking, does it mean that the sole focus of the Post-Millennial's attention will be on the work of the team. The penchants for multi-tasking and a preference for the flexibilities of telework from home (or the cottage or Fiji) could be seen by some as violating well established norms about where and how work is done.

Research has also shown that Millennials prefer a workplace that provides a team-setting that is representative of diversity (Deloitte, 2005; Espinoza, 2012; Lancaster & Stillman, 2002; Martin & Tulgan, 2006; Meister & Willyerd, 2010; NAS Insights, 2007). We believe the Post-Millennials will extend their predecessor's preference for a diverse and collaborative environment with increased emphasis on working in dynamic teams. They will have been prepared to do so having been provided learning opportunities incorporating team-based approaches since grade school. The focus on teams will extend to virtual contexts spanning national or cultural contexts. Thus, as highlighted earlier, cross-cultural competence will become an even more critical skill for Post-Millennials. Again, the connected

---

[9]See Social Media in the Workplace Around the World 3.0, accessible at: http://www.proskauer.com/files/uploads/social-media-in-the-workplace-2014.pdf.

nature of their digital livelihoods, shared global experiences and greater exposure to diversity, should ensure that the many Post-Millennials will be better prepared to meet this challenge than were the Millennials when they started work.

Our scan of the digital environment indicates that the influence of technology will change the nature of corporate collaboration far beyond the current Millennials use of social media in the workplace. New forms of teamwork will emerge as the participatory culture that the youth cohort will be used to increasingly influences the workplace (Linden, 2015). To link back to 'tight' versus 'loose' aspects, participatory culture is characterized by having low barriers to artistic expression, emphasizing creating and sharing one's creations, and having some type of informal mentorship (Jenkins, Purushatma, Weigel, Clinton, & Robison, 2009). It also stresses that each individual's contributions matter and that there is a social connection among the individuals. This emerging participatory culture will be a direct product of the digital age (Nielsen et al. 2009). It will arise through different forms such as affiliations and memberships in online communities; a social media presence; producing new creative forms of "expressions"; collaborative problem-solving, content creation such as Wikipedia; online gaming; and "circulations", with a focus on shaping the flow of media such as blogging and podcasting.[10] Where it develops, the nature of this participatory culture, with an emphasis on the individual within the context of deep collaboration, will be a marked departure from hierarchical structures and manager-led teams.

An important extension is the concept of self-forming teams: individuals who voluntarily select to come together to address a specific (and sometimes urgent) issue. These types of teams are enabled but not controlled: managers provide the culture and flexibilities for these types of teams to emerge but neither appoint team members nor provide specific direction or typical managerial controls (Hoda, Noble, & Marshall, 2010; Okros, Verdon, & Chouinard, 2011). To return to the consideration of Post-Millennials and gamers, those who have spent time in their youth playing multiplayer online games will have developed some of the skills needed to create, contribute to and disband self-forming teams; the challenge is whether managers are able to envision a future workplace with no managers. For the curious, we recommend a review of the Valve Corporation's New Employee Handbook especially the section title 'Welcome to Flatland'.[11] This suggests that a key question that employers should ask a new hire is: 'How extensive is your network and how good are you at harnessing its power?"

This democratization within teams will present a challenge in trying to maximize individual contributions (including reconciling differing viewpoints) while also optimizing team results. Drawing on their experiences since pre-school including their philosophy of 'no peer left out', many Post-Millennials will be seeking new ways to formulate teams; greater independence in choosing not only *how* to do work but *what* to work on and with *whom*; and, assurances that all will be recognized for their contributions to the collective effort. Thus, this evolution to a much more democratic work environment begs the question about how leadership

---

[10]See again Verdon's research and websites as well as Jenkins et al. (2006).
[11]Accessible at: http://www.valvesoftware.com/company/Valve_Handbook_LowRes.pdf.

of these teams will be decided; how they will operate, and how executives will still have an assurance that what they produce meets the corporate goals.

In this context, Drath et al. (2015) challenge the assumption that leadership requires leaders. Leadership is a process that emerges from a group when they achieve direction, alignment and commitment—and that this can develop within a team without anybody being formally anointed as the leader. It will challenge a host of taken for granted assumptions that have become deeply woven into organizational thinking including many aspects of the structural systems we presented earlier (job descriptions, hierarchical reporting relationships, managerial control) and will also require significant shifts in the operant culture in many workplaces.

Responsible Autonomy

> When you delegate work to the member of the team, your job is to clearly frame success and describe the objective—Steven Sinofsky

As an extension to the concept of self-organizing teams, the democratization of the workplace will also increase the emphasis across the organization for delegating authority down the corporate layers to the individual. The challenge here is that executives will still be influenced by the part of the Boomers legacy founded on MacGregor's 1960) Theory X, hence, will want to know that these employees are doing the management-approved right work the corporately-endorsed right way when granted independence.[12] Fairtlough (2005) describes the central tenet to enable delegation while maintaining a focus on the overarching objectives that he calls responsible autonomy. As autonomy means a high degree of independence and entails a tendency toward self-organization and governance, responsible autonomy suggests personal accountability for the outcomes of self-organization. To meet the expectations of future generations of workers, organizations will need to pay increased attention to generating the social fabric and stewarding the intrinsic motivations to provide conditions that allow people to function with more responsible autonomy and foster their mastery in a context of purpose and belonging. When established, this will lead to: greater engagement and enabled participation; a deeper trust-based social fabric (across both the virtual and physical spheres of action); more rapid scalable learning; and, more effective collaboration and self-organization.

Verdon et al. (2009) examined the application of responsible autonomy in the Federal public service and the military. While both are characterized by an emphasis on hierarchy and structural controls, the military can adopt the philosophy of 'mission command' (originally the German concept of *Auftragstaktik)* in which superiors provide sufficient guidance to ensure subordinates understand the

---

[12]The core of MacGregor's Theory X is that employees are not motivated to perform to a high standard at work hence need details rules, close supervision and threats of punishments to maintain a reasonable level of productivity. This philosophy is evident in many corporate approaches to the creation and enforcement of rules.

objectives to be achieved, the broad parameters for choice of actions and the central principles to guide complex decision making—and then let the team use the maximum of creativity and flexibility to achieve mission success. The application of mission command is a central tenet of the way in which elite Special Forces operate.[13]

Self-organization as a means of completing work is reliant on responsible autonomy as a social operating system (Wellman, 2001). Such an operating system is based on trusted personnel, agent-forum accountability, context/competence-based leadership and networked individualism. It is a process that enables an overarching order or coordination to emerge out of local interactions (that may initially be disordered). As developed in previous work on the 'meta-organization' by Okros et al. (2011), such a workplace paradigm challenges the traditional industrial enterprise that must reconfigure its organization charts, reporting relationships and physical accommodation to enact organizational change. Self-organization through responsible autonomy can be a spontaneous process that is not directed or controlled by hierarchical authority, managerial processes or rules-based structures but is possible when an organization is appropriately architected as a platform (PriceWaterhouseCooper, 2012). Such a platform enables the rapid and agile generation, assemblage and harnessing of knowledge networks, as and when needed. In this way a platform for self-organization harnesses the increasingly specialized skills, talent, knowledge, and motivations of people (Prensky, 2006).

This shift will enable empowered Post-Millennials (and others able to adapt to the new work realities) to exploit the new, unprecedented capacity for knowledge flow. To return to our introduction of the dominant models related to organizations structures and functioning, as the next cohort becomes more of a force in the office, the expectations of this generation are likely to push a change that represents fundamental shifts in corporate structures [14] as depicted in Table 7.2.

Information Control, the "Truth" and Challenges to Authority

> Information is power. But like all power, there are those who want to keep it for themselves
> —Aaron Swartz

Post-Millennials in general will have lived their lives with nearly unlimited and instantaneous access to the body of human knowledge.[15] The traditional "command-and-control" workplace is premised on the power that different levels hold over knowledge and the flow of information. Post-Millennial will not be satisfied with the old command and control motif that said: "we'll give you the

---

[13]Amongst many professional articles that describe the application in the context of Special Forces, see Flynn and Schrankel (2013).

[14]Again, see Okros et al. (2011) for a full discussion of these factors.

[15]Again noting that each person will exercise choice as to whether to access this body of knowledge and how to interpret or apply it.

Table 7.2 Changes in organizational functioning

From	To
Place-to-Place	Person-to-Person
Person-in-Job	Person-Best-Able
Principal-Agent Accountability Framework	Agent-Forum Accountability Framework
Hierarchy of Supervision	Hierarchy of Competence

amount of information you need to do the job and no more" (Lancaster & Stillman, 2002, p. 231). This approach has already been noted to be seen as a hindrance to Millennials (Meister & WIllyerd, 2010; Moss, 2011; Wiggins, 2012).

To return to our Chap. 2 discussion of transaction costs, adaptive Post-Millennials are likely to be frustrated by situations where there exists a significant cost in the time and effort involved in finding relevant information. This issue is particularly salient for hierarchical organizations such as government bureaucracies where the cost of looking for information that exists within the organization is estimated to be as high as 20% of an individual's time (Cross & Parker, 2004). Accordingly, information management will need to adopt more open sharing across the organization, even if it means increasing the risk of information "leaking" to competitors or the media (Hagel, Brown, & Davison, 2010).

We noted reports that Millennials are willingly breaking corporate policies on technology, partially in response to what they perceive as an outdated work environment but also because they believe that they better understand the needs of the organization (Jenkins et al., 2009). Further, the tendency of Millennials' to broadcast personal information has been identified as presenting a unique challenge (Accenture, 2008; Fritzon, Howell, & Zakheim, 2008). With the speed at which they communicate, some may not give sufficient thought to the ramifications of certain messages. Indiscrete publication of intimate personal and corporate details may become more frequent. We have already suggested that many Post-Millennials will be learning valuable lessons with regards to sharing too much personal information; however, it remains to be seen how they approach the sharing of work-related information. Particularly when it comes to problem solving, it will not be a surprise to see some apply a taken-for-granted assumption that the best ways of finding relevant information, developing creative solutions or checking to see if there are alternate views of the issue is to engage broadly across their community and friends. As these personal networks will extend far beyond corporate boundaries, there can be concerns that Post-Millennials may not be able to discern what corporate or personal information is inappropriate to share (Malloy, 2012).

The risk of information leakage, however, is somewhat buttressed by the transparency of the Internet, which creates conditions that can make accountability easier. Transparency enables a more participative and democratic form of accountability by shifting the problems inherent in the traditional principal-agent mechanism of accountability towards methods enabling an agent-forum accountability framework (Bovens, 2010). Pentland's ongoing research in social physics (which also supports the propositions of the 'wisdom of crowds') suggests that anyone can learn to become a good and/or better decision maker—a social decision maker. As we have stated, the key is the capacity to engage in social exploration to encounter a much greater diversity of people, types of thinking, domains of knowledge and ideas—a sort of designed serendipity. By assembling a set of potential strategies (the variety of behaviors others exhibit), Pentland argues that people can become better decision-makers.

Drawing on Verdon's contributions, we argue that social decision making enables people to avoid both the echo-chamber and the isolation-chamber and enables then to engage in social learning (copying a wider diversity of successful strategies and ideas) within a 'sweet-spot' that produces the highest rewards and best decisions. Similarly, social physics research has demonstrated that the most productive and creative groups create conditions for optimal idea flow: high engagement within a group balanced with high individual exploration outside the group. However, to optimize decision making, each individual has to have access to a different array of information—different examples of success and failure of others. As indicated in our initial digital scan, this suggests that the previous constraints upon identity that required an isolated, atomistic, anonymous individual for the industrial economies may no longer be adequate for the emerging economies of the digital environment. The idea of 'owing one's personal data as private property' may be a drastic barrier to 'wealth/value' creation in the digital environment. Thus, the threat of the "leak" may be trumped by the benefit of diffused, social learning.

Of greater importance than the issues surrounding control of information, we have identified that an important outcome of 21st Century education will be the perspective that all knowledge is contestable and all 'truth' comes with an expiry date. As a result, Post-Millennials who have adopted these views will expect to be able to challenge rules, operating procedures, declarative statements and executive decisions particularly when these do not fit how they have come to understand the world around them. While their interest will be to identify the most appropriate way of 'knowing' or understanding the information they are working with, this will most definitely be seen as a direct challenge to the authority (and privilege) of those in higher positions to set policies, rules and procedures that govern the workplace. Not only will managers and executives have to get used to the idea of engaged Post-Millennials challenging their authority to define the corporate world, they will also have to learn how to deal with the disruptive effects of them importing new ideas and different frames of reference. While many organizations proclaim that they encourage employee creativity, they do so based on the assumptions that their organization structures and espoused culture will constrain this creativity to being within defined limits; some Post-Millennials will use their capacities to push well beyond these boundaries.

Organizational Loyalty and Advancement

You hire the best people you can possibly find. Then it's up to you to create an environment where great people decide to stay and invest their time.—Gabe Newell

While the Boomers are characterized by their ambition and loyalty to the organization, Millennials are seen to be more loyal to individual managers and corporate visions but not necessarily to the organization itself (Alexander & Sysko, 2012; Ng, Schweitzer, & Lyons, 2010). Having witnessed the influence globalization, especially the lack of loyalty on behalf of employers to retain workers when 'outsourcing' jobs, most Millennials do not expect to stay in one job forever or, in fact, for long at all (Jayson, 2006). Further, their preference for collaboration leads many to identify with, hence have loyalty to, their team, but not the organization (Hogg 2002; Tanner 2010). Accordingly, the sense of loyalty that bound a Baby Boomer to the firm for a lengthy career is not likely to be shared by most 21st Century workers.

This tension extends to perceptions about the quality of work younger people produce: one US poll by Workplace Options found 77% of their co-workers believe Millennials have a different attitude toward workplace responsibility than older workers; 68% feel they are less motivated to take on responsibility and produce quality work; and 46% believe Millennials are less engaged at work than older employees.[16] In contrast to these views by others, research shows that the Millennials have high (likely unrealistic) expectations for advancement; Ng et al. (2010) reported they expected their first promotion within 18 months of joining a company.

These attitudes stand in contrast to those of the Boomers.[17] The dominant view is that this generation generally believes that achievement comes after paying dues and they value organisational commitment, loyalty and sacrifice to achieve success. More so, they have ideals that work equates to self-fulfilment especially through meeting targets and deadlines hence see hard work and long hours as key to success (Zemke et al., 1999).

We anticipate that many Post-Millennials will approach work commitment in a similar fashion as the Millennial peers. The challenge we see looming is with the operant culture and taken-for-granted assumptions related to loyalty, commitment and motivation. Those who have been enculturated to the dominant career employment model will continue to evaluate the motives and interests of younger workers using the behavioural indicators that have been valued in the past: hard work, long hours, time at the desk, complying with the rules and following the directions provided by managers. We anticipate that many Post-Millennials will have difficulty accepting these as the key indicators of job success. Their loyalty is more likely to be more to the project at hand than the organization per se and, in contrast to others, they are likely to give greater value to the outcome achieved rather than the output produced.

---

[16]http://www.workplaceoptions.com/polls/.
[17]Noting that there are differences across nations, the attitudes reported pertain to Boomers in the US and Canada.

Our key observation is that the interplay between Post-Millennials expectations regarding employer loyalty to them and employers' perspectives of lack of long-term commitment to the organization has the potential to generate a self-fulfilling prophecy with the actions of each contributing to reinforcing this negative cycle. A central conclusion is that this is most likely to continue in those firms that retain the Boomers preferred career employment model with the expectation that new employees have to prove their loyalty and commitment before the organization is prepared to offer them advancement or career tenure. Conversely, those employers who can demonstrate that Post-Millennials are valued members of the team will engender the type of organizational citizenship behaviours and affective commitment that leads to greater contributions by the individual.[18]

Supervision and Mentoring

The mediocre leader tells. The good leader explains. The superior leader demonstrates. The great leader inspires.—Gary Patton

The final area where we anticipate potential generational clashes pertains to the relationship between new hire Post-Millennials and their immediate supervisors. We expect the next cohort to extend the Millennials desire to have fun at work and develop not only trust but good relationships with their supervisors and even friendships with their coworkers (Lancaster & Stillman, 2002; Lowe et al., 2008; Meister & Willyerd, 2010; Moss, 2011; NAS Insights, 2007; Rainer & Rainer, 2011). Drawing on the coaching form of teaching they are now encountering in school, many Post-Millennials are likely to expect similar leadership styles from their bosses. Thus, where "Boomers see 'The Man' and Xers see 'authority hurdles', Millennials {and we offer, Post-Millennials} will see friends, life coaches and guides" (Shore, 2012).

To return to our differentiation between 'tight' and 'loose' cultures, the Boomer generation is seen to show deference to authority and not be comfortable voicing opinions to superiors—and expecting others to conform to these norms (Gentry et al, 2011).[19] Part of the criticisms of Millennials as workers is their perceived rejection of hierarchy; desire for involvement through having a say in the process; and, willingness to share information with all. The common description is that they value competence and skill, and prefer relationships based on caring, trust, and mutual respect rather than mere authority. Millennials tend to look for ethical behaviour and, those who do, are not afraid to challenge rules or the status quo to live according to their values (Rainer & Rainer, 2011). As we expect many

---

[18]See Nielson et al. (2009) for recent work examining OCBs and teams; and, Meyers and Allan (1991) for their original conceptualizations of organizational commitment.

[19]Noting that this is less a factor with Francophones in Canada; see our reports by Charbonneau & Garneau.

Post-Millennials to hold similar preferences, they too are liable to be seen by older workers to be violating implicit workplace norms by speaking up and speaking out.

We have, however, previously suggested that the Post-Millennials as a whole will be more aware of the expectations of others that they should fit into the organization and not stand out to the degree that the Millennials appear to have. To the extent that they do, the dilemma they will face will be to concurrently blend in while also finding a way to make their work personally meaningful and fulfilling. Thus, we expect that they will be more apt to actively seek feedback, advice and information. While seeking and accepting feedback is an integral part of most workplace cultures, we anticipate three potential problems in the future. First, researchers have already noted that the described Millennials sense of immediacy extends to the expectation of instantaneous feedback and recognition (Shandler, 2009). We anticipate that Post-Millennials will be seen to continue this trend, however, the challenge will be that supervisors are more likely to want to provide feedback at a time of their choosing not the employee's.

Second, research suggests that the new employees will be more interested in advice and coaching related to attaining their mid to long-term goals: promotions, tackling more challenging projects and finding ways to adapt work routines to fit the preferences we have already highlighted: unrestricted use of technology, working in collaborative teams, being delegated autonomy, open access to information and developing a map to career success (Lancaster & Stillman, 2002; Martin & Tulgan, 2006; NAS Insights, 2007; Rainer & Rainer, 2011). In contrast, supervisors are more likely to be prepared to provide feedback on how to follow the rules, which procedures to follow and how to make the boss look good. The third issue pertains to who these supervisors will be: mid-career Millennials. While we might anticipate that those advanced to this level will strengthen their interpersonal skills and that these two will find ways to harness social media and digital devices to facilitate new forms of mentoring, unless employers have assisted Millennials who have been promoted to higher levels to develop the full range of leadership skills, the Gen Xers in senior management and executive roles may have concerns over the effectiveness of supervisor-employee relations.

Conclusion

While we have suggested that, overall, the Post-Millennials will be more focussed than the Millennials have been on fitting into the organizational environment when hired, many will also bring a host of competencies, ideas and questions that will serve to challenge the status quo. Our central argument in this volume is that employers will be wise to harness the potential that the best of the Post-Millennials will bring thus, in particular, need to understand who they are and adapt accordingly rather than trying to force fit them into the existing organizational systems. We have, therefore summarized four key perspectives that those in the digitally engaged Post-Millennial cohort might like to share if they perceive that their managers are prepared to listen.

"It's not that I disagree boss; I know you're wrong". The way in which they will have learned to learn along with their unique use of social media will result in this cohort acquiring, creating and applying knowledge in dramatically new ways. This will result in them challenging not only day to day work processes including the use of digital technologies but the fundamental nature of work structures, management philosophies, bureaucratic control mechanisms, the application of rules and the authorities of those senior to them.

"Actually, we've decided to do it this way". Having continuously worked in collaborative ways with peers applying creative use of technology, an emphasis on exploring new ways to solve problems and belief that all truth comes with an expiry date; this cohort will constantly be sharing views with others to find alternate ways of accomplishing goals. Hence, they will frequently be challenging established procedures, experimenting with new approaches, sharing ideas with those outside the unit/team and developing unique solution sets and, conversely, having little patience with outmoded standard operating procedures or outdated technology.

"My moral compass is pointing in a different direction". Although most will be raised by sheltering parents, their direct access to evidence of the best and worst of human society, emphasis on fairness, nose for authenticity and experience sharing their opinions with the entire world will result in this cohort developing not only unique worldviews and assumptions about human nature but a strong sense of self-worth and confidence in their ability to exercise independent moral judgement. In this context, they will challenge managers to articulate the principles underlying their decisions or directions and, when these principles are not explained, decide for themselves or amongst themselves right versus wrong.

"I'm not who you think I am". Their exposure to diversity, active use of social media to present selected aspects of their identity to specific audiences and observations of their Millennial elders striving to fit in and succeed will result in this cohort developing unique ways of blending into their environment (the chameleons) and reflecting back to supervisors what the boss wants to see (the mirrors) while retaining an independent self-identity. This will result in them challenging corporate efforts to instill core values, the operant organizational culture and accepted norms of behaviour and the accuracy of performance appraisals through their ability to publicly 'fit the company mold' while privately retaining alternate values and beliefs.

References

Accenture. (2008). *Millennials at the gates: Results from Accenture's high performance IT research*. New York: Accenture Research.

Alexander, C. S., & Sysko, J. M. (2012). A study of the cognitive determinants of generation Y's entitlement mentality. *Academy of Educational Leadership Journal, 16*(2), 63–68. Retrieved from https://www.questia.com/library/journal/1P3-2750829131/a-study-of-the-cognitive-determinants-of-generation.

Bovens, M. (2010). Two concepts of accountability: Accountability as a virtue and as a mechanism. *West European Politics, 33*(5), 946–967.

Chowdhury, R. (2013). Evolution of mobile phones: 1995–2012. http://www.hongkiat.com/blog/evolution-of-mobile-phones/.

Cross, R., & Parker, A. (2004). *The hidden power of social networks: Understanding how work really gets done in organizations.* Boston: Harvard Business School Press.

Deloitte. (2005). *Who are the Millennials? A.k.a. Generation Y.* Oakland, CA: Deloitte Development LLC. Retrieved from http://www.mcosa.net/SPF-SIG%20TRAINING%20Folder/us_consulting_millennialfactsheet_080606.pdf.

Drath, W. H., McCauley, C. D., Palus, C. J., Van Velsor, E., O'Connor, P. M. G., & McGuire, J. B. (2015). Direction, alignment, commitment: Toward a more integrative ontology of leadership. *The Leadership Quarterly, 19,* 635–653.

Espinoza, C. (2012) *Millennial integration: Challenges Millennials face in the workplace and what they can do about them.* Unpublished Ph.D. Thesis, Antioch University: Retrieved from https://etd.ohiolink.edu/rws_etd/document/get/antioch1354553875/inline.

Fairtlough, G. (2005). *The three ways of getting things done: hierarchy, heterarchy & responsible autonomy in organizations.* Bridgeport, England: Triarchy Press.

Fritzon, A., Howell, L., & Zakheim, D. (2008). *Military of Millennials.* Toronto: Booz & Company. Retrieved from http://www.strategy-business.com/media/file/resilience-03-10-08.pdf.

Flynn, M., & Schrankel, C. (2013). Applying mission command through the operations process. *Military Review, 93*(2), 25–32.

Gentry, W. A., Griggs, T. L., Deal, J. J., Mondore, S. P., & Cox, B. D. (2011). A comparison of generational differences in endorsement of leadership practices with actual leadership skill level. *Consulting Psychology Journal: Practice and Research, 63*(1), 39–49.

Gilson, L. L., Maynard T. M., Jones, N. C., Vartiainen, M., & Hakonen, M. V. M. (2015). Virtual teams research: 10 Years, 10 themes and 10 opportunities. *Journal of Management, 41*(5), 1313–1337.

Hagel, J., Brown, J. S., & Davison, L. (2010). *The power of pull: How small moves, smartly made, can set big things in motion.* London: Basic Books.

Hoda, R., Noble, J., & Marshall, S. (2010). Organizing self-organizing teams. In *Proceedings of the 32nd ACM/IEEE International Conference on Software Engineering,* Cape Town, South Africa (pp. 285–294). New York: ACM.

Hofstede, G. (1998). Identifying organizational subcultures: an empirical approach. *Journal of Management Studies, 35,* 1–12.

Hogg, M. A. (2002). Social identity. In M. R. Leary & J. P. Tangney (Eds.), *Handbook of self and identity* (pp. 462–479). New York: The Guilford Press.

Jayson, S. (2006). Generation Y Gets Involved. *USA Today,* October 23, 2006.

Jenkins, H., Clinton, K., Purushotma, R., Robinson, A. J., & Weigel, M. (2006). *Confronting the challenges of participatory culture: Media education for the 21st century.* Chicago, IL: The MacArthur Foundation.

Jenkins, H., Purushatma, R., Weigel, M., Clinton, K., & Robison, A. (2009). *Confronting the challenges of participatory culture: Media education for the 21st century.* Cambridge: MIT Press.

Kunins, J. (2010, February 9). Windows Live Messenger—a short history [Blog post]. Retrieved from http://blogs.windows.com/windows_live/b/windowslive/archive/2010/02/09/windows-live-messenger-a-short-history.aspx.

Linden, S. J. (2015). *Job expectations of employees in the Millennial generation.* (Doctoral dissertation). Retrieved from ProQuest Dissertations and Theses. (Accession Order No. ATT 3722002).

Lancaster, L. C., & Stillman, D. (2002). *When generations collide: Who they are. Why they clash. How to solve the generational puzzle at work.* New York, NY: Harper Collins.

Lowe, D., Levitt, K. J., & Wilson, T. (2008). Solutions for retaining Generation Y employees in the workplace. *The Business Renaissance Quarterly, 3*(3), 43–58.

MacDonnell, R., O'Neill, T., Kline, T., & Hambley, L. (2009). Bringing group-level personality to the electronic realm: A comparison of face-to-face and virtual contexts. *The Psychologist-Manager Journal, 12*(1), 1–24. https://doi.org/10.1080/10887150802371773.

Malloy, E. (2012, October). Gen Y, and on to Z. *The Foreign Service Journal, 89*(10), 28–41.

Martin, C., & Tulgan, B. (2006). *Managing the generation mix: From urgency to opportunity (Expanded* (2nd ed.). Amherst, MA: HRD Press.

McGregor, D. (1960). *The human side of enterprise.* New York: McGraw-Hill.

Meister, J. C., & Willyerd, K. (2010). *The 2020 workplace: How innovative companies attract, develop and keep tomorrow's employees today.* New York, NY: Harper Collins.

Meyers, J. P., & Allan, N. J. (1991). A three-component conceptualization of organizational commitment. *Human Resource Management Review, 1*(1), 61–89.

Mintzberg, H. (1979). *The structuring of organizations: A synthesis of the research.* New York: Prentice Hall.

Moss, A. (2011). *Generation Y: An exploratory study of worker experiences, values, and attitudes in the Federal Government (Unpublished doctoral dissertation).* Cleveland, OH: Cleveland State University.

NAS Insights. (2007). *Recruiting & managing the generations.* Cleveland, OH: NAS Recruitment Communications. Retrieved from www.nasrecruitment.com/TalentTips/NASinsights/GenerationY.pdf.

Nielsen, T. M., Hrivnak, G. A., & Shaw, M. (2009). Organizational citizenship behavior and performance: A meta-analysis of group-level research. *Small Group Research, 40*(5), 555–577.

Ng, E. S., Schweitzer, L., & Lyons, S. T. (2010). New generation, great expectations: A field study of the Millennial generation. *Journal of Business Psychology, 25*(2), 281–292.

Okros, A. C., Verdon, J., & Chouinard, P. (2011). *The meta-organization: A research and conceptual landscape (DRDC CSS TR 2011–13).* Ottawa, ON: Defence Research and Development Canada.

Pelto, P. J. (1968). The differences between "tight" and "loose" societies. *Trans-actions, 5,* 37–40.

Pentland, Alex "Sandy". *Social Physics-Bitcoin-BM.* https://idcubed.org/chapter-1-social-physics-human-centric-society/.

Prensky, M. (2006). *Don't bother me, mom—I'm learning: How computer and video games are preparing your kids for twenty-first century success.* St. Paul, MN: Paragon House.

PriceWaterhouseCooper. (2012). *Millennials at work: Reshaping the workplace.* Retrieved from https://www.pwc.com/gx/en/managing-tomorrows-people/future-of-work/assets/reshaping-the-workplace.pdf.

Rainer, T., & Rainer, J. (2011). *The Millennials: Connecting to the largest generation.* Nashville, TN: B&H Publishing Group.

Shandler, D. (2009). *Motivating the Millennial knowledge worker: Help today's workforce succeed in today's economy.* United States: Axzo Press.

Shore, N. (2012, March 15). *Turning on the "no-collar" workforce.* New York: Media Post. Retrieved from http://www.mediapost.com/publications/article/170109/turning-on-the-no-collar-workforce.html#axzz2Q2S9b5kf.

Tanner, L. (2010). *Who are the Millennials?* DRDC CORA Technical Memorandum 2010-284. Ottawa, ON: Defence Research and Development Canada.

Verdon, J., Forrester, B. C., & Wang, Z. (2009). *The last mile of the market how networks, participation and responsible autonomy support mission command and transform personnel management.* (DGMPRA TM 2009-022). Ottawa: Defence Research and Development Canada.

Wellman, B. (2001). The rise of networked individualism. In Keeble, L. (ed.) *Community networks online.* London: Taylor & Francis.

Wiggins, G. L. (2012). *A descriptive analysis of generation Y employees working in Georgia State Government: Implications for workforce planning.* (Doctoral dissertation). Retrieved from ProQuest Dissertations and Theses. (Accession Order No. ATT 3544061).

Zemke, R., Raines, C., & Filipczak, B. (1999). *Generations at work: Managing the clash of veterans, Boomers, Xers, and Nexters in your workplace.* New York: AMA Publications.

Harnessing the Potential of Digital Post-Millennials

8

> *Employers generally get the employees they deserve*
> —J. Paul Getty

Introduction

The preceding chapters presented our analyses of the characteristics, expectations and goals that we have assessed many Post-Millennials will bring with them when they start their careers. The focus was on the potential generational and cultural clashes that may ensue when members of the digitally engaged Post Millennial cohort encounter the realities of the world of work—and employers encounter the realities of Post-Millennials in their organization. The focus will now turn to the implications for employers and how they can prepare for potential changes.

We fully understand the wide range of enterprises across the private, public and not-for-profit domains; the significant differences across and within market sectors; variations between regional and national contexts; and, unique aspects of local labour markets especially with regards to availability or competition for talent. Further, our conclusions are indicative only as any number of future events could alter either the characteristics of the Post-Millennial age group as a whole or the labour market they will be entering. Finally, variability will exist within the Post-Millennial generation and many will share some commonalities with older workers, however, we return to our focus of identifying the ways in which the younger generation may differ so as to provide early indications to employers that employee characteristics may be shifting in important ways.

We cannot offer detailed recommendations for specific actions employers should take to prepare for the arrival of specific Post-Millennials. Instead, we will consider aspects of organizational effectiveness (at a broad, generic level) with observations on some of the potentials and some of the tensions that the Post-Millennials are

© Springer Nature Switzerland AG 2020
A. Okros, *Harnessing the Potential of Digital Post-Millennials in the Future Workplace*, Management for Professionals, https://doi.org/10.1007/978-3-030-25726-2_8

likely to bring. The initial discussion will present and integrate two concepts that, together, are offered as a basic framework for understanding organizational effectiveness.[1] This framework will be used to provide recommendations that organization may wish to consider as they prepare for the arrival of the Post-Millennials and the concurrent threats and opportunities presented by the coming digital tsunami.

Organizational Effectiveness

> Organizational effectiveness does not lie in that narrow-minded concept called rationality. It lies in the blend of clearheaded logic and powerful intuition—Henry Mintzberg

As illustrated in the 'tyranny of the urgent over the important' executives are constantly juggling different issues, topics and objectives: running the business of today versus positioning the organization for success into the future; focussing on the firm's people versus its finances; enabling creativity and growth versus ensuring quality control and compliance; etc. This often involves finding a balance between optimizing the outcomes, benefits or returns in one domain against developing a minimally satisfying solution for all facets of the enterprise. Our framework for considering these dynamics starts by drawing on the work initiated by Quinn and Rohrbaugh, which is generally referred to as Quinn's Competing Values Framework.[2] We then add concepts drawn from the Canadian military leadership model which highlights two foci: leading the organization and leading people.[3] Together, these provide an integrative basis for considerations in addressing the Post-Millennials in the workplace.

Quinn's Competing Values Framework

Simplistically, the framework presented in Fig. 8.1 comprises four quadrants with the vertical axis reflecting a focus on flexibility versus control and the horizontal axis reflecting a focus either internal to the organization versus external. The reference to competing values reflects that tensions between the opposite quadrants. The External + Control focus on maximizing profit through productivity, efficiency and exploiting market opportunities is in tension with the Internal + Flexibility focus on enhancing human capital through training, development, team-building and attending to personnel issues. The External + Flexibility focus on adaptability

---

[1]We fully acknowledge the vast literatures on organizational management and leadership. The information presented in this section is a short précis based on work conducted by the author and various members of the research team.

[2]See Quinn and Rohrbaugh (1983) for the original conceptualizations.

[3]See Department of National Defence (2005) *Conceptual Foundations* for a full presentation of the Canadian Armed Forces leadership model and Okros (2010) for a summary of the key ideas and expansion of the implications for the Canadian military.

through creativity, innovation and embracing new ideas is in tension with the Internal + Control focus on managerial control through rules, procedures, accountability structures and measurement frameworks. We will refer to these four quadrants as: productivity (rational goal in the diagram), human capital (human relations), adaptability (open systems) and managerial control (internal process).

While the diagram includes the related aspects of organizational culture, in other work, we posit the four quadrants to provide the outcome values: the objectives that leaders are focussed on attaining while, when properly articulated, there is an independent factor of conduct values embedded in culture that provide the guidance for how these objectives are to be achieved.[4] We will, therefore, refer to five dimensions: Productivity, Human Capital, Adaptability, Control and Culture. While any particular firm may be more focussed in one area than another,[5] all executives, regardless of the nature of their business, have to deal with finding the optimum balance across these dimensions or, conversely, avoid going too far in any one direction to create what Quinn has labelled negative value zones: overemphasis on productivity leads to the oppressive sweat shop, over attention to human capital $\rightarrow$ the irresponsible country club, unrestricted adaptability $\rightarrow$ tumultuous anarchy or over-control $\rightarrow$ frozen bureaucracy (Quinn, 1991).

Leading the Organization and Leading People[6]

The second aspect we offer draws on two broad facets of leadership. *Leading the Organization*[7] is based on the strategic positioning/change management literatures that emphasize the requirements for executives to, first, assess the future environment to determine changes needed to ensure success and then, second, apply systems perspectives to implement integrated initiatives to align all aspects of the organization for the envisioned future state. *Leading People* is based on the task cycle and daily supervisory duties in which leaders provide direction, inspiration, correction and clarity to individuals or small groups as well as investing in developing individual and group capacities. The outcome of leading the organization is setting the conditions for individual and small group success. Front-line supervisors will focus more on *Leading People* activities although they still have to engage in *Leading the Organization* functions especially when implementing change while the executive cadre will spend most of their time on *Leading the*

---

[4]See *Conceptual Foundations* Chapter Two for a detailed presentation.

[5]Cameron and Quinn (2011) provide illustrations of different organizational cultures using the Competing Values Framework.

[6]This section is developed from research led by the author when responsible for developing the leadership framework for the Canadian Armed Forces as well as Okros (2010).

[7]In the Canadian Armed Forces, the first is referred to as Leading the Institution as the military represents both an organization operating within government bureaucratic systems and, concurrently, a profession seeking to regulate its own affairs. See Freidson (2001) *Professionalism: The Third Logic* for his presentation of the bureaucratic and professional ideologies as well as the third which dominates the private sector; the market ideology.

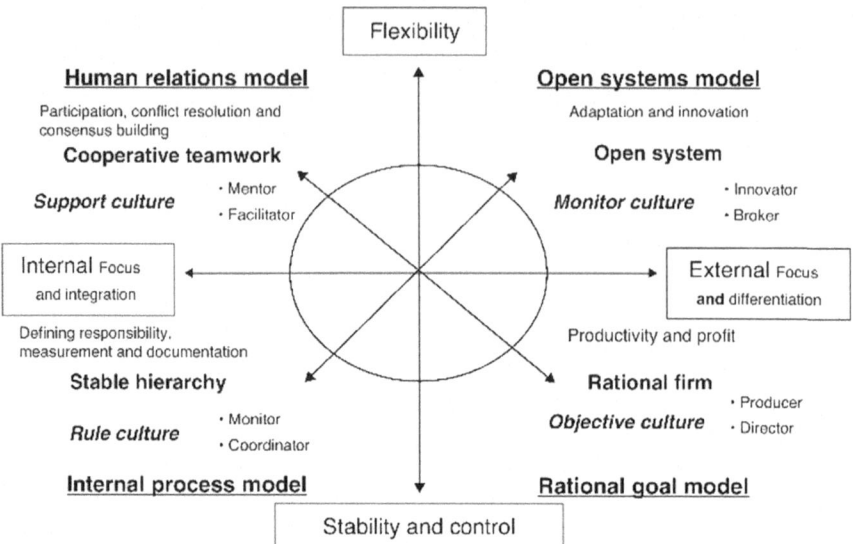

Fig. 8.1 Quinn Competing Values Framework (Developed from publicly accessible information at: https://www.quinnassociation.com/english/) (Note: copyright not required: https://www.quinnassociation.com/en/disclaimer_en)

Organization but still need to attend to *Leading People*. The following Table 8.1 summarizes how the Quinn quadrants (productivity, human capital, adaptability and managerial control) plus establishing a values-based culture are integrated with the dual leadership foci.

The table indicates the types of leadership required for each of the dimensions with differentiation between the objectives when one is engaged in *Leading People* versus *Leading the Organization* (e.g. Results Focus versus Strategic Direction for Assertive Leadership associated with Productivity).

As an extension of the different leadership foci, these can be expanded to provide more specific information on the leadership or managerial responsibilities associated with each of the ten areas outlined in this table. The following Table 8.2 has been adapted to provide a short summary of the key duties of leaders across the full spectrum of organizational responsibilities.[8] This framework with exemplar responsibilities for the different leadership function will be used to illustrate the types of decisions or actions that executives should consider when anticipating the Post-Millennials entering the workforce. We will use the five primary foci of Productivity, Human Capital, Adaptability, Control and Culture with amplifying comments for the relevant aspects under Leading People or Leading the Organization.

---

[8]For a more comprehensive presentation of factors which have been tailored for the Canadian military context, see Table 4 in *Conceptual Foundations*.

Table 8.1 Differentiated Leadership Styles

Leading people	Leading the organization
Productivity: Assertive leadership	
Results focus	Strategic direction
Human capital: Supportive leadership	
Employee motivation	Workplace practices
Adaptability: Innovative leadership	
Creativity and innovation	Manage change
Control: Accountable leadership	
Structure and accountability	Systems alignment
Culture: Values-based leadership	
Ethics and values	Corporate stewardship

Developed by the author from the research conducted to produce *Conceptual Foundations*

Table 8.2 Differentiated leader responsibilities

Focus	Leading people	Leading the organization
Productivity	Clarify objectives Solve problems, make decisions Plan, organize, task, delegate Manage resources	Establish strategy and goals Set priorities, allocate resources Develop corporate assets Empower leaders at all levels
Human capital	Mentor, educate, develop Resolve interpersonal conflicts Ensure workplace fairness Motivate individuals and teams	Accommodate personal needs Listen, provide mechanisms of voice Ensure fair complaint resolution Recognize and reward performance
Adaptability	Seek information, keep current Anticipate the future Support innovation, creativity Learn from experience	Analyse environment Seek competitive advantage Develop 'brand' Initiate and lead change
Control	Structure and coordinate work Establish routines and SOPs Develop and enforce rules Keep everybody informed Monitor, inspect, correct	Develop coherent policies Support intellectual inquiry Clarify ideas, manage meaning Communicate effectively Maintain audit systems
Culture	Socialize new employees Articulate core values Lead by example Establish a climate of respect	Enforce accountabilities Reinforce corporate identity Articulate core principles Establish an ethical culture

Developed by the author from the research conducted to produce *Conceptual Foundations*

Accommodating Adaptability

> There are no rules here—we are trying to accomplish something—Thomas Edison

In assessing the potential impact of Post-Millennials arriving in the workforce, the clear overarching tension comes from the Quinn model axis of flexibility versus control. From there, the most significant issues will be in the domain of adaptability as engaged members of this cohort will be seeking to bring new ideas, different perspectives and, especially, creative uses of digital technology into the workplace. This pressure for greater adaptability will be in opposition to the desire in most organizations to maintain managerial controls. To use Quinn's negative zones, the concern from the C-suite will be on preventing an outbreak of the "tumultuous anarchy" that could be seen to cause significant internal disruption and confusion while also taking the organization down the wrong paths resulting in erosion of competitive advantage. In contrast, enthusiastic Post-Millennials will see themselves trapped in the 'frozen bureaucracy' that prevents them from moving the organization forward. Thus, the first of our major conclusions is for executives to pay particular attention to the tensions between adaptability and control.

In assessing how to balance these two domains, it will be important to recognize that competent Post-Millennial, aided by their Millennial supervisors, will be quite prepared to contribute to some of the Leading People responsibilities for adaptation: keeping current with new developments, anticipating what the future might look like and engaging in creativity and innovation. In this area, it will be essential for their supervisors to apply the wisdom that comes with experience to provide some basic constraints on the wild enthusiasm of new workers who believe they have just solved all of the firm's problems. Thus, one of the initial areas of focus should be developing the capacity of middle managers and front-line supervisors to engage in the creative challenge function to ensure that the bright ideas put forward by front-line Post-Millennials are valuable and attainable. As many of these managers will be Millennials, the corollary suggestion is to invest in developing managers' coaching and counselling skills but, as another aspect of adaptation, allowing Millennials supervisors and their new Post-Millennials trainees to determine how digital technology and social media might facilitate these exchanges.

At the more senior levels, the focus shifts to two other areas. The first comes from the *Leading the Organization* facets of Adaptability that are related to conducting the long-range analyses of how the company needs to be positioned for success in the future as well as then capitalizing on the bright ideas and innovative approaches that employees will offer as the catalyst for important organizational change initiatives. It will be important to create an environment where individuals and teams are encouraged to bring novel ideas forward. Activities similar to the TV shows Dragons' Den or Shark Tank provide one avenue; the establishment of 'collaboratories' where individuals are encouraged to work together on new projects is another, and allowing individuals unstructured time to work with others on ideas of their own choosing would be a third.[9] As we have highlighted, we anticipate that many Post-Millennials will be interested in team-based approaches including the ability to pick the teams that they join—or, in fact, being a member of multiple teams with a portion of their time divided amongst many different projects.

---

[9]At a Strategic Leadership Forum held at Canadian Forces College, Mr. Jim Leech, CEO Ontario Pension Plan, described the multiple benefits achieved by allowing selected employees to work together have one day per week free to work on any topic they choose. Cited with permission: Mr. Leech/Dr. Okros, 5 June 2014.

These types of flexibilities in work arrangements may challenge the current approaches to structuring tasks in many organizations but will enable the types of pre-adaptation needed for future success.[10]

Establishing fora for creativity also means authorizing individuals to challenge taken-for-granted assumptions, disrupt the status quo, undermine existing authorities (and privileges) and introduce new ideas that may be difficult for established members of the organization to accept. Incorporated in the Dragons' Den or collaboratory ideas is that these are 'bounded' spaces where individual can engage in innovative thinking without disrupting the remainder of the establishment.[11] Thus, to harness Post-Millennial potential, it is vital to create zones where they are comfortable uttering heresy. From there, to return to our earlier comments that more senior employees (especially late Boomers) may interpret these activities as challenging authority (and not respecting their status), it will also be important to create buffers to prevent alarming those uncomfortable with creative (wild and crazy) new ideas. As an extension of the benefit in developing coaching skills for managers, it will be beneficial to develop programmes such as reverse mentoring where executives can pass on wisdom to new employees and Post-Millennials can provide new ideas to the seniors.

Counterbalancing Control

> It's not wise to violate rules until you know how to obey them—T.S. Eliot

As a response to the focus on Adaptability, we suggest that the second area of executive focus needs to be in the Quinn Managerial Control quadrant. Here, the most important aspects are the *Leading the Organization* responsibilities of developing coherent policies; communicating effectively; and, clarifying ideas and managing meaning. It is important to recall the discussion in the previous chapter on organizations having both structural and social systems. Part of developing coherent policies will include overseeing changes across the structural systems: perhaps shifting from hierarchical reporting relationships to enabling open teams or, as in the case of Valve Corporation, moving as far as 'Flatland' with no managerial level at all.

Similarly, the ability to influence social systems and, especially the operant culture, is through effective communications and, in particular, providing clarity around ideas, concepts or frames of reference as well as managing the meaning that

---

[10]See Okros et al. (2011) for a short discussion of preadaptation and exaptation, see the academic exchange by Cattani (2006) and Dew (2007) for considerations when applied to technological advancements.

[11]This is not a new idea as the origins are attributed to US aircraft manufacturer Lockheed's creation of 'skunk works' during the Second World War; our suggestion is to ensure that many new Post-Millennial employees are able to participate rather than reserving this only for experienced employees.

individuals extract from their work. To return to the ways Post-Millennials should have learned to learn and engage in social construction, it will be valuable to recognize that formal announcements or comments from seniors will be but one of many inputs that they will draw on to make sense of what they are encountering. Those who assume that the company memo sent to all will be the last word on the issue are likely to be disappointed. Feedback mechanisms and, in particular, opportunities for senior executives to gain an accurate understanding of how front-line employees have interpreted policy changes are critical to success. While new Post-Millennials employees will be focussed on fitting into the organization, they are likely also going to use opportunities to interpret decisions in a way that will allow them to make work fit them. Our summary statements of 'we've decided to do it this way' and 'Boss, I know you're wrong' are indicators of the (quiet) approach that they are likely to take.

In clarifying how Adaptability is being balanced with Control and especially articulating what will change and what will remain much the same, it will be beneficial for executives to recognize two factors. First, the "Nike" leadership model (Just do it) won't be effective. Drawing on the lesson most parents learn with their children that 'no' and 'because' are rarely sufficient answers, it will be important for executives to not only make decisions but, on many occasions, to explain the rationale behind these decisions. When we have important points in law, we turn to the Supreme Court looking for a simple answer: yes or no—however the Justices typically take several hundred pages to provide the response as they have to articulate two ideas: the logic and principles that led to their decision and the acknowledgement that they fully considered the opposing points of view. One of the benefits of open feedback mechanisms or reverse mentoring programmes is that these can help executives present their logic in a way that the newer employees will understand.

Second, executives need to appreciate the differing career perspectives for those at middle management or just starting their employment as compared to those who are reaching the pinnacle of their career. A goal of any change initiative is amending what executives expect from those across the organization. New employees are typically quite willing to adjust to changes and, especially when these changes involve embracing digital technologies and open inquiry, many Post-Millennials will quickly be comfortable with the 'new normal'. Those at the mid-level, however, will be heavily invested in their careers and career success. At a basic level, they have probably just figured out what types of decisions will earn them rewards—or sanctions. They may hold a variation of the view of young children when at play: you can't change the rules in the middle of the game. Thus, an important aspect that executives need to consider is how they are changing the implicit career employment model including whether decisions to amend policies such as for workplace practices, reporting relationships, delegated authorities, assigned responsibilities etc. might be interpreted as signalling new criteria for career success. Changes in these domains could lead to unintended consequences should middle managers not accurately assess the new path to advancement.

Investing in Human Capital

> The growth and development of people is the highest calling of leadership—Harvey Firestone

Second to Adaptability, it is clear from our research that the Human Capital domain will be the other major area in which engaged Post-Millennials will be pushing for greater flexibilities. We have already highlighted the likely interest in *weisure* time amongst many with a much greater desire for employers to accommodate individual preferences for work arrangements. This could easily extend to expectations for greater flexibility in other areas seen as employment benefits or 'perks'. While a range of cafeteria benefit plans are available, most are focussed on the traditional issues of a financial nature such as healthcare, retirement plans, leave entitlements, etc.[12] As these plans are intended to generate motivation and reward performance (rather than just being part of the compensation package), it is recommended that employers take a more expansive view as to alternates that may be more valued by younger workers: shifting from fulltime to part-time work to allow more time for young families or continued education; flexible work hours including blended time in office and telework; allowing individuals to combine work travel with leisure pursuits; representing the organization at volunteer or charity events as part of a desire to contribute to the community; etc.

While flexibility in work arrangements and benefits programmes is fairly obvious (and are already under pressure from Millennials), a number of other facets drawn from our framework are important. All areas in the *Leading the Organization* domain of Human Capital will require attention. We have already suggested that fairness and ethical behaviours will matter to many Post-Millennials—and that they will speak out through social media and widespread external networks if they do not perceive that seniors are paying attention to their views. Thus, effective mechanisms of voice will be of value. Many corporations rely on organizational loyalty to ensure that concerns and complaints are dealt with internally. As this loyalty may be weaker in the future, those organizations that do not have effective ways for employees to be heard when they have a complaint or concern (including whistleblower protection) will run the risk of being subject to unfavourable publicity including broad social media campaigns. As with all facets of culture, our reference to effective mechanisms pertains to the views held by junior workers not executives.

In early discussion, we highlighted the shift from the current implicit corporate model of rewarding individual performance to the growing preference for team-based recognition. Just as the reference to employment benefits can include a wider range of non-monetary perks, performance recognition can be more than promotions or financial bonuses—but these also need to be more than just a name on the "employee of the month" plaque. This is one of the areas where facilitating

---

[12]Noting that differences across countries make some of these more important for one context versus another. As an example, benefits related to health care will be of greater importance in the US than in Canada.

the engagement of Post-Millennials will be valuable as they will be able to propose creative ways to identify and reward outstanding individual performance (and it is unlikely to be through supervisor's performance appraisals). An illustration of an alternate approach is the growing use of 'badging' to recognize competencies—whether acquired at work, through schooling or elsewhere such as volunteering in the community.[13]

In turning to the domain of *Leading People*, all facets here will also be of import. The most critical will be the supervisory responsibilities to optimize the contribution of each person and develop them to achieve their full potential. While we expect Post-Millennials to be looking for the traditional supervisory feedback on how to perform assigned work effectively and to develop job-specific skills, there are several reasons why we believe they are more likely to be interested in organizational and career mentoring. Our research suggests that many will be concerned with fitting in and in finding a workplace that fits their personality. Thus, attention to the fit between person and organization will be important so it should be expected that the individual or supervisor may quickly recognize when this has not been achieved. The promising Post-Millennials are unlikely to stay in work environments where they do not fit in hence this should be an aspect of early mentoring. Similarly, they will probably maintain the reported Millennial expectations that they will be able to move up quickly in the organization—or, at a minimum, be given increased responsibilities relatively soon after joining. Those seeking advancement will be eager for managers to provide guidance on how to achieve these early career goals; however, executives will be expecting these supervisors to also be providing some words of wisdom to align expectations with corporate realities.

It will also be important to ensure sufficient attention is given to addressing interpersonal conflict in the workplace. As highlighted in the comparison between tight and loose cultures, those who are most comfortable with aspects of the first (clear norms, defined roles, high respect for supervisors, consistency in language, dress and behaviour) can easily be upset when newcomers do not follow well established organizational customs. As those with longevity may just assume that these always have been, hence always will be, the way business is conducted, the potential for workplace conflict will be high and supervisors seeking to address these issues will need some 21st Century negotiation skills to do so. The complaints by co-workers of Millennials not complying with corporate norms in language, use of technology, etc. are illustrations of the types of minor conflicts that will need to be addressed.

Supervisors will need to have a repertoire of effective leadership styles. They will need to shift from giving comprehensive instructions, direction and corrective feedback on work to be done to using participative coaching as part of skill development and conflict resolution to providing supportive mentoring to assist new Post-Millennial employees in aligning their expectations for career success with corporate realities. Again, it will be beneficial to enhance these capacities in supervisors and managers and, especially, as these will be rising Millennials, to

---

[13]As an illustration of badging, see: http://openbadges.org/about/.

develop methods to do so through digital media in addition to face-to-face interactions.

An additional issue to be addressed pertains to the type of work that the Post-Millennials will be seeking to perform. Given the nature of their 21st Century learning environment and especially the penchant some will have to explore multiple topics, a number of Post-Millennials may wish to get involved in a wide range of work activities rather than sticking to the narrow area of work that corresponds with their job description. Those with an interest in working at the intersections of different corporate divisions or business lines can be a significant asset in breaking down the "silos of excellence" that often exist and in helping to identify the types of radical shifts in business practices that will be critical in optimizing (or surviving) the digital tsunami. Programmes offering short job rotations during initial employment could be one way to facilitate the Post-Millennials interest in doing a bit of everything and can provide a more holistic understanding of the organization relatively quickly.

The final issue related to Human Capital comes from our earlier comments on social construction and the expectation that Post-Millennials are likely to extend the areas where the Millennials have been reported to be redefining social norms and roles. We suggested that some of those in the next age group will move beyond having a more fluid understanding of marriage, parenting and the markers of adulthood such as home ownership to redefining the concepts of work, employment, job and career. To prepare for new employees, employers might want to consider options in areas such as task swapping (having a friend in a different firm do part of my assigned tasks while I do a part of theirs as we're each better at the other); personal sub-contracting (paying somebody to do part of my work); co-working (two people doing one job and splitting the pay); internal contractors (employees with no job description who sell their services to different supervisors); or blended employers (working for multiple organizations at the same time).[14]

Throughout these considerations of how executives may want to address issues related to enhancing Human Capital, we offer two broad conclusions. First, those organizations seen by enthusiastic Post-Millennials to be paying attention to this domain are more likely to attract the top talent. Second, once convinced to join the company, the initiatives that may be considered in the Human Capital domain should be integrated and aligned to ensure that the firm can harness the full potential that these new employees will bring.

Maintaining Productivity

> There are no secrets to success: it is the result of preparation, hard work and learning from failure—Colin Powell

As with balancing adaptability with control, there is a clear requirement to ensure that flexibilities introduced in the Human Capital domain do not erode the ability of the organization to deliver on core business. The main comment offered in this

---

[14]Or, at a minimum, have a well-articulated rationale for why these are not deemed viable.

regard is to recognize that all organizations provide fairly consistent messages (written, oral and symbolic) that continually remind individuals that productivity and attainment of corporate objectives matter. We anticipate that new Post-Millennials employees will generally be focussed on fitting into the organization and demonstrating their worth, hence, will be attentive to messages that are intended to ensure that they are doing the right work the right way. Our general observation is to suggest that, while some with experience may be concerned that the suggestions in the preceding discussion would, indeed, create the "irresponsible country club", it will also be easy for Post-Millennial employees to perceive the focus on productivity as representing the "oppressive sweatshop". Thus, in the *Leading People* aspects of Productivity, it will be of value to pay attention to communications surrounding all of the facets of clarifying objectives, providing direction and tasks, making decisions and managing resources to ensure that new employees understand what is expected of them—and why. In doing so, it will be important to recognize significant differences amongst any cohort particularly with regards to work structure: some people will be looking for a high degree of structure with clear rules, defined responsibilities and articulated standard procedures; others will be seeking the greater flexibility, creativity, and independence of an open organization. Differences such as these explain the basic leadership maxim: know your people.

The most important functions under Productivity will come from the *Leading the Organization* activities of establishing strategic goals and developing corporate assets. While the dynamics will vary by sector and country, all executives are concerned with optimizing outputs and outcomes for the current business while concurrently investing in new capacities and new business lines to prepare for the anticipated future. Whether viewed as changing the tires on the truck while speeding down the highway or doing a heart transplant while the patient is running a marathon, there is a balance to be struck between the focus on today as opposed to tomorrow. In many cases, the approach taken is to buffer most of the organization and, in particular, more junior front line workers from future changes and only roll these out when properly developed by the hand-picked (and usually senior) change team. To the extent that executives recognize that some of the Post-Millennials will be the ones to bring the new ideas, critical analyses and creative suggestions needed to survive the coming digital tsunami, it would be of value to determine how their ingenuity and enthusiasm can be harnessed to assist in developing long term strategies and developing new capacities. Those who do believe that seniors value their inputs will be more engaged and committed; those who don't are not likely to be around long and may take the keys to future success to the competition.

Integrative Culture

Culture eats strategy for breakfast—attributed to Peter Drucker

In terms of organizational culture, we have previously referred to espoused versus operant culture: the ideal that is intended to exist as compared to the reality of what individuals actually believe, value and do. There are always gaps between the two and the instances of bending rules, cutting corners, accidental amnesia, seeking forgiveness rather than permission and other forms of working around the articulated standards are most visible at the junior levels not the senior ones. As Post-Millennials are likely to amplify the Millennials' desire for increased flexibility, the C-suite will benefit from an accurate understanding of the operant culture and the areas where significant gaps exist between espoused ideals and actual practice. Further, as many organizations engage in active processes to create a brand identity (externally and internally), we note that this involves a degree of 'myth making' hence our caution is that those who are part of constructing this myth should not to start to believe it without clear evidence.[15] Thus, ensuring an accurate understanding of the operant culture takes time and effort, starting with ensuring executives are comfortable hearing negative news.

The primary purpose of creating a broadly shared culture is to influence employee identity, especially the values and principles that they will draw on when making decisions in dynamic or ambiguous settings. It will, therefore, be important to assess the degree to which new employees choose to become mirrors and chameleons. Many Post-Millennials will be comfortable acting in a manner that is consistent with what the organization has signaled is preferred (mirroring back what they believe the boss wants to see) or avoiding standing out (blending in as chameleons especially when there are inconsistencies in what is expected in different contexts or with different supervisors). As suggested in our summative 'I'm not who you think I am', we caution that these external behaviours may not reflect their personal views or values. Particularly when the issues involve ethical principles and broader social responsibilities, these individuals may either be thinking or acting on the premise that "my moral compass is pointing in a different direction". An additional facet of socially aware Post-Millennials seeking to fit in is that they may exhibit one set of behaviours in one setting and a different set in another: the pit bull in the sales meeting can be the kindler-gentler buddy in the team meeting.

As our focus is on Post-Millennials when they enter the workforce, the primary conclusion we offer is that organizations should pay close attention to the signals and messages sent to new employees. Firms that rely on a 'welcome to the company' pamphlet and 'orientation by walking around' may want to consider a more intentional process of initial socialization featuring two-way communications: sit and listen sessions featuring "death by Power Point" will not achieve the effects intended. While it is unlikely that commercial enterprises will go to the efforts of the military to inculcate a shared identity, common value system and strong links to the profession, it may be worthwhile to examine whether some of the associated practices might be considered: small group activities to create team bonds, rites of passage to mark the transition from probationary status to welcomed member of the work community, exposure to exemplary leaders or personal attention from those in the C-suite.

---

[15]And the plural of 'anecdote' is not 'data'.

In assessing the effectiveness of new employee orientation or onboarding activities for executives should apply the process of institutional analyses utilized by Ouellet and Balakhnina as part of our research.[16] Those who would seek to establish some form of order (social, political, corporate, professional, etc.) must maintain legitimacy in the eyes of those who must comply with the imposed order. This can be assessed by examining the alignment—or often disconnects—across three institutional domains: regulative, cognitive and normative. Regulative refers to the rules and regulations that are invoked to justify and legitimize the decisions of the institution, whether they are formal or informal, and the reward and punishment systems that underwrite them. Cognitive encompasses shared conventions, systems of thought, and individually-shared mental schemas used to provide legitimacy for decisions. As we have highlighted earlier, this extends to what is considered to be true, correct, meaningful or proven. Normative includes common behaviours, values, deeply held beliefs and elements that underwrite ethics in a particular community. These norms and values specify the way in which things should be done and the manner in which decisions should be made so that they are socially perceived as acceptable, good, right, desirable, or just. The normative dimension is also the foundation that ultimately defines the identity of a particular group or community as every human collective self-defines itself, consciously or not, to be unique, special, or superior in some respects to others. To the extent that there are disconnects in how the regulative, cognitive and normative domains are perceived by new employees, the potential exists for cultural chaos.

In assessing the operant culture and the tensions that may be revealed through institutional analyses, it is important for executives to consider the issue of toxic leaders (Lipman-Blumen, 2004; Reed, 2004). These individuals can exist at the mid (or senior) levels of an organization by projecting two images: one upwards to their seniors and another to their subordinates.[17] Toxic leaders use dysfunctional behaviors to deceive, intimidate, coerce, or unfairly punish others to get what they want for themselves but disguise their actions as necessary to achieve their assigned duties. To return to the Quinn model, these types of leaders often exist in contexts where C-suite executives focus heavily on outputs and outcomes (the bottom line Productivity component) but do not pay sufficient attention to either the demoralizing consequences in the Human Capital domain or the corrosive effects on organizational values or principles in the Culture domain. We anticipate that most Post-Millennials are going to be less tolerant of such individuals or be willing to suffer in silence. There are several mechanisms to detect toxic leaders including the use of 360° assessments however the most effective is another basic principle: leadership by walking around.

---

[16]For the broader conceptual considerations, again, see Scott (2008).

[17]The common analogy is to a totem pole: those looking down see smiling faces, those looking up see another part of the anatomy.

References

Cameron, K. S., & Quinn, R. E. (2011). *Diagnosing and changing organizational culture: Based on the competing values framework*. San Francisco: Wiley.

Cattani, G. (2006). Technological pre-adaptation, speciation, and emergence of new technologies: How Corning invented and developed fiber optics. *Industrial and Corporate Change, 15*(2), 285–318.

Department of National Defence. (2005). *Leadership in the Canadian Forces: Conceptual Foundations*. Ottawa: Canadian Defence Academy.

Dew, N. (2007). Pre-adaptation, exaptation and technology speciation: a comment on Cattani (2006). *Industrial and Corporate Change, 16*(1), 155–160.

Freidson, E. (2001). *Professionalism: The third logic*. Chicago: University of Chicago Press.

Lipman-Blumen, J. (2004). *The allure of toxic leaders: Why we follow destructive bosses and corrupt politicians–and how we can survive them*. London: Oxford University Press.

Okros, A. C. (2010). *Leadership in the military context*. Kingston: Canadian Forces Leadership Institute.

Okros, A. C., Verdon, J., & Chouinard, P. (2011). *The meta-organization: a research and conceptual landscape*. (DRDC CSS TR 2011-13). Ottawa, ON: Defence Research and Development Canada.

Quinn, R. E. (1991). Mastering competing values: An integrated approach to management. In D. A. Kolb, I. M. Rubin, & J. S. Osland (Eds.), *The organizational behavior reader* (5th ed.). Englewood Cliffs, NJ: Prentice-Hall.

Quinn, R. E., & Rohrbaugh, J. (1983). A spatial model of effectiveness criteria: Towards a competing values approach to organizational analysis. *Management Science, 29*(3), 363–377.

Reed, G. E. (2004). Toxic leadership. *Military Review, 84*, 67–71.

Scott, R. W. (2008). *Institutions and organizations*. Thousand Oaks: Sage Publication.

Surf's Up

9

The only place success comes before work is in the dictionary
—Vince Lombardi

As we presented in the introduction to this volume, the focus of our research has been to examine the implications of todays youngsters being raised from birth immersed in an increasingly omnipresent digital environment. Although efforts to peer into the future can be problematic we are fairly confident in suggesting that the 'Internet of Everything' will produce significant changes to many facets of our lives. The choice for employers is not a matter of *if* they will need to change business practices but *how* and *when*. Our integrative assessment of emerging digital developments led us to conclude that these will lead to changes in the conditions of change: in certain key areas, the digital environment will produce disruptive breaks from the present. As with the early stages of the Industrial Revolution, we are beginning to see shifts away from well-established ways in which we live our lives to what are best seen as the transitional phases of new possibilities: technological advances such as driverless cars, 3D printing, biotechnologies and cheap energy; societal shifts through social media, enhanced global awareness and new forms of political participation, and, adverse personal consequences due to erosion of privacy, cyber-hacking and malicious trolls are all just hints of what is yet to come. We foresee a coming digital tsunami with the potential to cause significant disruptions. Some businesses are in the lead in developing and exploiting these new opportunities hence are likely more aware of some of the potential implications, however, we suggest that all employers, including in the public and not-for-profit sectors, should be anticipating the digital Black Swans that may suddenly appear to be able to make requisite adjustments.

As a critical component of success into the future, we have provided a comprehensive assessment of the characteristics that many members of the Post-Millennial age group are likely to bring to the workplace when they embark on their careers. Our rationale and our philosophy are clear: the youth of today will build the future thus we should pay attention to who they are and enable them to

© Springer Nature Switzerland AG 2020   171
A. Okros, *Harnessing the Potential of Digital Post-Millennials in the Future Workplace*, Management for Professionals,
https://doi.org/10.1007/978-3-030-25726-2_9

make the maximum contributions possible as they enter the workforce and ultimately lead our social and business affairs. We acknowledge that our analyses and predictions are optimistic but all must recognize that, if we do not set the conditions to harness their potential, the fault will lay with their elders not them.

In our assessment of generational theory and cohort analyses, we concluded that, while it is highly unlikely that we can predict key characteristics of the next generation, some plausible suggestions can be offered by examining areas where those of a similar age have had broadly shared similar experiences and where these experiences differ from those before them. Of course, age alone explains little of who a person is as the many facets of identity, family, community and individual circumstances all combine to make each individual individual. Nonetheless, generational descriptions are important as a range of media are contributing to the creation of generally held assumptions or stereotypes concerning different age groups including the Post-Millennials and, whether accurate or not, these stereotypes will influence attitudes and expectations concerning this group as well as how members of this age group see themselves. Not all young people will be afforded the opportunity to benefit from digital technologies. Still, we concluded that a sizable cohort of the Post-Millennials will be able to do so in one form or another. Our examination of education and learning indicated that updates in curricula and pedagogy designed to develop 21st Century skills are changing the ways young people are learning to learn with implications for the competencies they will bring to the workplace. Further, we assessed that an enhanced collaborative teaching environment will yield a more cooperative youth cohort than their elders.

Our second section then presented the characteristics that these young people are likely to bring into their adult lives. While we recognize both continuity as Post-Millennials will share many aspects that generations before have held and variability across those of similar ages, we have focussed on areas where we anticipate differences particularly between Post-Millennials and their Millennial elders. Although our conclusions are inherently speculative generalizations, the skills, values, and traits we identified are logical consequences of a digitally enhanced upbringing. Accordingly, many of the traits expressed by Millennials—having experienced adolescence during the digital revolution of the late 20th and early 21st Century—will be similar in many respects to their Post-Millennial successors. The greater lessons for employers, however, pertain to how these two groups are likely to differ.

Our consideration of the cognitive skills and competencies indicated that the skills these young people will be able to develop should position them well for the 21st Century knowledge economy, including apparent strengths in traditional competencies such as critical thinking, problem solving, adaptability, and creativity. While many hold the view that Millennials struggle with social interaction at work, we suggest that the Post-Millennials who have benefitted from the opportunities afforded them in their youth will have several desirable competencies: considerable soft skills; an ability to sift through immense amounts of information to deliver results; effectiveness in applying multi-tasking to deal with disrupted work requirements; and, the potential to strengthen their skill sets during their careers through their capacity for lifelong learning.

When we examined the generally shared sense of identity and social skills that most Post-Millennials may carry into adulthood, we concluded that the power of the digital tsunami is not in its ability as a tool—as Millennials see it—but as the means for social interactions especially the establishment of social norms and the processes of social construction. While family, community, and socioeconomic conditions will factor into any child's socialization, we concluded that the Internet and social media, in particular, will play a significant role in the construction of the "self," as the medium represents an ongoing, global conversation that can serve to develop social norms by consensus while also exposing youngsters to the adverse aspects of human existence. We suggest that employers pay close attention to how teens are making sense of their world and, when hiring, seek to identify those who have developed a keen sense of individualism and an enhanced capacity to present different images of themselves to others.

Finally, we considered the expectations that Post-Millennials may have regarding work and life as they enter adulthood. Notwithstanding the variability that will exist across this group, a picture nevertheless emerges of the potential Post-Millennials when they arrive at work for day one. We expect many to be ready and able to contribute and will be expecting immediate, meaningful work. Even before that first day, the engaged Post-Millennials who have developed the ability to communicate via multiple platforms, the propensity to "do their homework" on an employer, and the understanding of their image in the eyes of others—particularly in response to stereotypes older generations may hold of them—will allow them to mold their persona to their employer: a 'chameleon' using 'mirrors' to succeed. These skills may serve new Post-Millennial employees as they encounter possible workplace culture clashes we presented in Chap. 8. Here, Post-Millennials have the potential to be out front in demanding changes to how "work" is conducted. In particular, as Boomers retire, the structures and processes they leave behind may be antithetical to the values and worldviews that digital generations will bring. Employers who are not anticipating changes will be challenged to alter the structures and assumptions behind the "Boomer workplace" to obtain and retain a competent team.

The success of any enterprise will hinge on shifting from a workforce comprised of knowledge workers to one with expert thinkers: individuals able to apply the independence of thought and creativity required to not only identify a novel way to solve an emerging problem but to do so by analyzing the context and by challenging assumptions to first understand what the problem is. Thus, employers will not only have to identify the skills needed for future work requirements but to also create the types of work environment, organizational policies, managerial and leadership styles and reward systems needed to first, attract the best and the brightest, then, focus their efforts on the organization's goals and, finally, to retain the right mix of talent over time. All of these will require a significant degree of re-thinking and, in many cases, will present challenges to the workplace legacies the Boomers will have left behind. Given the time needed to implement effective culture change initiatives, employers will need to examine how they will do so.

In conclusion, we offer four key ideas to guide employers into the future. First, re-examine corporate agility and be prepared to expand the focus from agile business processes to agile leadership and supporting HR functions. Second, pay attention to who is being hired to ensure the firm really does get the 'right' people and to apply the same techniques used to identify and target ideal customers to doing the same for ideal new employees. Third, balance the competing tensions between communicating who you are and what you expect from recent employees with also listening to their questions, comments and bright ideas thus ensure a focus on optimizing their contributions not forcing conformity. Finally, prepare supervisors and managers now for changes that will be implemented in the near future.

To draw from the professional military literature, in their volume titled *Military Misfortunes: The Anatomy of Failure in War* Cohen and Gooch (1990) identify three problems: failure to learn, failure to anticipate and failure to adapt. One of these can cause corporate headaches, two can produce major problems and all three can result in catastrophic disasters. This volume has provided the information to assist executives in learning more about the Post-Millennials, anticipating who they will be and starting to adapt to harness their potential.

Reference

Cohen, E. A., & Gooch, J. (1990). *Military misfortunes: The anatomy of failure in war.* New York: Free Press.

Printed by Printforce, the Netherlands